SPIRIT IN DARKNESS

St. John is a terrifying friend,
but the more you know him,
the more you will love him.

Spirit in Darkness

A Companion to

Book Two

of the

"Ascent of Mt. Carmel"

BY THE

REV. FR. BRICE, C.P.

Author of "Journey in the Night"

FREDERICK PUSTET CO., INC.

Publishers

NEW YORK AND CINCINNATI

1946

Nihil Obstat
  CONELL DOWD, C.P., S.T.D.
    Censor Deputatus

Imprimi Potest
  HERMAN J. STIER, C.P., J.C.D.
    Provincial

Nihil Obstat
  ARTHUR J. SCANLAN, S.T.D.
    Censor Librorum

Imprimatur
  ✝ FRANCIS CARDINAL SPELLMAN, D.D.
    Archbishop of New York

New York, Jan. 15, 1946.

To

CONRAD,

CECILIA AND

SR. M. BERNADELLE, S.S.N.D.

CONTENTS

CONTENTS

ABBREVIATIONS

A.   Ascent of Mount Carmel

D.N.   Dark Night of the Soul

S.C.   Spiritual Canticle (second redaction)

L.F.   Living Flame of Love (second redaction)

S.T.   Summa Theologica (St. Thomas Aquinas)

All references to the Works of St. John of the Cross are to the translation of E. A. Peers, published by Burns Oates and Washbourne, London, to whom I acknowledge my gratitude for permission to quote therefrom. In all quotations the *italics are mine.* If not otherwise specified, the reference is to Book Two of the "Ascent of Mount Carmel." Large Roman numbers refer to Book; small Roman numbers refer to chapter or stanza; arabic numerals refer to paragraph numbers in Peers' translation. Thus, A.,I,iii,1 means "Ascent," Book One, ch. iii, paragraph 1, S.C.,v,3 means "Spiritual Canticle," stanza v, paragraph 3.

CHAPTER I

Introduction

ST. JOHN of the Cross loved the darkness. Along with his love of nature went the tranquillity and satisfaction which he felt in the thickening gloom of night. Not content with climbing the mountains and gazing upon the lovely and luxuriant forms of green that towered in the heights or mingled with the lowly flowers of the meadows; not content even with losing himself in contemplation among the rocks during the revealing light of day, John would go out in the evening with his Religious at Calvario and scatter them in solitary places to make their evening prayer. Having bought a plot of land on the bank of the Guadalimar, he would go there for perhaps a week at a time. With a companion he would sit in a verdant meadow banking the stream, and would speak of the beauty of the heavens or the harmonious movements of the celestial spheres. The night was sometimes far advanced before the Saint, at the insistence of his companion, would consent to seek shelter and retire.

It was here at Calvario, when he was about thirty-six or thirty-seven years of age, that this mystical writer began the commentary on those verses which begin:

En una noche obscura,	On a dark night,
Con ansias en amores inflamada,	Kindled in love with yearnings —
Oh dichosa ventura!	Oh, happy chance! —
Sali sin ser notada,	I went forth without being observed,
Estando ya mi casa sosegada.	My house being now at rest.

The verses themselves had probably been composed

1

during his imprisonment at Toledo, and often afterwards John had interpreted them at the request of the Carmelite nuns and friars, for most everyone knew the eight stanzas by heart. But so deeply was the doctrine of this Saint loved, that he was compelled, at the insistence of his spiritual children, to commit the interpretation of them to writing. We might well imagine John, then, betaking himself to some lonely spot, and in the cool of evening planning the divisions of his commentary on the poem of "The Dark Night." How often he must have gazed silently into the waters of the Guadalimar, where the stars of immeasurable serenity, now focused into white sparks, quivered and tossed inextinguishably on the hissing waves! How quickly the time would pass, while the tranquil points of light, forgetful even of the years, seemed to glow more brightly in the breath of midnight, like beacons of faith in eternal things.

In the mind of John of the Cross the veil of night, drawn across the trivial shadows of day, had a particular significance. Night was like the obscurity of faith, and for this reason he was attracted to the poetic imagery of darkness as a symbol. One of his first poems dealt with the theme of faith, and its re-echoing refrain was "Although 'Tis Night." In the stanzas of his *Canticle of Love*, it is in "the tranquil night" and in "the serene night" that the Bride-soul contemplates her Beloved. And in the eight verses of "The Dark Night" it is the concept of darkness or some equivalent idea, that gives a striking unity to the poem, especially in the first five verses, where this symbol of faith takes, if I may say so, the *leading* role, and then disappears before the light of the Beloved, after having guided the soul safely to Him.

It may be inferred, therefore, that the beauties of night had a particular charm for John of the Cross. But what about his readers? Can they appreciate the radiant obscurity of "The Dark Night"? Will the stars of faith be sufficient illumination to guide them through day's eclipse? Will they not be frightened as the glowing sheen of day gradually fades into the soft, serene effulgence of starry blue? John himself felt that the spiritual night was the most secure condition or means for travelling the way of the spirit. He seems not to have anticipated any paralyzing fear on the part of his readers. He even flaunts, as it were, the difficulty and darkness of the road, before the eyes of the reader. In the first chapter of this Book Two he tells us that the soul must travel "in darkness and concealment." This darkness is deeper, and consequently more terrifying, than that of the night of the senses, because when St. John spoke of the night of the senses in Book One, he was employing the imagery of dusk (the beginning of night) when the objects of the world are only beginning to disappear from the sight of the soul, whereas by "darkness" he means the darkness of midnight when the soul has progressed into the starlit fields of *pure* faith. But let us explain this a little more.

St. John of the Cross delineates the movement and progress of the soul towards God as a journey in the night. "A journey?" you will say. Yes, that is a good metaphor, a most useful rhetorical contrivance, and has been used by a multitude of writers and preachers. But why "journey *in the night*"? The answer is: because the journey to God is not by means of the *light* of reason only, but also, and primarily, by the *obscurity* of faith. That faith is obscure is known to everyone who understands the meaning of supernatural faith, for this virtue does not reveal God in clear vision, but darkly, as when one looks at the sun through a negative film. This simile of night is used by our author throughout the commentary of the poem of "The Dark Night," which, by the way, comprises both the "Ascent of Mount of Carmel" and the "Dark Night of the Soul." In another work St. John referred to this journey as the "Dark Night of the Ascent of Mount Carmel," [1] which indicates the unity of the two titles. If formerly the "Ascent of Mount Carmel" and the "Dark Night of the Soul" were thought by some to be two separate works, now it is certain that St. John planned both as one work and one doctrine. The *Ascent of Mt. Carmel* is dark because it is made in faith, and the *Dark Night of the Soul* is also an ascent, because its goal is the summit of perfection. That there are distinctions between the two works cannot be denied, but the point to be stressed here is that the concept of night or darkness is continued from the time the soul sets out on the upward climb until it reaches the summit at dawn of day.

What is the interpretation of *Night*, which was so poetically attractive to St. John, but is so prosaically repulsive to souls who do not understand his doctrine? The author of the "Ascent" has defined this term in the third chapter of Book One. *Night* is a figure of speech taken from the operation of the visual faculty. When the eyes are closed, the privation of light is as night to our faculty of vision. The blind man may be said to be in a perpetual night. So also the mortification of the natural desires may be called a night of the soul. For even as the visual faculty is nourished by light and fed by objects that can be seen,

[1] L.F.,i,25

so the soul is fed and nourished by the senses; and when these senses are mortified and deprived of their objects, they may be said to be in darkness or night. As the coming of dusk gradually removes from our sight the many objects around us, though they still remain in the darkness, so also the mortification of the senses removes the objects of the world from the soul and seems to place both them and the soul in a night. It was with this meaning that John of the Cross treated of the *Night of the Senses* in Book One. In the *Night of the Senses* the soul detached its senses and desires from all the natural objects of sense perception. In other words, it departed, in affection and desire, from the things of the world, in order to journey towards God. Deep though its desires of worldly pleasure were, it courageously shut its eyes against them, because it knew that the joys of sense are contrary to true spirituality and perfect love of God.

One might think that by this detachment from exterior objects the purification of the soul would be complete. But, not so! There may be interior apprehensions and preternatural perceptions of things that are not of this world, and which, consequently, are more deceptive and dangerous than worldly things, or, at least, do not constitute the true road to Divine union. It is necessary, therefore, that not only the senses but the interior faculties also be placed in the spiritual *Night*.

Yes, we may speak of a *Night* of the interior faculties as well as of the senses. Because of the close relationship of *all* the faculties of man, we may easily apply the term *Night* to the spiritual operations of knowing, remembering and loving, as well as to the sensible operations of seeing, hearing, etc. Men universally agree in speaking of the "light of the understanding" or in calling ignorance a "darkness." Scripture also employs this manner of speaking, for Christ is called the "Light of the world," and concerning those who shut their spiritual faculties against Him it is written that "the darkness grasped it not." [2] It is entirely natural, then, to speak of a *Night* of the faculties when the understanding, memory and will are deprived of their proper objects.

For the sake of greater precision, John of the Cross makes a distinction between the "Night of the Senses" and the "Night of the Spirit." The *Night* of the senses is that emptiness or idleness of the senses which results from their being mortified and detached from the things of the world. The *Night* of the spirit is that emptiness or idleness which results from the mortification, detachment or purification of the soul's spiritual faculties (intellect, spiritual memory, and will) from the objects of their *natural* opertion. According to this division, John planned the parts of the "Ascent of Mount Carmel," which explains what the soul itself can do toward placing itself in this *Night*. Book One treated of the darkening of the exterior senses; Book Two, with which we are now concerned, treats of the darkening of the understanding (intellect); Book Three will expound the darkening of the memory and the will — (logically, St. John should have given a fourth Book to the treatment of the will).

As we were saying previously, John of the Cross was not at all dismayed by the terrors of the *Night*. He even proved himself rather unfeeling, by telling the reader in the very first chapter (Book Two) that the things which he is going to expound gradually "are somewhat obscure." He reas-

[2] John i,5

sures us, however, that though it will be necessary to proceed attentively, some things will pave the way for others, and in the end they will all be quite clearly understood. He is also heartless in warning us that the darkness of the spirit is by far greater than the dusk which the senses entered. Indeed, John prefers the term "darkness" in this connection to that of "night." "For, however dark a night may be, something can always be seen, but in true darkness nothing can be seen; and thus in the night of sense, there still remains some light, for the understanding and reason remain, and are not blinded. But this spiritual night, which is faith, deprives the soul of everything. . . ." [3] And that is why we speak of the spirit being in darkness.

But you shall not frighten us, John of the Cross! We know why you say that the darkness of the spirit is greater than that of the senses. Since the interior and spiritual faculties (understanding, memory and will) are deeper and more expansive than the exterior senses (eyes, ears, etc.) it must naturally follow that the darkness of the spirit will be more deep and penetrating. A larger vessel has a greater emptiness than a small one when the contents of both are poured out. Since the capacity of the spiritual faculties is deeper than that of the senses, so also must their emptiness be more profound. As the light of the spiritual faculties reaches higher and more penetratingly than that of the senses, so also must their darkness be more profound and interior. But if this is so, how bright must be that faith, and how abundant that love, which are to illumine and fill them!

If the understanding, memory and will are to be dark-

[3] i,3. (If not otherwise specified, the reference is to Book Two of the "Ascent of Mount Carmel.")

ened (or emptied) of their natural capacities, that is only because we wish to fill them with faith, hope and love. Yours is not a doctrine of darkness, St. John. Yours is rather a doctrine of light — supernatural light! And, therefore, we shall not be terrified — as some have been — by the dark night of the soul. We may not, perhaps, understand everything that St. John wrote in Book Two, the first time we read it. A little patient consideration will clear up everything. And even though we do not understand all the intricacies of faith, visions, etc., that would not hinder us from grasping the essential lesson which you, St. John, wish us to learn and practise, namely:

We must love God alone. We must remain in darkness to all that is less than God. Only by pure faith can the understanding be united to God.

In the present work, as in Book Two of the "Ascent," we are concerned principally with one faculty: the understanding (or intellect). But, since all the powers of the soul are intimately united and mutually influence one another, we shall know how to purify them all, if we learn the instructions given for the understanding. Indeed, so fundamental are the principles herein treated, that the reader who masters them will be able to read all of St. John's works with as much ease as delight. It may also be well to warn the reader that it is not necessary for him to have experienced the things of which St. John treats herein. All that is necessary is to learn the sublimity and importance of pure faith, as our author understands it, and to gather from the succeeding chapters this one guiding principle: THE ORDINARY AND PROXIMATE MEANS OF

UNITING OUR SOULS TO GOD IS BY DARK AND PURE FAITH
AND THE LOVE ENKINDLED THEREBY.

As we take up Book Two, then, we find that John of
the Cross (irrespective of our fears) begins to interpret the
second stanza of his poem, and to tell us that the understanding must be placed in darkness by means of the virtue of faith, which is as midnight to the soul.

> *In darkness and secure,*
> *By the secret ladder — disguised —*
> *Oh, happy chance!*
> *In darkness and in concealment,*
> *My house being now at rest.*

The allegory has literal reference to a maiden who es-
capes from her home while her household is asleep, and
in disguise, descends a secret ladder, while the darkness
affords her concealment and security. Far away on the
lofty mountain of perfection her Beloved awaits her coming, so that they may be united in the transformation of
love.

The mystical interpretation of the stanza is briefly as
follows. The one, supernatural means of uniting the intellect to God is faith. Faith is a secret ladder by which
the intellect may escape from its natural imperfections
and ascend the steep slopes toward Divine union. Disguised in the vesture of the theological virtues, the bride-
soul may mount in darkness, concealed from the world
and the devil who wish to stop her, to union with her
Beloved. The importance of faith is manifest in the many
references to it, even in the two introductory chapters of
Book Two, in such terms as "pure faith," "Divine ladder

of faith," "light of faith," "darkness of faith," "spiritual night, which is faith," "rays of His Divine light."

Every Christian is familiar with those terms which signify the elevating effect of faith, or its purity. What is not so well understood, even by Religious, is that faith is a spiritual night, that is to say, faith causes darkness in our natural understanding. Just why this is, and how it must affect our spiritual life, are questions to be answered in this Book of the "Ascent," as only a John of the Cross could answer them. But, in order to prevent our becoming too involved in the obscurities of faith and to avoid confusion, let us proceed step by step, treating of ideas familiar to every Christian, and thus establishing ourselves on solid ground and making sure of our direction, before the shades of evening gather around us. Then when we begin to comprehend the simplicity and security of this darkness, and the restfulness and joy in this journey towards God, (Oh, good fortune!), it will not seem to us such a horrifying thing to place our own SPIRIT IN DARKNESS.

In the following chapter we shall, therefore, speak of the union of the soul with God through sanctifying grace. St. John writes of this union in chapter five, where he interrupts his discourse on faith, in order to clarify his subject by the doctrine of grace. We shall do well, consequently, in taking up the doctrine of grace at the very beginning.

Attentive reading of the following pages will suffice to give the reader a clear knowledge of Book Two of the "Ascent." However, to those who wish to make a study of St. John, I suggest either of the following two methods, or both: first, to familiarize himself with the text of Book Two of the "Ascent"; secondly, to read the chapters of St. John in connection with the related parts of the present work. The studious reader will find, moreover, references to the works of St. John in the footnotes, and these will help toward a fuller knowledge of his doctrine.

CHAPTER II

The Divine Union

IN CHAPTER FIVE of this Book Two, St. John describes in detail for the first time the Divine union to which he desires to lead the soul. In the First Book of the "Ascent" there were only occasional glimpses, as it were, of the union of the soul with God. Now that he is treating of the spiritual night, and in particular of that part of the night which is faith, St. John thinks it well to interrupt his treatment of faith and the understanding, to explain what he means by union with God. This prepares the way for what he shall afterwards say in the following chapters.

There is a certain natural union of God with the soul, by which He conserves it in being. If God were to cease thinking of the soul, and this union of Creator and creature were to fail, the soul would at once become annihilated and cease to exist. God's infinite power is necessary to preserve everything in existence, and according to this power of conservation God dwells and is present substantially in every soul, even in that of the greatest sinner in the world. This union is intimate, necessary and continual, but it is not the greatest. There is another union, which, though unfortunately it is not being wrought continually in all souls, is much more sublime. The union of the soul with God through sanctifying grace is a higher life by which the soul becomes a sharer in the Divine Nature. Whereas the former is a natural union, this is a supernatural union. And although God is united to the soul here too, as its Author and Cause, this union is most remarkable in that it brings God to the soul, not only as the preserver of its existence, but even as the object of its operations. In the soul in grace God is present as the object known is in the knower, and as the object loved is in the lover. God is now called, not merely Creator, but the Light of the soul and its Beloved. If previously the union of the soul with God was like that of the canvas and the artist, now it is the union of a child embracing his father. Yes, the union of which John of the Cross has written is the sublime union of grace.

But the life of grace may be conceived in two ways: strictly, as its exists in the essence of the soul, or dynamically, as it blossoms forth in the faculties. Grace, as it is in the soul of the newly baptized infant, is more of a mystery than even the soul itself. Both are unseen, unknown in themselves, and without blossom or sign of fruit, until, like the seed that sprouts forth in new life, they show themselves in activity. It is by activity that both the soul and grace are manifested and known. I do not mean merely external activity, the hammering and forming of matter. I refer to the acts of the faculties, the acts of knowledge and love, for it is these that are most intimately related to the soul and to grace. The nature of a living thing is known by its operations: a good tree is that which brings forth good fruit; the animal shows that it has a sentient principle of life by the lowly acts of knowledge and the material appetites that set it in motion; so also man proves himself to have a spiritual soul by the fact that he has spiritual ideas and spiritual desires. The very fact that man understands the spiritual proves that he has a spiritual soul; and because he can love the beautiful as such, he knows that the life within him partakes of spiritual beauty, and that life he calls his soul.

But not only do the acts or faculties of the soul prove its nature. They also constitute the perfection of the soul, naturally. The soul of a child is imperfect. Even its rational life lies latent in it for some years before development. Speaking only of natural life — it will depend on the use to which the faculties are put, whether this or that soul will become a cultured soul. The very words "culture," "education," "development" denote that the perfecting of character comes about through the powers inherent in one's being, *i.e.*, the faculties of the soul. We speak of certain refined and cultured persons and we say that they must have had a good education, excellent environment or much experience. We admire a gentle and patient spirit and say that such a one must have gone through the crucible of suffering. What is this but to say that the soul is perfected through its acts of knowledge and will?

Speaking philosophically, it means that the intellect is informed in a spiritual way by the species of its object; that the will becomes like that which it embraces — for love makes like, as St. John insists [1] — and the soul is transformed into the object of its love, as St. Thomas agrees.[2] If a soul is to grow in natural perfection, its faculties must attain to their most noble natural objects. This is not a sudden transformation, for perfection comes gradually. The child puts away the toys of youth one by one, and sets its gaze upon the ideals of more lasting worth. "When I was a child, I spoke as a child, understood

[1] A.,I,iv,3
[2] III Sent. d.27, q.1, a.1

as a child, thought as a child. But when I became a man,
I put away the things of a child." [3] There are some, however, who never grow out of childhood: they will not put
away the things of childhood, and consequently, they
never attain transformation into the beautiful and noble
things of life. The state of perfection is not for them.
What is to be regretted is that, very often, persons do not
reach the full age of human life, not for lack of opportunities, but simply because they are attached to the tin-
selled toys of sensual pleasure, and will not put away the
things of a child. Refusing to give up their imperfect
habits of living, they chose not to ascend by the steps of
higher acts and habits, and so fail to attain a more perfect
manner of living.

So it is with the *natural* soul. The soul *in grace* shows a
remarkable similarity to what we have described. Baptized
in Christ, it now bears the image and likeness of God; it is
a partaker of the Divine Nature, and has within itself the
seed of eternal life. But the true image and likeness of
God must eventually become dynamic, even as God is not
mere potency, but most Pure Activity terminating in
Wisdom and Love that are eternal persons. And it is not
only a partaker of the nature of God, but also of the life
of understanding and love which is a unity or totality in
God. Nor can it be content to bury this seed of eternal
life within itself forever, but this seed must sprout, grow,
blossom and bear fruit under the rays of the Divine Sun.
"Now this is eternal life: that they may know Thee, the
only true God, and Jesus Christ, whom Thou hast sent." [4]
We were made to know and love God, even in this life, as

[3] 1 Cor. xiii,11
[4] John xvii,3

the catechism insists. The soul is enabled to do this by means of a supernatural organism: grace, the theological virtues and the gifts of the Holy Spirit. Grace dwells in the essence of the soul; faith, hope and charity in its faculties. And as the soul is the remote principle, and the spiritual faculties are the proximate principles of *natural* knowledge and love, so grace is the remote principle and faith and charity are the proximate principles by which we know and love God *supernaturally*. And the gifts of the Holy Spirit are necessary for the soul to reach perfection in faith and charity.

As the nature of the soul is proved by the spiritual operations of its faculties, so the supernatural beauty of the soul may often be judged by the acts of its faculties, and spiritual directors can, to some extent, measure the sanctity of a soul by its interior acts. But it is chiefly with the progress of the soul that St. John is concerned, and he knows how great a part the faculties must play in the eternal destiny of our spirit. One must know how to use — or not use — one's faculties. Perhaps it may seem strange to say that, if the soul is not to be hindered on the road towards perfection, the non-use of the faculties is a more important matter than their use.

As with natural life, so also with the supernatural, the soul of a child is imperfect. Grace dwells within it, as it were, dormant. Only with the development of the spiritual faculties, can the full life of grace increase, for it is in the intellect and will that faith and love reside. In the soul of a normal child, the natural and supernatural grow up together, the human and the divine take their turn in its knowledge and love. As faith and love grow more and more, the soul is transformed supernaturally (in a limited sense), for here, as in the natural order, the intellect is illumined by spiritual light, the will becomes like that which it embraces, and the soul is transformed into the object of its love, which is God. This is not a sudden transformation, for perfection comes slowly. Neither is it complete or pure transformation, for that is the state of perfection or the "Mount" toward which the soul ascends. Even more true is it here that the child must put away the trifles of youth, and set its gaze upon ideals of more lasting worth. In order to reach spiritual manhood, it is necessary to put away the things of a child. There are some, however, who will not put away the things of spiritual childhood, and, consequently, it is impossible for them to reach the state of perfection or transformation in God.

In the second paragraph of this chapter five of Book Two, St. John says that he intends to treat only of the "permanent and total union according to the substance of the soul and its faculties with respect to the obscure habit of union." Why does he say that this union of the soul and its faculties is *permanent*? Because he is speaking here of the *habit* of union; the habit of sanctifying grace, and the habits of the theological virtues, which may all be considered as one habit of union with God, are permanent in that they abide continually; while the *acts* of union, *i.e.*, the *acts* of knowledge and love, are transient, as he says — ". . . there is no permanent union in the faculties, in this life, but a transitory union only." St. John does not mean that this union of grace and the virtues cannot be lost. They are permanent so long as mortal sin does not drive them from the soul.

And, why does St. John call this union a *total* union? Because it is not only a union of the soul in its essence, but a union of the soul in the fullness of its power, a union of the soul with power to know and love God supernaturally. It is rightly called a *total* union because of the unity of the soul and its faculties. In distinguishing or emphasizing the separate work of the faculties, one is apt to forget that the soul with its faculty of understanding and its faculty of loving are not separate entities, but form a total. It is the soul that understands and loves. Rightly, then, does St. John speak of a total union, because the habits of grace, faith, hope and love are intimately united like the different parts of a tree. Let us compare grace to the roots of a tree, faith to its trunk reaching toward the sky, hope to its branches, as it were, seeking to embrace the heavens, and love to the delicious fruit, towards which all the rest form a preparation or means. The deeper the roots, the higher the trunk may grow; the stronger the trunk, the more numerous or extensive the branches; the larger and more healthy the tree, the more abundant the fruit. So it is with the supernatural organism within the soul: grace is the root striking into the very soil and substance of man's being; and the deeper the root of grace, the higher the trunk of faith; the higher the trunk of faith, the stronger the branches of hope, and likewise, the more abundant the fruit of charity. The supernatural habits are infused, grow and develop together. This is what is meant by the permanent and total union of the substance of the soul and its faculties, with respect to the obscure habit of union.

Now, what is meant by the "obscure habit of union"? Since the soul and its faculties form a totality, their habits too must form a certain totality, and therefore, one may speak, in the singular, of *the habit* of union. But why "obscure" habit? The reason why our author calls this habit *obscure* cannot be fully appreciated until the doctrine of this Book Two has been digested. Let it suffice to say that this habit acquires its obscurity from the nature of faith, which theologians commonly call obscure because it does not fully reveal its object as does the glory of heaven.

John of the Cross quotes and expounds a certain text of his namesake, the apostle St. John; which text in full reads thus:

> He came unto His own, and His own received Him not. But to as many as received Him He gave the power of becoming sons of God; to those who believe in His name: who were born, not of blood, nor of the will of the flesh, nor of the will of man, but of God." [5]

This is a passage that clearly proves the supernaturalness of our sonship and of the grace which transforms the soul into a son of God. Christ gave us the power of becoming sons of God. Not that we are to be born again in a physcial way, as Nicodemus thought, but our rebirth is spiritual. We are born again, not of flesh and blood this time, not even according to the spiritual will of man, but we are born of God. Nothing of earth has anything to do with this second birth, except the sacramental waters of Baptism. It is wholly the work of the Holy Spirit. Unless a man is born thus of the Holy Spirit, he will not be able to see the kingdom of God.

But notice how St. John interprets this passage — mystically, perhaps, but nevertheless in a very real and satisfying way. Not those are to be called "transformed in God" who have only now received sonship in Baptism.

[5] John i,11

These are mere children in the spiritual life. Only those truly possess the kingdom of heaven here on earth, who, being born again through grace, die first of all to everything that is of the old man, attain to great purity of life with no admixture of imperfection, are raised above themselves to the supernatural mode of communion with God which is the state of perfection or pure transformation. In other words, St. John is speaking, not merely of the union of the soul with God by grace in the strict sense, but of the *total* union of both the soul and its faculties, the union of the soul perfected in pure faith and love — (paragraph 5).

That this is a very sublime union may be gathered from the fact that God communicates to the soul His supernatural Being, in such wise that it appears to be God Himself, and has all that God has. All the things of God and the soul are one in participant transformation; and the soul seems to be God rather than a soul, and is indeed God by participation. This is not to say, however, that the soul loses its identity. The soul remains distinct from the Being of God, as it was before, but now it is transformed in God's love, even as the window is transformed by the light of the sun (paragraph 7).

What a sublime union! To learn more of this possible union of the soul with its God, the reader must refer to the "Spiritual Canticle" and the "Living Flame of Love." St. John uses the same terms to designate this union in nearly all his works. We will pick out only a few typical ones from the first two Books of the Ascent:

"pure union with God and transformation in Him" (I,iv,3)
"pure transformation of love" (I,iv,3)

"high estate of union with God" (I,v,2)
"mount of perfection" (I,v,6)
"Divine transformation" (I,xi,6)
"supernatural transformation" (II,iv,2)
"union and transformation of the soul" (II,v,3)
"transformed into a state of perfection" (II,xv,4)
"transformation and union with God" (II,xvi,15)
"Divine and substantial union with God" (II,xxiii,4)

These and many other terms are used to designate
either the ultimate union itself or one of the stages
towards that union. This state of transformation in God
is never long absent from our author's mind. But now we
may ask, "How does the soul reach this mount of perfection?"

In reply it must be said that, ordinarily, union with God
flourishes or increases through love. The habit of grace
and the habits of faith, hope and charity are all ordained
towards the act of love, just as the life of the tree is ordered towards its fruit. But there is also reciprocal action.
The leaves and the blossoms nourish the tree itself, and
so help to increase the very roots to which they owe their
existence. In like manner, the acts of love which spring
from the roots of grace and the stem of faith, cause in
turn an increase of grace in the soul. The tree is a totality: each part of it can increase only as the whole increases.
So it is with the supernatural organism of grace, the theological virtues and the gifts. It increases as a unit; and
since this unit is no other than the total union of the soul,
of which St. John speaks, this total union is increased
through love.

According to this perspective, the spiritual *will* is
supreme, for it is the throne of love. Even in the natural

order, the cultivation of the faculties and the growth of the soul depends on the will, which loves the goal set before it and orders the other faculties as its servants. The will itself is perfected, not only by its own habits, but also by the habits of the other faculties. In these comparisons of the natural and supernatural orders, one thing must not be forgotten: if in the natural organism habits are increased by the perfection and repetition of acts through the inherent power of nature, in the supernatural organism increase and perfection come from God, who gives grace through the merit of charity. These words of St. John (paragraph 4) are to the point:

> Wherefore, although it is true that, as we have said, God is ever in the soul, giving it, and through His presence preserving within it, its natural being, yet His presence does not always communicate supernatural being to it. For this is communicated only by love and grace, which not all souls possess; and all those that possess it have it not in the same degree; for some have attained more degrees of love and others fewer. Wherefore God communicates Himself most to that soul that has progressed farthest in love; namely, that has its will in closest conformity with the will of God.

Love is therefore supreme. Even the Sacraments depend upon love for their greater fruitfulness. But love is both affective and effective. Affective love has God for its sole object, being a participation of that love with which God loves Himself. Effective love has secondary objects, namely, those things within or without ourselves which require our attention and effort. This might be called a participation in God's providence or rule over created things. By both affective and effective charity, we conform our will with the Divine will. I think that it is in this fullest sense that St. John speaks of conformity to the Divine will — not in the ordinary sense of merely keeping the Commandments. In other words, conformity to the Divine will means that the human will participates in the form of God's will, that is, it is supernatural in habit and act. Thus, St. John says that perfect Divine union takes place "when the two wills — namely that of the soul and that of God — are conformed together in one, and there is naught in the one that is repugnant to the other. And thus, when the soul rids itself totally of that which is repugnant to the Divine will and conforms not with it, it is transformed in God through love." "And the soul that has attained complete conformity and likeness of will is totally united and transformed in God supernaturally" (paragraphs 3 and 4).

The soul that hopes to attain perfect union with God ought to remember two things: first, that its perfection depends upon God as its Cause; second, that the soul can and must dispose itself for the degree of union which God desires to give it. As regards the first, John of the Cross tells us that not all souls reach the same degree of union, since this depends upon what the Lord desires to grant each one. Some receive more, some less; but all are content, if they attain to the fullness of their capacity. Even here on earth, as it will be in heaven, souls in the state of perfection enjoy equal peace and tranquility, and each is satisfied, although some of them may be many degrees higher than others. The reason is that each one's capacity is satisfied. Until a soul reaches that measure of purity of which it is capable, it never attains true peace and contentment (paragraphs 10 and 11). The second thing to be remembered is that God requires certain dispositions on the part of the soul. Besides having humility and earnestly praying for God's grace, the soul must rid itself of all that is contrary to Divine union. But, to speak of this will require another chapter.

CHAPTER III

Contrarieties

WE HAVE seen so far that the Divine union to which St. John wishes to lead his readers is a *total* union, that is, a union of the soul in the state of grace acting with its supernaturalized powers. This supernatural life of the soul is infused by God, as everything truly supernatural must be. The spiritual will of the soul is supreme, since the other faculties are subject to it as to their master, and also because it is through love that the soul is transformed. It is necessary, therefore, that the will be conformed — be made one form with — the will of God. This means that there must be nothing in the one that is repugnant to the other. When the soul rids itself entirely of whatever is repugnant to the Divine will, it is transformed in God through love.

God is Love, as St. John the Apostle says. Or, to be psychologically precise, God's will is one infinite, eternal act of purest love. If the human will is to be transformed in God's will, it must become inflamed with a perfect habit of supernatural love. But for the will to possess the purity of love, or to love God purely, is nothing else than to possess the habit of charity perfectly. Many souls are capable of making *acts* of pure love; but this is not the same as having the *habit* of love perfectly. The soul that has not the *perfect habit* of love can make *acts* of perfect love occasionally, but its day's record will show much that falls short of perfect love. Now, love makes like, and when the soul has attained the habit of love perfectly, it becomes like God to such a degree that its state is called Divine transformation.

But since the will depends upon the understanding or intellect, it is necessary that this faculty be also perfected, which happens through enlightenment or illumination. This supernatural enlightenment comes from God, and, striking the intellect as a ray of sunlight strikes a window, it illumines it to a lesser or greater degree, according as it is purified from the mists and stains of creature knowledge. By such supernatural illumination (which is faith) the soul may become so transformed by the ray of light as to seem to be itself a ray of light. The understanding of the soul is like a window upon which is ever beating the Divine light of God.

Again, the understanding may be compared to the power of vision. A picture may be most perfect, with many and most sublime beauties and delicate and subtle delineations, so that its delicacy and excellence cannot be appreciated by all in an equal manner. Less beauty and delicacy will be seen in this picture by one whose vision is imperfect. He whose vision is better will see greater beauty in it. The person whose vision is most perfect will be able to see the most perfections in the picture, although there may remain higher degrees of attainment. Thus the perfection of the soul depends on the purity of its vision, and the more pure the soul is, the more will God enlighten it (paragraphs 6 to 9, chapter five).

What, then, must the soul do to prepare itself? The soul must rid itself of all that is contrary to the illumination of the understanding and the conformity of the will. This is to be understood of that which is contrary not only in

₁action, but likewise in habit, so that not only do the voluntary *acts* of imperfection cease, but even the *habits* of
imperfection have to be annihilated. This is no small task.
As a matter of fact, it is impossible for the soul by its own
efforts to uproot the imperfect habits that are contrary to
the total union of the soul with its God. The Dark Night
of the passive purifications is necessary to eradicate and
burn away these imperfections so opposed to the perfect
habit of love.

What are these *habits* of imperfection? — for it is only
with habits that we are now concerned. What is it that im-
pairs our vision and prevents us from seeing all the delicate beauties in the picture of Divine loveliness? What
are these mists and stains that prevent the window of the
soul from being transformed by the Divine rays? What is
it that is repugnant to the Divine will, and so prevents
perfect conformity of the human will with the Divine?
It is creatures! But, not merely creatures as they are in
themselves. It is our own preoccupation with creatures:
the employment of our natural faculties of understanding
and will upon created things. " . . . the more completely
a soul is wrapped up in the creatures and in its own abilities, by habit and affection, the less preparation it has for
such union; for it gives not God a complete opportunity
to transform it supernaturally."

St. John calls these imperfections "natural dissimilarities and contrarieties." [1] They are natural dissimilarities
because natural habits are wholly dissimilar from supernatural habits: there is no comparison between natural
habits of knowledge and love and the supernatural habits

[1] St. John employs the word "contrarieties" again in D.N.,
II,ix,3.

of faith ad charity. And he calls them contrarieties because, not only do the habits of faith and charity transcend
the natural habits of our faculties, but they are contrary
to them, that is, they are adverse to them. First, the natural operations of our understanding and will are not
able to attain to God in Himself. " . . . no creature whatsoever, or any of its actions or abilities, can conform or
can attain to that which is God . . . " (Paragraph 4). (This
principle was expounded in the first Book, chapters 4 and
5, where it was explained how God transcends every creature and all natural knowledge and every natural desire.)
Secondly, the natural habits are contrary to supernatural
habits, in that these war against each other. "For the flesh
lusts against the spirit, and the spirit against the flesh," as
St. Paul says.[2] (This principle was treated more at length
in Book One, chapters 4 and 6.) Even in the natural order,
certain habits are adverse to each other. For example, the
habit of ignorance is opposed to the habit of wisdom;
gentleness is opposed to severity; justice to injustice. And
what ardent lover will tolerate within his heart any other
image than that of his beloved? There are instances of
musicians, inventors, artists and philosophers who scarcely
thought of eating and sleeping, so deeply were they transformed into their objects, so jealously exclusive were the
habits they had formed. Much more contrary are the
natural and supernatural orders, because the latter is infinitely above the former, and each is extremely jealous of
the other, as is proven by experience as well as by psychology. Therefore, habits of imperfection must be cast out,
in order that the habit of perfection may reign. Childish
things must give way to higher ideals. When one is a child,

[2] Galatians v,17

one may think of and desire the things of a child, but in order to reach spiritual manhood, the things of a child must be put away.

> This is to be understood of that which is repugnant, not only in action, but likewise in habit, so that not only do the voluntary acts of imperfection cease, but the habits of those imperfections, whatever they be, are annihilated. And since no creature whatsoever, or any of its actions and abilities, can conform or can attain to that which is God, therefore must the soul be stripped of all things created, and of its own actions and abilities — namely, of its understanding, liking and feeling — so that, when all that is unlike God and unconformed to Him is cast out, the soul may receive the likeness of God; and nothing will then remain in it that is not the will of God, and it will thus be transformed in God. . . . The soul, then, needs only to strip itself of these natural dissimilarities and contrarieties, so that God, Who is communicating Himself naturally to it, according to the course of nature, may communicate Himself to it supernaturally, by means of grace (paragraph 4).

If the reader desires to know what these imperfections are in particular, let him read again the eleventh chapter of Book One, which explains very well how even the smallest habits of voluntary imperfection are a hindrance to Divine union, and gives some examples of these imperfections.

Before concluding our study of this fifth chapter, let us answer a certain question which someone might ask, namely: "Is this total union of the soul, herein described, a mystical union?" Most of the description in this chapter could, no doubt, be applied to the supernatural life of the commonplace Christian. There are several passages, however, which prove that St. John of the Cross has in mind a mystical union, *i.e.*, a union attained through infused contemplation.

Those who have read the "Spiritual Canticle" and the "Living Flame of Love" will readily see, at least a similarity between the Divine union described here and the exalted states described there under the similes of spiritual marriage and flames of love. Note the use of the terms "transformation," "pure transformation," "perfect transformation" in this chapter, and the frequency of this term in those places. And since the "Ascent" and the "Dark Night" are one, leading to the same union, notice, if you will, the description of perfect souls, their assimilation to God and their participation in the Divinity, (D.N. II, xx, 4,5) and also the simile of the Bride (D.N. II, xxiv, 3,4).

Then, there are indications that this union is attained through the supernatural mode of the gifts of the Holy Spirit or infused contemplation. When St. John describes the perfect as those "who being born again through grace, and dying first of all to everything that is of the old man, are raised above themselves to the supernatural...," what can he mean by placing that phrase on mystical death between the two states of grace and the supernatural? From his whole doctrine we know that he means that the soul is: first, born to the life of grace and the virtues; secondly, it dies a mystical death to itself and to human ways of dealing with God; thirdly, it is raised to the *supernatural mode* of the gifts of the Holy Spirit. This is substantiated by several phrases that tell us about this mystical death of human ways:

... the soul must be stripped of all things created, and of its own actions and abilities — namely, of its understanding, liking and feeling — so that, when all that is unlike God and unconformed to Him is cast out, etc. (v,4)

... the more completely a soul is wrapped up in the creatures and in its own abilities, by habit and affection, the less preparation it has for such union; etc. (v,4)

As though he had said: He gave power to be sons of God — that is, to be transformed in God — only to those who are born, not of blood — that is, not of natural constitution and temperament — neither of the will of the flesh — that is, of the free will of natural capacity and ability — still less of the will of man — wherein is included every way and manner of judging and comprehending with the understanding. (v,5)

... the preparation of the soul for this union, as we said, is not that it should understand or experience or feel or imagine anything, concerning either God or aught else, etc. (v,8)

Let not the reader be discouraged if he does not as yet understand the meaning of such language. This second Book and those that follow were written to teach just what this means, for this is the spiritual night of faith which still remains to be explained.

Summing up this chapter five of Book Two, we say that the union herein described is:

1st, a union by grace.

2nd, a total union, that is, a union of the soul considered in the fullness of its faculties. This union is brought about by the (entitative) habit of grace and the (operative) habits of faith, hope and charity.

3rd,   a union of perfection, transformation or deification.

4th,   an obscure union (by reason of the obscurity of faith).

5th,   a mystical union, in that it is reached or actuated by the superhuman mode of the gifts of the Holy Spirit. Because of the influence of the gifts, a mystical death takes place in the natural faculties and abilities of the soul.

CHAPTER IV

Divine Vesture

IN CHAPTER FIVE of the second Book of the "Ascent" St. John discussed the *total* union of the soul with God, by which he meant the union of the soul considered in the fullness of its powers. He spoke of grace as being the means by which God communicates Himself to the soul, for grace is the soul's sharing in the nature of God and also the root of the supernatural activity of the faculties. But the faculties, although very intimately united to the soul, are nevertheless distinct and require distinct habits to enable them to operate supernaturally. And since, as we have said, increase of grace and Divine union comes to us principally through our faculties, St. John goes on to discuss, in chapter six, the soul's spiritual faculties and the virtues by which they participate in Divine life. So important is the life of these faculties that Books Two and Three were written to teach the soul how to purify and supernaturalize them; and elsewhere in his works, St. John speaks frequently of the work of the faculties.

The faculties are three: understanding (or intellect), memory and will. The theological virtues are likewise three, one for each faculty. This is not the place to discuss whether John of the Cross maintained that the memory is a distinct faculty ontologically, or whether the virtue of hope inheres in the memory in the same manner as faith in the intellect and charity in the will. Suffice it to say that St. John treats of the memory as playing an important part in the spiritual life, and hope as being very intimately connected with the memory. Perhaps this may be best explained by their relation to the idea of possession, for things are said to be possessed by the memory because of its retaining power, while hope regards things that may be possessed only in the future. At any rate, the memory is purified by hope, just as the intellect is purified by faith and the will by charity.

The theological virtues have God as their direct object. Faith unites the intellect to God as the First Truth; this is a truly supernatural act by which God dwells in the intellect — "That Christ may dwell by faith in your hearts." [1] Hope unites us to God as our future possession; this is a truly supernatural act by which God might be said to dwell in our memory so that we do not forget our "hope of the glory of the sons of God." [2] Charity unites the will to God as our Beloved; this is a truly supernatural act by which God dwells in the will — "the charity of God is poured forth in our hearts." [3] If the reader will consult a concordance of the New Testament, he will be surprised to see how numerous and beautiful are the passages on faith, hope and charity. It is because these three virtues, rooted in the soil of grace, form an organism of Christian life. With this supernatural organism the soul is able to live by participation the kind of life that belongs by nature to God alone. Much that we associate with religion is purely natural; not so the infused habits — they make us lead a heavenly life even here on earth; they are the beginning of eternal life and the seed of glory.

[1] Ephesians iii,17
[2] Romans v,2
[3] Romans v,5

Horticulturists seem to perform miracles in the plant kingdom, by engrafting flowers or fruit of a superior quality on a sturdy stock and roots. Thus grow flowers or fruits which could never have evolved from the natural powers of the stock, no matter how carefully it was nourished and pruned. The Divine Horticulturist does something far more wonderful to our souls, by making them bring forth fruits truly Divine. He not only engrafts the stem of faith, the branches of hope and the blossoms of charity in our souls, but he changes the roots themselves — the essence of the soul — by infusing into it the quality of grace, so that a celestial plant may grow in the garden of His kingdom — a plant that may bring forth an abundant harvest of the Divine fruit of love, if it is well cultivated and pruned. And so, John of the Cross may well insist that the theological virtues are the means by which the "soul is united to God according to its faculties," and that the "soul is not united with God in this life through understanding, nor through enjoyment, nor through the imagination, nor through any sense whatever; but only through faith, according to the understanding; and through hope, according to the memory; and through love, according to the will" (paragraph 1). St. John is relentlessly logical in this matter, for it is a question of supernatural life or death. If the supernatural virtues are the Divine life of the faculties, then nothing else apart from these, not even the most beautiful natural virtue, can save them from death. And not only must these Divine virtues be cultivated carefully, but all the shoots that suck away their sap, must be mercilessly pruned. We say "mercilessly" because the reader will find St. John adamant in the chapters to follow, as regards the pruning that is to be done.

The second point to be considered in regard to the theological virtues is that they lead the soul into the dark night of the spirit. Their first and essential work is to unite the faculties to God. Secondarily, and as a negative result, the powers are led into darkness. Does this mean that the faculties are being smothered or annihilated? No, but they are being set in darkness as regards their *natural* objects. However dark, empty and cold the soul may feel when led into this night, it is really basking in the light of faith, and filled with the substance of hope, and warmed with the fire of charity. If the soul is unconscious of its gain, that is because of the immense chasm stretching between the natural and supernatural orders, and because it is not as yet prepared to enjoy its new treasure. Later on, as the Divine sun begins to dawn, things will change, and then natural light will be as darkness to it, the hope of natural possessions as emptiness to it, the warmth of natural affections as coldness to it.

Why must faith, hope and charity cause darkness and emptiness in the soul's powers? First, as regards faith, this virtue unites the intellect with objects which it cannot reach naturally. For, as St. Paul tells us, faith is the substance of things to be hoped for, the evidence of things which the natural understanding cannot see. As regards heavenly things, we walk by faith and not by sight. The things of faith are not revealed to the natural understanding, but are darkness to it. Thus, though faith brings us certainty, it does not lift the veil of obscurity. The union of faith is an obscure union; that is why the soul is united to God by the *obscure habit* of union.

As regards hope and charity, because of their relation to faith they participate in this obscurity. The things that faith reveals only obscurely are the things that we hope for. Hope is not possession, but we hope for the things that we do not yet possess. Hope and emptiness are correlative. If we already possessed God in the light of glory, we should no longer have hope. Since, St. John habitually attributes possession to the memory, it is fitting that he speak of a relation between hope and the memory. The shadows of the things we hope for have a way of lingering in the memory, according to the depth of our hope.

Similarly, charity causes emptiness in the will. But notice that St. John does not say that the reason of the emptiness of the will is because the soul does not as yet possess God as it will in heaven, but this emptiness is an emptiness of all things that are less than God, since we are obliged to withdraw our affection from them all, in order to center them upon God alone. In other words, perfect charity drives out purely natural affections (paragraphs 2,3,4).

It will be noticed, however, that St. John says that these virtues empty the soul of *all things* and that the virtue of hope "renders the memory empty and dark with respect both to things below and to things above." It is clear then, that the spiritual night is a darkness to all things, both to the things of earth and the things above, though for different reasons. If faith reveals supernatural things only obscurely, it also obscures natural things, for we cannot make an act of faith and an act of natural understanding at the same time. So also with hope: if hope presupposes an emptiness of the things hoped for, it also brings about an emptiness of the things on earth, since we cannot make an act of supernatural hope and an act of natural hope at the same time. Similarly, with charity, which does not now fill us with the joy of heaven, but, nevertheless, demands an emptiness or detachment from natural loves, since charity is contrary to natural affection. This helps us to understand why earthly things are contrary to heavenly habits, and why habits of imperfection are called "contrarieties." [4] We may say, therefore, that the total union of the soul and its faculties is an obscure habit for two reasons: first, because it does not unite the soul to God in clear vision and possession; secondly, because the supernatural virtues, in the state of perfection, raise the soul above, and detach it from, the things of earth. For, in order to reach the summit of the mount of perfection, it is necessary to cast aside the old desires and human pleasures, and to enjoy a new state of knowledge and delight; and to quell the aptitude of the natural self, and be clothed with a new supernatural aptitude according to all the faculties, so that the soul's operation, which before was human, now becomes Divine, as St. John said even in the first Book.[5]

It is necessary, then, to inform the three faculties with these virtues, if they are to live a Divine life, as any Christian will admit. But in order to attain to the perfection of Christian life, it is necessary to lead the faculties into the dark, spiritual night, where they are stripped of all things save only these three virtues. This night with which we are at present concerned is called "active," for the soul must do that which it is able to do in order to enter therein. As in the night of sense, St. John prescribed

[4] Cf. A.,I,iv and v; A.,II,v,4

[5] A.,I,v,7

a method of voiding the sense-faculties of their sensible objects and desires, so that the soul might advance towards pure faith, so here, in this and the following Book, he describes a method whereby the spiritual faculties may be purified of all that is not God, and set in the darkness of pure spirituality. The three supernatural virtues and the darkness that necessarily follows are the means and preparation for the perfect union of the soul with God (paragraph 6).

In this method which our author is about to describe, there is found the greatest security against the crafts of the devil as also against the deceits of self-love, which usually hinder spiritual persons on their road when they do not know how to govern themselves according to the purity of faith, hope and charity. Thus, many souls, as was mentioned in the Prologue of the "Ascent," never reach the substance and purity of spiritual good, or at least do not journey by so straight and short a road as they might (paragraph 7).

It will not take us out of our way if we examine the symbolic description of these virtues given in another place in this same work. Expounding the second verse of his poem, he says that the soul goes forth to its Beloved "disguised." A person may assume strange clothing for two reasons: first, to show forth, beneath the symbolism of a garb or figure, the affections and desire that are in one's heart; secondly, to hide oneself from those who would like to frustrate one's designs. The soul, then, wishing to go forth to meet its Spouse, Jesus Christ, puts on a white tunic, which is faith, to symbolize the purity of its love and to dazzle the eyes of the devil, for the devil is blind and helpless before the purity of faith. Next, over this white tunic of faith, the soul puts on a green vestment which is hope. Having set aside its worldly garments, the soul receives the greatest courage from this green garment of hope in God alone, thus lifting itself up from any danger that may come to it from the world. Thus, too, its Beloved is pleased with it, and will grant the soul as much as it hopes for from Him. Lastly, the soul dons a splendid garment of purple, which denotes charity. This adds such grace and beauty to the other two colors, that the heart of the Beloved is captured by it, and the soul, engaged wholly in loving its Spouse, loses all thought of self, being thus freed from the dangers of self-love. Journeying thus disguised, the soul is freed from all dangers and attains to union with God, its highest Good.[6]

Thus, with poetic beauty, John of the Cross insists again that the theological virtues are essentially necessary for Divine union. Whatever else may be added, we have in this a proof that the passive night of the spirit (in which the above passage occurs) is the same fundamentally as the active night of the spirit, though marking a further stage in progress. From this it may be understood how important it is for the reader to remember that the foundation of the doctrine of the "Ascent" and the "Dark Night" is grace and the theological virtues. So far we have encountered nothing in our author that is outside the normal order of the Christian life.

[6] DN., II,xxi. (Dark Night, Bk II, ch. xxi.)

CHAPTER V

Faith

ST. JOHN told us that he was about to describe a method whereby the soul may enter into this night of the spirit, voiding and purifying its faculties of all that is not God, and setting them in the darkness of the three virtues which are the means and preparation for the union of the soul with God.[1] This is the theme and purpose of Books Two and Three of the "Ascent." In the third Book he treats of hope and charity, but with these we are not concerned in this work. In the Book with which we are dealing, St. John takes up the matter of faith, a question not as easy to understand as it is important to master. The reader may well spend time and effort in the study of this matter, for it will prepare for, and simplify, what is to follow. On the other hand, the careful reading and digesting of the principles of Book Three might serve very well as a preparation for those who find difficulty in understanding these chapters on faith.

The first question we have to ask is this: "Is faith supernatural?" We recall that there are two kinds of faith: human faith, by which a man may believe, for example, that a foreign country exists although he himself has never seen it, but believes this truth on the authority of another human being like himself, in whose veracity he trusts. Such faith we see every day, and we know that it is merely natural, for natural social life would be impossible

[1] vi,6

without it. The second kind of faith is Divine faith by which we believe in things revealed by God on His authority as Absolute Truth Itself. Now there are two reasons why this faith is supernatural: first, because the things which are proposed for our belief are above nature — it is the City of God which we believe in; secondly, because, the motive of our belief is the First Truth Itself — only God could reveal to us the existence of that eternal City. Since, then, both the matter and the motive of our belief are above nature, we rightly conclude that the act itself of belief is above nature; in other words, the act of faith is supernatural, even in its principle. This is equivalent to saying that, since our faith attains to the Divine truths by the revelation and authority of Divine Truth Itself, there must be something Divine about it, even though it springs up within ourselves, like a fountain of eternal life. Every Catholic knows that faith is the gift of God. "No man can come to Me unless the Father Who sent Me draw him. . . . He who believes in me has life everlasting." [2] He who believes has eternal life within himself even as he believes, because belief is nothing else than a participation of eternal life on the part of the intellect. "Faith draws Divine things to us." "By faith Divine things abide in us." [3] The acts of knowledge of the greatest natural genius cannot compare with the least act of faith in a child. Even the natural understanding of the loftiest angel cannot reach what a sinner on earth reaches, so long as he preserves his faith. This is what it means to say that faith is supernatural.

The next question is: "Is faith infused by God into our

[2] John vi,44-47
[3] "De Potentia" of St. Thomas, II,q.6,a.9.

souls?" Since it is not in us by nature, it is necessary that
God infuse it. This is how God draws us to Himself,
namely, by pouring into our minds the light of faith which
guides us along the supernatural road. "For by grace you
have been saved through faith; and that not from your-
selves, for it is the gift of God. . . . " [4] Two things are
ordinarily necessary for faith: first, that the dogmas of
faith be proposed to us — and this is a common notion of
faith, *i.e.*, the number of truths to be believed; secondly,
that the mind assent to the things to be believed. As regards this assent, we observe that the doctrines of faith
are proposed to believers and unbelievers alike, so that
the assent comes from the interior of man. Some, who
have the most precise knowledge of doctrine, and even an
admiration for its beauty, are without faith. The Pelagians
said that faith was caused by nothing more than man's
free will, and that man requires only the revelation of
things to be believed; but this has been rejected, for, since
faith is the road leading towards eternal life, it must arise
from a supernatural principle moving man inwardly. It
is God who infuses faith into us.[5] It need not surprise us,
then, when St. John speaks of faith as being supernatural
and infused. Though he applies these terms especially to
contemplation, it is because he thinks of contemplation
as being purest faith.

Allied to these notions of the supernaturalness and infusion of faith is that principle which he invokes so frequently in this Book, namely: "Faith alone is the proximate and proportionate means of union with God." He
does not mean, of course, faith to the exclusion of love,

[4] Ephesians ii,8,9
[5] S.T., II II,q.6,a.1

but as was seen in chapter six, faith is the first of the supernatural virtues and the stem that supports hope and love. Faith alone is this proximate and proportionate means, because in this life, the understanding cannot attain to God except through faith. Our natural faculty of understanding extends only to natural knowledge and could never of itself elicit a supernatural act unless God should be pleased to bring it to a supernatural action.[6] According to a rule of philosophy, all means must be proportioned to the end, that is, they must have some connection and resemblance to the end, such as will serve to attain the end. For example, to reach a certain city, it is necessary to use, not *any* road or means of transportation, but only such as connect with that city. Or again, if a cold and wet log of wood is to be set on fire, it is necessary that it be warmed and dried out by means of heat, which is the means by which the log will have a greater resemblance and proportion to the fire.[7] Perhaps the best comparison is that of light. Rays of light proportioned to the power of the eyes are necessary in order that a person may see. Red or green light is not a proximate and proportionate means of sight for a man who is color-blind. Likewise, there are rays of light by which no one can see. Such rays may affect a photographic plate and so serve as a remote means of seeing. But no object can be visible to the eye of man unless the light is proportionate to the power of sight. So it is with the understanding: by its natural power we "see," as we say, natural truth; but in order to know *supernatural* objects, the Divine light of faith is the only medium which has some connection and resemblance to

[6] The soul has an obediential potency for the supernatural.
[7] viii,2

them in this life. The light of faith is the proximate and proportionate means of being united to God through the understanding, for such is the likeness of faith to the beatific vision, that there exists no other difference except that which exists between seeing God and believing in Him, and faith does not represent God to us other than He is: infinite, transcendent, triune. And so, by this means alone, which surpasses all understanding, God manifests Himself to us in Divine light. And therefore, the greater the faith of the soul, the more completely or perfectly is it united to God. So, St. Paul said: "But, without faith it is impossible to please God. For he that cometh to God, must *believe* . . ." [8]

This makes it easy to understand why the soul calls faith a ladder, and in the very first paragraph of this Book St. John uses the term: "Divine ladder of faith"; and a little later speaks of faith as the "true guide" of the soul.[9] Wherefore faith is greater than miracles, as can be plainly proved from the New Testament.[10] According to the purity of faith will be the increase of hope and love in the soul, and thus the soul is led *essentially* and *directly* toward perfect union with God.[11] It is no wonder, then, that God, desiring purity of faith, should withhold sensible consolations and sweetness in the reception of the Holy Eucharist.[12] The anguish of the passive nights of sense and spirit are the price of increased purity in faith.[13]

[8] ix,1
[9] iv,3
[10] A.,III,xxxi,8,9
[11] A.,III,xxxii,4
[12] D.N.,I,vi,5
[13] D.N.,I,xi,4

The dark night of the soul, especially, is designed to purify the soul of its low manner of understanding and its
weak mode of loving and to prepare it for intense, pure
and strong spiritual communications through pure faith.[14]

Elsewhere in his works, the same concept of faith is to
be found. For example, God is the substance of faith, and
through faith God reveals Himself in secret and in mystery. Faith is like feet which lead the soul to its Spouse.[15]
Faith is a crystalline fount from which spring up the waters of everlasting life; on the silvered surface of this
fount are outlined eternal truths; the gold of the vision
of God is now hidden with plate of silver, which is faith,
but, although faith covers this gold with a surface of
silver, it does not fail for that reason to give us God in
truth, since a golden vessel covered with silver is a golden
vessel nevertheless.[16] Rational understanding of God is
not necessary; faith suffices, for, by means of infused faith,
God infuses also charity.[17] By faith in the understanding,
and by no other means, the soul comes to union with
God.[18]

Summing up our treatment of the virtue of faith, we
say that: first, it is supernatural; secondly, it is infused;
thirdly, it is the only proximate and proportionate means
of union with God. These principles are important, because it is upon them and others that flow from them, that
St. John bases the doctrine of the "Ascent" and the "Dark
Night." Not that he speaks only of faith. Hope has its

[14] D.N.,II,ii,5;iv,1
[15] S.C.,i,10,11
[16] S.C.,xii,3-6
[17] S.C.,xxvi,8
[18] L.F.,iii,48

part; and charity is the fruit of both, completing the work done by faith and hope. The gifts of the Holy Spirit, too, play their role, and much is to be said about Contemplation. But all of these are founded on faith which elevates the initial spiritual faculty of the soul.

But let us continue our study of this theological virtue, and consider what are the principles which John of the Cross draws from this certain and secure doctrine of faith. This we shall proceed to do in the following chapter.

CHAPTER VI

Knowledge of God

FAITH IS the only proximate and proportionate means to Divine union in the understanding. This is the fundamental principle of Book Two. It follows from this that all other things are not proximate and proportionate means; at most they are remote and ineffective means; and much there is that constitutes a positive hindrance to Divine union.

Can creatures lead us to God? To this question we cannot answer an unqualified yes or no. For the truth is that creatures can lead us to God, but *remotely*. When the soul first starts its journey toward its Beloved, it sets out on the road in the bright sunlight which is the consideration and knowledge of the creatures, in order that it may raise its mind to the knowledge of their Creator. This consideration of the created universe is the first step on the road to the knowledge of God. For as St. Paul tells us, the invisible things of God, such as His eternal power and Divinity, can be clearly seen in the visible things that He made. In reverent meditation, the soul walks among the elements of the earth, admiring in the waters the innumerable differences and species among the fish, in the woods the numberless varieties of animals and plants, in the air the great diversity of birds. All of these were set in their places by the creative hand of the Beloved. Raising its eyes to the heavens, the soul gazes upon the unfading beauty of the stars and celestial planets, which in turn bring to its mind the angels and holy souls that adorn heaven. All these speak to the spirit of man, giving testimony of the many beauties and powers with which God has endowed them, thus leaving in creation some trace of Who He is, revealing His greatness, power, wisdom and other Divine virtues. Seeing all the things of earth clothed with such marvellous loveliness, the soul is wounded in love by this trace of her Beloved which is reflected in creatures, and yearns to behold that invisible beauty of the Creator. With this love and desire of God comes a dissatisfaction with the creatures, and the soul no longer desires to use created things as means of mounting to God, for such knowledge is far distant from God, and naught on earth or in heaven can now give the soul the knowledge which she desires to have, since these are intermediaries, and are, as it were, a mockery.[1]

In the beginning the things of earth seem to have great loveliness and are eloquent in speaking the praises of God. Later, the soul realizes that, although the creatures bear some resemblance to God, God is not like created things, for He is infinitely above them. If the beauty of creatures is truly similar to God, His dissimilarity is truly infinite. A statue may be said to resemble a man, but man is far removed from the statue. The creature is like a signpost bearing the name of the city toward which it points but giving no promise of the beauty or wealth contained therein. So created things point the direction towards God, but the distance still to be traversed is without limit.

On the basis of this truth, John of the Cross is eloquent about the nothingness of creatures. All the things of earth and heaven, he says, are as nothing compared to God. All

[1] S.C., iv-vi

the beauty of creatures, compared with the infinite beauty of God, is the height of deformity. All the grace and beauty of the things of earth are supreme misery and unattractiveness in comparison with the infinite grace and loveliness of their Creator. All the goodness of the creatures of the world, in comparison with the infinite goodness of God, may be described as wickedness. All the wisdom of the world and human ability, compared to the infinite wisdom of God, are pure and supreme ignorance, as St. Paul wrote to the Corinthians, saying, "The wisdom of this world is foolishness in the eyes of God." All the liberty and dominion of the world, compared with the liberty and dominion of the Spirit of God, is the most abject slavery, affliction and captivity. All the wealth and glory of all the creatures, in comparison with the wealth which is God, is supreme poverty and wretchedness.[2] Which is an eloquent way of saying that, although the workmanship of the Creator does participate in His being, its being is infinitely below and entirely dependent upon the Self-existence which is God.

Things may be similar to one another in different ways. For example, two things may be alike in form and in measure, as when they are *equally white.* Or again they may be alike in form, but not in measure, as when one is *less white* than the other.[3] Again, the similarity may be wholly analogous, as when we call the lion a king of the forest, comparing the superiority of his animal strength to the rational dominion of a king. Also, the amoeba may be likened to a man because both have life, but what a difference in the concept of life! A grain of dust may be

[2] A.,I,iv
[3] S.T., I,q.4,a.3

compared with an angel as regards the attribute of existence, but their dissimilarity is such as to prevent frequent
comparisons of this nature. And yet this dissimilarity is
not infinite. The grain of dust is not as remote from the
loftiest angel as any creature in heaven or earth is remote
from the infinite God. That is why all that is less than
God is not a proximate but a remote means of uniting the
understanding with God, for, having no proportion to
God in themselves, how can they be a proportionate
means of union for us?

"Here it must be pointed out," says John of the Cross,
"that, among all the creatures, the highest or the lowest,
there is none that comes near to God or bears any resemblance to His Being. For, although it is true that all
creatures have, as the theologians say, a certain relation
to God, and bear a Divine impress (some more and others
less, according to what is more or less dominant in their
nature), yet there is no essential resemblance or connection between them and God; on the contrary, the distance
between their being and His Divine Being is infinite.
Wherefore it is impossible for the understanding to attain
to God by means of the creatures, whether these be celestial or earthly; inasmuch as there is no proportion of
resemblance between them. . . . What angel will there be
so exalted in his being, and what saint so exalted in glory
as to be a proportionate and sufficient road by which a
man may come to Thee?"[4]

St. John's reference to creatures "celestial or earthly,"
whether "angel" or "saint," is not merely a rhetorical
flourish, but he is hinting here, as he will prove very
clearly later in this book, that the popular type of sanctity

[4] viii,3

in which visions and revelations of things both celestial and earthly abound, is not really sanctity at all, but at most the concomitant of true spirituality. The same must be said of any "supernatural apprehension or knowledge" by which is meant the different types of *preternatural* knowledge, which may come from God or the devil, and cannot compare with faith.

It is not difficult to understand that created objects, especially the material contrivances of this world, have no proportion or similarity to God. For to what graven image shall we liken its Creator? What silversmith shall be able to sculpture Him Who is without form? What material thing can compare with Pure Spirit? Likewise, in the realm of spirits, which of them, mingling potentiality with actuality in his borrowed being, shall consider himself something in the sight of Absolute Reality? Every creature is as nothing before *Him Who Is*. However, one may readily admit this, but object that the understanding itself has means of knowing God. For the understanding is a spiritual faculty having spiritual ideas, and is independent in its being, even of the body where it dwells. It is true that the understanding has for its object all being, and that it has a passive capacity even for the vision of God. In this life, however, the soul has no capacity for receiving the clear knowledge of God. When Moses entreated God for this clear knowledge, he was told, "Thou canst not see My face: for man shall not see Me and live." [5] John of the Cross, following in the footsteps of St. Thomas and St. Augustine, believes that some, such as Moses and St. Paul, saw God clearly but fleetingly. Such a favor is

[5] viii,4; cf. also xxiv,2

truly extraordinary and granted to but few.[6] These are exceptions to the conditions of natural life, and it seems that the soul must be rapt out of its corporeal life to enjoy this favor, and the natural understanding must be suspended.

The knowledge of our natural understanding cannot serve as a proximate means to union with God. The reason is that our ideas are derived from the things of this world, and always remain proportioned to the things which we know through them. All that the imagination can imagine or the understanding receive in this life, comes under the category of forms or images received through the bodily senses. And since, as we said, external things cannot serve as a proximate means of union, it stands to reason that our ideas, which are limited and proportioned to those things, cannot raise us to the direct and clear knowledge of God. Thus our natural faculties, by the very fact that they are conditioned by the bodily senses, are naturally limited to the objects of those senses. Wherefore all that can be understood by the understanding, that can please the will, and that can be invented by the imagination, is most unlike God and bears no proportion to Him. The intellect, the memory and the will may be likened to workmen in iron and silver and gold. Shall they be able to form a graven image that is like to Him? Neither the understanding with its intelligence will be able to understand anything that is like God; nor can the will taste pleasure and sweetness that bears any resemblance to that which is God; neither can the memory recall anything that might represent Him. It is clear, then, that none of these kinds of knowledge can lead the

[6] xxiv,3; L.F.,I,14

understanding direct to God.⁷ For God has only one substantial image, His Son, Jesus Christ.

It will help us to understand this if we recall what St.
Thomas wrote of our knowledge of God. He tells us that
it is by a negative method that we reach the knowledge of
God through reason. The Divine substance is above every
form which our intellect can attain, and so we cannot
understand what God *is*, but only what He *is not*. In human knowledge and speech, we define objects according
to their classes, and point out how they differ from other
objects of the same class. For example, we speak of a certain kind of tree, and describe how it differs from other
trees by its form, its fruit, the size of its leaves, etc. And
so our knowledge is perfected by showing how the object
is different from others of a certain genus or species. But
God is above genus or species; therefore we have nothing
with which to compare Him. Since He cannot be classified
with created things, we can know Him only by His difference or dissimilarity from them. For example, we say that
there is no matter in Him (His spirituality), there is no
change in Him (His eternity), there is no potency in Him
(His actuality), no limit of any kind (His infinity), and so
on. All our most learned terminology is negative; and,
although it is true that we can predicate of Him certain
concepts such as perfection, beauty, justice, goodness, it
is because such terms are capable of infinitude. Thus, to
say that God is infinite goodness is to say that His goodness is an infinite distance above our conception of goodness. When we say that God is Beauty, we implicitly mean
that He is *not* the limited beauty of which we have positive knowledge. The more we know of God's dissimilarity

⁷ viii,5

and disproportion from created things, the less imperfect is our knowledge of Him. But our knowledge of God in this life shall not reach perfection until we have removed from our mind every idea that may limit Him.[8] In our present state, human knowledge of God is perfected in that we understand that He is separated from all things and above all things.[9]

"But," as St. John reminds us, "we should never end, if we continued at this rate to quote authorities and arguments to prove and make clear that among all created things, and things that belong to the understanding, there is no ladder whereby the understanding can attain to this high Lord. Rather it is necessary to know that, if the understanding should seek to profit by all of these things, or by any of them, as a proximate means to such union, they would be not only a hindrance, but even an occasion of numerous errors and delusions in the ascent of this mount.

"It is clear, then, that the understanding must be blind to all the paths to which it may attain, in order to be united with God. Aristotle says that, even as are the eyes of the bat with regard to the sun, which is total darkness to it, even so is our understanding to that which is greater light in God, which is total darkness to us. And he says further that, the more profound and clear are the things of God in themselves, the more completely unknown and obscure are they to us. This likewise the Apostle affirms, saying: The deepest things of God are the least known to men."[11]

[8] Contra Gentiles, I,xiv
[9] III Sent., dist. xxxv, q.2, a.2, sol.2
[10] viii,7
[11] viii,6

To sum up briefly the matter of our last two chapters: all the knowledge of our natural understanding can be no more than remote, dissimilar and disproportionate means to union with God. Faith alone is the ladder, the proximate and proportionate means to Divine union. See how important it is, then, to distrust our understanding, to make use of supernatural, infused faith, to increase and purify our faith! Since the "just man liveth by faith," [12] it is necessary that we know how to make progress in faith, which science St. John is anxious to teach us.

[12] Romans, i,17

CHAPTER VII

The Obscurity of Faith

THE REASON why we speak of the spirit being in *darkness* and of the *obscure* habit of union rises from the obscurity of faith. Faith is obscure, say the theologians, and St. John calls faith an obscure habit.[1] Why do we speak of faith as being obscure? Not because there is any uncertainty or weakness in faith, for we have already shown how faith is supernatural and infused and constitutes the only proximate means of Divine union in the understanding. Faith is obscure because it does not reveal to us in clear vision its own supernatural object. Though we have been truly raised to the supernatural order, our intellect does not directly attain to its supernatural object. Our imagination attains through proportionate images to the external world, our understanding penetrates the natural mysteries of being, but the veil that obscures the Divine object of our understanding cannot be pierced save by the light of glory.

But why must faith remain obscure? Does not faith unite our minds to Divine truth? Have we not said that faith is supernatural and infused? If faith is from above, how is it that we must remain in the darkness of this our exile? "We see now through a glass in a dark manner ... "[2] In faith we can distinguish two parts. The proper object of faith is the First Truth: it is the Divine Truth to which

[1] iii,1
[2] 1 Cor. xiii,12

our intellects adhere. It is in this that our minds perform
a truly supernatural act, being moved by Divine Truth
to assent to what it does not understand. To our natural
intellect it belongs to doubt and to err; to God alone it
belongs to be one with the Eternal Truth: and so, when
it is given to our intellect to participate in Unchangeable
Truth, our intellect thus receives a strength and certainty
that is above its nature. Such is the act of faith: a movement in the human mind receiving impetus and direction
from God toward the Truth Which is Himself. St.
Thomas Aquinas is very insistent on this point, that
Divine Truth is the proper object of faith.[3] Defectible of
itself, the human mind is made indefectible by being
joined to the Divine Truth. Faith joins man to the Divine
knowledge through assent. The object of faith is simple;
if the articles of faith are complex, that is because we do
not see God as He is; nevertheless, the object of faith remains simple, for we assent to complex propositions only
insofar as they reflect, like broken pieces of mirror, the
one and undivided Truth. The propositions that we believe, such as the resurrection of the flesh or the Passion
of Christ, sublime as they are, are not the formal object of
faith. That which faith attains is the Divine Truth in
them — the Infinite Truth revealing the truths we believe. It is under this aspect, then, that faith is supernatural, namely, that our intellect receives the power of
participating in Divine Truth. The virtue of faith is at
the basis of our faculty of knowledge, transforming it,
focusing its lens toward the inaccessible light of glory for
which it is now being prepared. One might feel inclined
to doubt that faith is other than natural, if we did not

[3] De Veritate, xiv,8

know that even here on earth our minds contain the seed of eternal life — "This *is* eternal life: that they may know Thee, the only true God, and Jesus Christ, whom Thou hast sent." [4] "He that believeth in the Son, *hath* life everlasting ... " [5]

The material object of faith is that which we believe on the authority of the First Truth. We do not see the First Truth in Itself. But rather we cling to it as it is manifested in those phases of truth which are the articles of faith and make up the Catholic creed. Not all of them have to do with God Himself. Some of them have to do with temporary events or contingent truths such as the Passion of the Saviour or the resurrection of our bodies. But each of them reflects the Eternal Truth in some way: for example, the Passion of Christ was foreseen by the prophets of Eternal Truth, and after it came to pass, in conformity with the eternal decrees, was recorded by the Evangelists under the inspiration of Divine Truth. Likewise with the resurrection of human bodies. Although this belongs to the mysterious future, for those who have the faith it is absolutely certain. Under the impulse of Divine Truth Itself, our minds adhere to the future resurrection of the body because of the certainty of that Truth to Whom all things are present, and from Whom Divine Power is not distinct. Therefore, that which is supernatural in the material objects of our faith is precisely the Divine Truth in them; and that which is supernatural and infused in us is the Divine power in our intellect, and the Divine persuasion in our will, which bring about our voluntary and certain adhesion to eternal verities.

[4] John xvii,3
[5] John iii,36

But what has this to do with the *obscurity* of faith? I have insisted thus far on the supernatural and infused element of this virtue, so that we may now safely consider the *darker* side of the picture, so to speak. Considering now only the material aspect of faith, we see that the truths which are revealed are written and preached in language proportionate to our natural knowledge. As regards historical and human events, such as the life and death of Christ, this is as it should be, for in them there is the human element as well as the Divine. But as regards Divine objects, such as the mysteries of the Blessed Trinity and the Incarnation of the Son of God, the element of mystery enters in. It is this element of mystery and the unknown that constitutes the obscurity of our knowledge and the darkness of our understanding.

We insisted previously that all creatures are as nothing in comparison with God, and that all the concepts of the natural understanding, whether of celestial or earthly beings, are not proportionate to God and cannot, therefore, be a proximate means of knowing God. This we readily granted when it was a question of reasoning; for our knowledge is by symbols or analogy, and as St. Thomas says, we perfect our knowledge of God by removing from our mind every concept insofar as it is limited to creatures. We know God best when we know that He is separated from all creatures and above them all. Now, here is the point: it is this same deficient knowledge which we employ in faith. We take the meager concepts of earth, our ideas of material and created things, which previously we said are remote, dissimilar, disproportionate, and use them to attain to God by a supernaturalized intellect. For example, we say that God is three Divine Persons. Our idea of a person is taken from a human person, created and finite, and never have we seen three of them in one nature. Our idea of Divine is also composed of the thoughts and limitations of earth. There is, of course, a new element of knowledge in the proposition of three in one, but this rather adds to our darkness. If Scripture tells us that God is infinite, we must use the same concept of the infinite which we derived from unaided reasoning. When St. Paul describes God as "a consuming Fire," [6] we may think of the fire in the kitchen stove or the house that we once saw burn down. Again, when we read how St. Paul speaks of God as "Light inaccessible," [7] the best we can think of is the sun giving us illumination from an unimaginable distance. St. John, speaking of Christ's divinity, calls Him the "Word" [8] of God the Father; and perhaps, many picture their father moving his lips, while even the philosopher does scarcely more justice to Christ in applying to Him our finite term of "idea." We are like the Samaritan woman, who, when our Lord revealed to her eternal life under the symbol of living water, asked Him, "Sir, thou hast nothing wherein to draw, and the well is deep; from whence then hast thou living water?" [9] Or, again, we are like Nicodemus, who, when our Lord spoke to him of a supernatural regeneration, could understand nothing but a physical birth.[10] Such, then, is the obscurity of faith. It is because we must liken God and the things of God to that which is proportionate to our na-

[6] Hebrews xii,29
[7] 1 Timothy vi,16
[8] John i
[9] John iv,11
[10] John iii,4

tural understanding. Even when we adhere to God Himself in His interior life, we must call to our aid the gross thoughts of earth, that they may be to us as symbols veiling the inaccessible light. The obscurity of our faith lies in this, that we do not know God precisely as He is, but faith gives Him to us in shadows.

In all this, we must be careful not to diminish the value of faith or to make of it merely a natural virtue. Faith is supernatural and infused, as we said, because its shadows and symbols come down from God Himself, and, though dark and mysterious because written in the language of earth, they are nevertheless Divinely true, and our soul has, through faith, the Divine faculty of knowing their Divine truth. We know as sons of God, even though our inheritance has not been revealed to us except in the hinting tongue of symbolism. "Dearly beloved, we are now the sons of God; and *it hath not yet appeared* what we shall be." [11]

To children the articles of faith seem luminous and clear. God is our Father and the child can see him with his kindly old face and white beard and can almost feel the warmth of his embrace. Is this our Father in heaven? Is this the God from whose creative fingers of pure spirit have tumbled the myriads of stars? And God is our King whom the child can see enthroned in colorful majesty with a sceptre of gold. Is this the King of creation? the King whose rule extends over the immeasurable universe and does not disdain to enforce His laws within the tiny atom? And the child thinks of God as a Trinity, but it is the trinity of the clover leaf, which, though one, is divided

[11] 1 John iii,2

in three separate parts. Is this the ineffable Trinity in
Whom three subsistent relationships or persons, though
distinct from one another, are nonetheless *the One?* — a
unity or oneness so simple that there is not even a division
of intellect and will, of nature and powers, or of potency
and actuality. To children the articles of faith are luminous and clear, but that is because the child does not as
yet attain to the reality undisguised. As the soul becomes
spiritually mature, it begins to realize that its concepts,
though true, are analogous. The hidden reality of the
Divinity is infinitely above all that the dogmas of our
faith make *clear* to our understanding; and, if our concepts are clear, this is a proof that our understanding is
not perfectly attuned to the hidden reality, since that is,
and must be, darkness to our natural faculty.

For this reason the soul in the Spiritual Canticle ad-
dresses her Spouse, the Son of God: "O Word, my Spouse,
show me the place where Thou art hidden." John of the
Cross explains that in these words the soul

> begs Him to manifest His Divine Essence; for the place
> where the Son of God is hidden is, as S. John [the
> apostle] says, 'the bosom of the Father,' which is the
> Divine Essence, the which is removed from every mortal
> eye and hidden from all human understanding. For this
> cause Isaiah, speaking with God, said: 'Verily Thou are
> a God that hidest Thyself.' Hence it is to be noted that,
> however lofty are the communications of a soul with God
> in this life, and the revelations of His presence, and how-
> ever high and exalted is its knowledge of Him, they are
> not God in His Essence, nor have aught to do with Him.
> For in truth He is still hidden from the soul, and there-

fore it ever beseems the soul, amid all these grandeurs, to consider Him as hidden, and to seek Him as One hidden, saying: 'Whither hast Thou hidden Thyself?' [12]

Since God is hidden and secret, faith, which is the means of union with Him, is also hidden and secret. It is more secret than our powers of reasoning. It would be a mistake to explain faith merely as an assent to dogmas: a heretic, convinced by the power of his own reason, may profess belief in certain articles of the creed together with the Christian, and yet that which is essential to faith would be lacking in him. If the heretic's knowledge is luminous, that is because he is basking in the natural light of his own intellect; he sees the dogma merely in a human light. The Christian, on the contrary, does not stop at the surface of the dogma, but his faith terminates in the reality which cannot be other than darkness to the natural intellect, and his assent is a participation in the hidden but Divine Truth instead of a superficial knowledge of symbols. In both the heretic and the Christian there can be an assent to dogmas, but in the Christian there is the secret mirror of faith in which he sees the Divine Truth of that to which he assents.[13] So hidden and secret a thing is this gold of faith that a person may deceive even himself, mistaking the power of his reason for faith. But faith is hidden and secret, being far deeper in the soul than reason, and having regard only for the authority of God. If a man is not prompt to believe on Divine authority alone, but seeks reasons to move his will toward faith, he lessens his merit in that measure in which he mixes the impure light of

[12] S.C., i,3
[13] S.T.,II II, q.5, a.3

reasoning with the pure darkness of supernatural belief.[14]
So secret and hidden, we repeat, is this theological virtue,
that a spirit may seem to have it and yet be totally without
it. For example, the devils have the appearance of faith
so that they tremble for fear of Divine things,[15] but their
assent is only the result of intellectual acumen, and not of
the secret power of faith.[16] The motive of their intellectual
assent is not less than the Christian's, namely, the authority of God, and yet there is lacking to them the secret and
infused light of grace.[17]

Let us take one more illustration to show the tran-
scendance of faith. Man is a rational animal, as they say.
The beast is an animal inferior to man in that it does not
share his powers of intellection. In the order of animality,
however, the beast is not inferior; nay, its powers of sense
are often superior to man's. In the field of sense perception and sense memory, the animal may outdo the
philosopher; yet the animal ever remains in an inferior
order, because he has not the faculty of knowing by ideas
and thought. On the other hand, the man with his gift of
intellect, using a stock of possibly inferior sense-perceptions, builds and develops a spiritual life that associates
him with the angels. Why? Because God has given to man
an interior and secret faculty, which, though it feeds on
sense-knowledge, is almost infinitely superior to it. The
animal grasps the surface of things; man *adheres to the
truth* of that which he perceives like an animal. Make a
similar comparison between the unbeliever and the man

[14] S.T.,II II, q.2, a.10
[15] James ii,19
[16] S.T., II II, q.5, a.2
[17] De Veritate, q.14, a.9, ad.4

who has the virtue of faith. The unbeliever has senses and memory as good as the believer; he also hears the truths of the gospel and the disproportionate or symbolic descriptions of God; he may even have a better knowledge of the articles of faith because of his intellectual acumen. In the field of luminous natural knowledge the unbeliever may outdo the believer; yet the unbeliever ever remains in an inferior order, because he has not that supernatural faculty of adhering to Divine Truth as such. On the other hand, the man with the gift of faith, though his sense-perceptions be enfeebled (so as to make it difficult, for example, to see and hear the preacher of the gospel), and even his reasoning powers be anything but sharp, can build and develop a spiritual life that associates him with the Blessed Trinity itself. Why? Because God has given to this man an interior and secret faculty, which, though it employs and assents to propositions couched in human language, is nevertheless Divinely superior to them. The faithless man adheres to the *natural* truth of what his senses and reason grasp; the believer adheres to the *Divine* Truth of the dogmas brought into his interior by natural senses and faculties. His ability to adhere to them *Divinely* is the power of faith.[18] Faith is secret, hidden and obscure precisely because it is supernatural.

As John of the Cross says, on the authority of the theologians, faith is certain but obscure:

> And the reason for its being an obscure habit is that it makes us believe truths revealed by God Himself, which transcend all natural light, and exceed all human understanding, beyond all proportion. Hence it follows that, for the soul, this excessive light of faith which is

[18] Cf. In Boetium de Trinit., q.3, a.1, ad.4

given to it is thick darkness; for the greater light disables
and overcomes the lesser,[19] even as the light of the sun
overwhelms all other lights whatsoever, so that when *it*
shines and disables our powers of vision, *they* appear not
to be lights at all. Thus the sun blinds our vision and
deprives it of the sight that has been given to it, inasmuch
as the sun's light is great beyond all proportion and surpasses the powers of vision. Even so the light of faith,
by its excessive greatness, oppresses and disables that of
the understanding; for the latter of its own power, extends only to natural knowledge, although it has a faculty
for the supernatural, when Our Lord may be pleased to
bring it to a supernatural action.[20]

This "faculty for the supernatural" of which he speaks,
means nothing more than this, that the human intellect
is capable of being raised to supernatural action through
the infused habit of faith and actual grace.

After describing the spiritual night in the first two
chapters of this Book Two of the "Ascent," John of the
Cross proceeds in the third chapter to explain how the
dark night is the result of faith, insofar as this virtue is
obscure. To make this clearer, he explains how we obtain
knowledge in this life. All the ideas and thoughts of our
understanding come to us through the senses by means of
phantasms or images. When a child is born into the world,
his intellect is as dark as an unchalked blackboard, since
no light of knowledge has as yet touched it. The knowledge of this child grows from the presence of material
objects, for these are transmitted through the senses to
the intellect, which receives them in a mysterious, spirit-

[19] I have departed in this sentence from the translation of Peers.
[20] iii, 1

ual manner. The point we are making here is merely that, in the natural order, a person receives no knowledge except that which he thus receives from the things or persons around him. "From the object that is present and from the faculty, knowledge is born in the soul." Wherefore, if one should speak to a man of things of which his mind had no previous knowledge, he would have no more illumination from them than if naught were said of them. For example, if one should say to a man that on a certain island there is an animal which he has never seen, and give him no description of that animal in order that he may compare it with others that he has seen, he will have no more knowledge of it than before. Or again, if one should describe to a man born blind what is meant by white or yellow or any color, he could understand little of it, however much one might describe it to him. For, as he has never seen colors, he has nothing by which he may judge them; only their names would remain with him, and for want of the experience of light or of that to which it can be compared, he must remain in darkness.

This is the way with faith. It tells us of things which we have never seen or understood. There is nothing on earth — and nothing created, to be exact — which can compare to the Blessed Trinity to Which we desire to be united. Thus we have no light of natural knowledge concerning the Trinity, since that which we are told concerning this mystery has no relation to any sense or faculty of ours; we know it by the ear alone, in disproportionate, human language, but we believe it, though we must remain in darkness like the blind man. Faith is not knowledge which enters by any of the senses, but it is only

THE OBSCURITY OF FAITH

consent given by the soul to that which, as St. Paul says, enters through hearing.[21]

St. John goes on to say that "faith greatly surpasses even that which is suggested by the examples given above. For not only does it give no knowledge and science, but, as we have said, it deprives us of all other knowledge and science, and blinds us to them, so that they cannot judge it well. For other sciences can be acquired by the [natural] light of the understanding; but the science that is of faith is acquired without the illumination of the understanding, which [natural illumination] is rejected for faith; and, in its own light, it [the natural understanding] is lost, if that light be not darkened." [22] In what sense can it be said that faith "deprives us of all other knowledge and science, and blinds us to them"? St. Thomas says that the same thing cannot be the object of both faith and natural science in the same person. That which has been demonstrated by natural reason cannot be the object of faith. The reason is that faith makes one adhere to a revealed truth that has no evidence in our world of nature: "faith is the evidence of things that appear not," as St. Paul says.[23] For example, if a man knows from philosophy that God is *one* and undivided, this cannot be an object of faith for him. For another man, to whom this is not evident, it may be an article of faith. To both, the mystery of the Blessed Trinity is a matter of faith, for that is above philosophy. So, science and faith cannot coexist in the same person as regards the same object considered under the same re-

[21] iii,2,3
[22] iii,4
[23] Hebrews xi,1

spect.[24] In this sense, faith "deprives us of all other knowledge and science," taking this to mean that faith is incompatible with *other* knowledge and science — *other*, that is, than the knowledge and science of faith, for faith, too, is knowledge and science. In other words, faith is incompatible with the evidence of reason in regard to one and the same object. In this sense, it can also be said that faith "blinds" our natural faculty, which mode of expression is used several times in this chapter three. This interpretation makes clear what follows. "For other sciences [than faith] can be acquired by the light of the understanding; but the science that is of faith is acquired without the illumination of the understanding, which is rejected for faith; . . ." If a man should have the evidence of sight or science concerning an object, he could not, by that very fact, have faith concerning it, (St. Thomas would say). The soul must be in darkness, therefore, in regard to one or the other. If it have the light of clear vision or understanding, it cannot have faith; if it have faith, the light of the natural understanding must be "lost" or "darkened." "It is clear, then, that faith is a dark night for the soul, and it is in this way that it gives light; and the more it [*i.e.*, the soul in its natural understanding] is darkened, the greater light [of faith] comes to it." [25]

Even though not all theologians agree with St. Thomas, all will agree that it is impossible for a man to have both natural certainty and faith at the same time as regards the same object. Or, to put the matter more concisely, it is impossible for an act of natural knowledge to coexist with an act of faith. The intellect is one and simple, and there-

[24] S.T., II II, q.1, a.4 and 5
[25] iii,4,5,6

fore capable of but one act at a time. The same is true of
the will. It follows that, at any given moment, the soul
cannot adhere to both natural and supernatural truths.
When the soul is occupied with an act of faith, it must be
deprived of other knowledge and science — of all other
knowledge and science whatsoever. In this sense, it can be
even more truly said that faith blinds the soul and places
it in darkness.

We must admit, then, with John of the Cross that "in
the presence of faith the soul is deprived of its natural
light and is blinded." This is what is meant by the obscurity of faith, and this is the reason why, in treating of
the total union according to the soul and its faculties —
since that union is founded in faith — we spoke of the
obscure habit of union.

CHAPTER VIII

Light and Darkness

It is a terrible thing for a spirit to be torn between light and darkness. Nowhere in the universe are light and darkness so much at home as in the soul of man. In every corner of the world light is at swords' points with darkness. As light recedes, darkness, like a criminal in the night, lurks at its heels. When light returns, the darkness must flee. There is no give and take between them: no compromise, no compact, not so much as even a temporary and treacherous handshaking. Where light chooses to dwell, darkness can find no content. Only when light is beaten off or at least held back, by the defense of thick walls, can darkness seize a moment's rest in some uncertain citadel.

Only in man can these belligerents abide together — in the same soul — in the same faculty even. The reason that they consent to dwell in the same house is that *this* light and *this* darkness are not enemies but strangers. For *this* light is from another world, a supernatural world; the darkness permits its guest to dwell in the higher part of the castle, so to speak. For the light of which we are speaking is the light of faith, and the darkness is the deprivation of natural understanding: that is why they dwell peaceably together.

It is a terrible thing for a spirit to be torn between light and darkness — when it is a question of the light of virtue and the darkness of sin. But here it is not with virtue and sin that we are primarily concerned, but with faith and its power over the natural understanding. There are two aspects of faith with which we ought to be familiar in order to understand John of the Cross: first, faith is light; second, faith is darkness.

SECTION 1: FAITH IS LIGHT

The image of light, which plays a great part in the literature of faith and contemplation, besides being founded on psychological analogy, is used frequently in the gospels. "The people that sat in darkness, hath seen great light: and to them that sat in the region of the shadow of death, light is sprung up," [1] because of the coming of Christ. Not all were able to comprehend the light that shone in darkness. Christ was the true light that was to enlighten every man that comes into the world.[2] This light that came into the world was Truth; if men loved darkness rather than the light, that was because their works were evil, for anyone who does evil, hates the light.[3] "I am the light of the world," Christ had said, "He that followeth Me, walketh not in darkness, but shall have the light of life. . . . Whilst you have the light, believe in the light, that you may be the children of light." [4] Since the life which Christ came to bring was supernatural, the light, too, must be supernatural. Those who have the faith are known as the "children of light." [5] The Cause of this light is God, for "God is light" and "God, who hath commanded the light to shine out of darkness, hath shined

[1] Matt. iv,16
[2] John i,4-9
[3] John iii,19-21
[4] John viii,12; xii,36
[5] Luke xvi,8; Ephesians v,8; 1 Thess. v,5

in our hearts, to give the light of the knowledge of the glory of God . . ." [6]

This simile of light was constantly used in the Christian tradition. St. Thomas used it frequently, comparing three different species of light: first, the light which makes it possible to see material objects; secondly, the light by which we understand intellectual objects and recognize the first principles of being; thirdly, the light of faith, by which we recognize the Divine truth of certain propositions revealed by God. By the first light, material objects are impressed upon the brain; sense-perception assents, as it were, to the existence and truth of external objects. By intellectual light, man assents to the first principles of knowledge; such knowledge is impossible to animals, although they see the external world through the light of day; and the fact that man has this intellectual knowledge and science, proves that there shines within him a light more perfect than the rays of the sun. And just as the light of the sun is a simple thing in itself, but is broken up in the reflection of a multitude of objects, so man's intellectual light is simple, but is able to comprehend a multiplicity of partial and complex truths. To the animal the external world remains complex and without harmony; to man the world is unified and harmonious in his light of truth.

By the light of faith, believers assent to the truths revealed in the world through the prophets, Christ, the Apostles and Holy Scripture. Such knowledge is impossible to unbelievers, even to those who lived with Christ, who knew the Old Testament, who saw the first elements of the Church, because faith is a distinct and higher light

[6] 1 John 1,15; 2 Cor., iv,6

than that of the sun or of natural reason. Faith, too, is a
simple light, and although it may illuminate various and
complex dogmas, and seem, through reflection, to be itself broken up into shades and colors, still it remains itself
undivided, being the light of the unwaning Truth.[7]

How is it, if the proper object of our faith is the First
Truth, that we do not see this Truth in clear vision, as do
the saints in heaven? If, in the early morning, just before
the sun rises over the hills, a man gazes in admiration at
the sky, the various clouds, and the tree tops, all illuminated by the rays of the yet invisible sun, he is like the
man of faith, who, though he does not see the proper object of faith as It is in Itself, still may rejoice in reflected
and shadowy truths that participate in its illumination.
And inasmuch as the sun's rays are visible to us, although
by reflection in multifarious objects, so also the Divine
Truth may be said to be the object of faith, since it is by
the illumination of that Divine Sun that we are able to
see the eternal truthfulness of the articles of the creed.[8]
For faith is a spiritual light by which we see those things
which we believe.[9] The light of our belief is certainly a
higher light and has greater effects than any natural light.
And if this infused light does not bring us a clear vision of
supernatural truth, as the sun manifests material objects
or intellectual light reveals spiritual objects, the reason
is because we participate in the Divine Light here on
earth only imperfectly; in heaven we shall receive it perfectly and see the First Truth in clear vision.[10]

[7] Cf. De Veritate, q. xiv, a.8, ad 5
[8] Cf. De Veritate, q. xiv, a.8, ad 4
[9] S.T., II II, q.1, a.4, ad 4
[10] De Veritate, q. xiv, a.9, ad 2

Coming now to John of the Cross, we see that he speaks of faith as light even when he is most anxious to prove its obscurity. Although faith may be called a dark night for the soul, "it is in this way that it gives light; and the more it is darkened, the greater light comes to it. For it is by blinding that it gives light . . ." [11] Faith is comparable to that cloud in Scripture which gave light by night, for it gives "light and illumination" to the darkness of the soul.[12] This "excessive light of faith" overcomes the lesser light of natural understanding, since this light of faith is great beyond all proportion and surpasses the powers of vision.[13] The soul must approach towards union with God, in darkness, for in this way faith "wonderously illumines" it.[14] To the soul, faith is a "guide and light," [15] while to the devil "the light of faith" is more than darkness.[16] By faith the soul will "see the light," that is to say, "will see supernaturally," [17] and God will manifest Himself in "Divine light" which passes all understanding.[18] Again, faith may be compared to the lamps of the soldiers of Gideon, which could not be seen because they were concealed in dark pitchers; but when the pitchers were broken, the light was seen. Just so does faith contain within itself "Divine light" which will show forth the glory and light of the Divinity, when the pitchers of this life are broken.[19]

[11] iii,4
[12] iii,5
[13] iii,1
[14] iv,6
[15] iv,2
[16] i,1
[17] iv,7
[18] ix,1
[19] ix,3,4

The above passages are sufficient to prove (if that be necessary) that this mystical Doctor of the Church did not regard the first theological virtue as being essentially darkness. Many other examples might be given to show this. And now, keeping in mind that faith is really lightsome, let us see in what sense it is darkness to the soul.

SECTION 2: FAITH IS NIGHT

Faith is not a night in itself, as we have seen. Rather it is "a light that shineth in a dark place, until the day dawn, and the day star arise in your hearts . . ." [20] The dark place is the natural understanding which is deprived of its natural light by the operation of faith. The intellect or understanding is darkened for three reasons, we may recall:

1st, Our intellect does not attain to the clear vision of God in this life.

2nd, The revelation of God, or the material object faith, is written and preached and known by us in the obscure symbols of human language.

3rd, Acts of faith are incompatible with purely natural reasoning. Or, in other words, the evidence of philosophy cannot elicit the supernatural adherence to Divine Truth which is proper to faith.

I hope that I may be pardoned for delaying somewhat on this matter, for it is indeed important. This necessary obscurity of faith is the very foundation of St. John's doctrine, and it is the point where he is most likely to be misunderstood. This Doctor was denounced to the Inquisi-

[20] 2 Peter, i,19

tion in his day for saying, "And this second night, which is faith, belongs to the higher part of man, which is the rational part, and, in consequence, is more interior and obscure, since it deprives it of the light of reason, or, to speak more clearly, blinds it." [21] These words are capable of an erroneous interpretation, but the three principles given above show us their true meaning.

Since, faith is, so to speak, a dark night to the soul, let us see now what practical conclusions may be drawn for the spiritual life. But, let us briefly review our principles:

1st, Divine union or transformation of the soul is attained through grace and love.

2nd, This is a total union of the soul and its faculties. Therefore, the theological virtues must perfect the faculties.

3rd, Faith is the only proximate and proportionate means to union with God.

4th, All that is less than faith, *i.e.*, no creature nor any concept of the understanding, can be more than a remote and disproportionate means of Divine union.

5th, Faith is light; nevertheless it causes darkness in the understanding.

Realizing that faith alone can unite the understanding to God, and that to have faith purely, *i.e.*, without any admixture of anything less than faith, the soul must be in darkness, the soul ought, indeed, to prefer the darkness in order that it may be guided by faith alone. But what is this darkness which the soul must have, in order to enter

[21] ii,2; also Peers translation, Vol. III, p. 392

into the abyss of faith? [22] First, there is the sensual part of the soul which has to do with creatures and temporal things. Of this St. John already treated in book one, speaking of the night of the senses. It is clear that the soul cannot attain to God by means of the senses, and therefore it must be in darkness with respect to all that can enter through the eye, and to all that can be received through the ear. And since the imagination (or fancy) cannot picture anything but what comes through the senses, the imagination, too, ought to be in darkness. But the spiritual faculties depend upon the senses and imagination, and therefore, the understanding, memory and will must also be darkened. St. John mentions the understanding frequently, as being the principle of knowledge, but he also speaks of the will and the desire or any other sense. It is clear, then, that *all* the natural faculties must be darkened. "He that would attain to being joined in one union with God must not walk by understanding, neither lean upon experience or feeling or imagination, but he must believe in His Being, which is not perceptible to the understanding, neither to the desire nor to the imagination nor to any other sense, neither can it be known in this life at all." [23] The soul must not cling to any "will or manner of its own, or to any other act or to anything of its own," if it will attain to Divine union in its perfection. [24] In a word, the soul must be in darkness in regard to *all its natural operations*. This is extreme darkness, indeed! But, let it be understood that St. John is speaking of darkness or detachment "according to the affection and will — so

[22] iv,1

[23] iv,4

[24] iv,4

far as this rests with itself." Union with God is consummated in the *will* through *love*; what wonder, then, that
the soul must be detached in *affection* and *will*? Moreover, this is a *supernatural* transformation to which he is
leading the soul; that which is *natural* must therefore be
left in darkness. The soul must be voided of all such
things as can enter its capacity — must completely and
voluntarily void itself of all that can enter into it through
affection and will, not only in the lower and sensual part
of the soul, but also in the rational and higher part — must
be set in darkness and carried far away from all that is
contained in its nature. The reason is that union with
God, being supernatural, is something that cannot be
comprehended by human ability.[25]

Faith alone is the soul's guide and light. All the natural
abilities of the soul will cause it to stray. As a consequence
it must be in total darkness to all that it understands and
experiences and feels and imagines; else it cannot be
guided by faith alone. Take the example of a blind man.
If he is not quite blind, he may refuse to be led by a guide.
Seeing a little, and being able to distinguish a certain
direction, he may think it better to go in whatever direction he sees, because he is not able to see a better way.
Thus the blind man can lead astray a guide who sees more
than he, since the power of choice lies with himself, and
not with the guide whom he hires. So also the soul that
relies on its own feeling, experience or knowledge of God
will easily go astray, since it will not be guided by faith
alone.[26] But the soul that blinds itself in its natural faculties upon this spiritual road will be able to see superna-

[25] iv,2
[26] iv,3

turally. Those difficult words of our Lord are easily interpreted in this sense: "For judgment I am come into this world; that they who see not, may see; and they who see, may become blind." [27]

The reader without theological knowledge will find a great difficulty in St. John's use of the word "supernatural," which, however, is easily explained. He says that if the soul have courage to pass beyond its natural limitations, it will enter within the limits of the "supernatural." In this sense he means that which is supernatural in substance, such as grace, the theological virtues and the gifts of the Holy Ghost. In other places he says that the soul must remain detached from "supernatural" things and that "no supernatural apprehension or knowledge in this mortal life can serve as a proximate means to the high union of love with God." [28] By "supernatural" is here meant knowledge which comes outside of the course of nature, e.g., visions, which may be produced by God or the devil. The more proper term would be "preternatural." The later chapters of this Book Two of the "Ascent" are given over to the explanation of such "supernatural" apprehensions. It seems that sometimes he uses the word "spiritually" in this sense (cf. iv,6).

With relentless logic, John of the Cross goes a step further and says that the soul must pass beyond everything to "unknowing." [29] See to what a state our logic has led us! Let us quote John of the Cross from several sources:

> Right well doest thou, O soul, to seek Him ever in His hiding-place, for greatly dost thou magnify God,

[27] iv,7
[28] Cf. A,I,v,2; A,II,iv,2; viii,5
[29] Cf. A,I,iv,5; also A,II,iv,4

and closely dost thou approach Him, when thou holdest Him to be far more lofty and profound than all that thou canst reach; remain thou not, therefore, either partly or wholly, in that which thy faculties can comprehend. I mean, be thou never willingly satisfied with that which thou understandest of God, but rather with that which thou understandest not of Him; and do thou never rest in loving and having delight in that which thou understandest or feelest concerning God, but do thou love and have delight in that which thou canst not understand and feel concerning Him; for this, as we have said, is to seek Him in faith. Since God is unapproachable and hidden, as we have likewise said, however much it seem to thee that thou findest and feelest and understandest Him, thou must ever hold Him as hidden, and serve Him after a hidden manner, as One that is hidden. And be thou not like many ignorant persons who hold a low conception of God, understanding God to be farther off and more completely hidden when they understand Him not and have no consciousness or experience of Him; the truth being rather the contrary, that, the less clearly they understand Him, the nearer they are approaching to Him, for, as says the prophet David, He made darkness His hiding-place. Thus, when thou drawest near to Him, thou must perforce be conscious of darkness because of the weakness of thy sight. Well doest thou, then, at all times, whether of adversity or of temporal or spiritual prosperity, to hold God to be hidden and thus to cry to Him, saying: "Whither has Thou hidden Thyself?" [30]

In order to reach Him, a soul must rather proceed by not understanding than by desiring to understand.[31]

[30] S.C., 1,12
[31] A.,II,viii,5

The perfections of God, since they are things unknown after a human manner, must be approached "by unknowing and by Divine ignorance." [32]

> For, as we say, the goal which it seeks is beyond ... even the highest thing that can be known or experienced; and thus a soul must pass beyond everything to unknowing.[33]

Does this Carmelite friar mean that our concepts of God are worthless? Does he mean that, because the language of God's revelation is human and symbolic, it does not approach to God or benefit us? Does he mean that the meditations of spiritual persons, since they are composed of the inadequate images and thoughts of created things, are useless? Certainly not! Meditation, properly made, is profitable and necessary, at least for beginners. It is difficult to say how often merely *natural* meditations are made. Certainly, there need not necessarily be anything *supernatural* about a meditation, for example, on the existence or power or beauty of God, since natural reason alone is sufficient to grasp and juggle these concepts. May not a merely natural meditation be made on Jesus Christ as a perfect human character, since even an atheist should admit the authenticity of the gospels and the nobility of their central character? And even when the thoughts are garnered from the articles of the creed and we adhere to them through Divine faith, how easy it is to cast the natural light of our puny minds merely on their surface, so that we seldom think and love God as the transcendent, incomprehensible Good, hidden in thick darkness! The point which St. John is stressing here is that the soul can-

[32] D.N.,II,xvii,7
[33] iv,4

not reach the perfection of faith unless it proceed in darkness. We do not adhere to the symbols of our creed merely,
but to that which is hidden beneath them. Images and
thoughts are not the proper object of faith, but they are
the glass through which the eye of faith looks towards its
object: "We see now through a glass in a dark manner." [34]
There is no getting away from this principle: the soul
cannot perfect its faith except in darkness!

"But," someone will object, "to proceed in darkness is
to be without thought. And, to be without thought, is to
be without love. Therefore, such darkness is nothing else
than a lack of activity. To be in the dark is to be in idleness." This is a good objection. We must admit that ordinary faith (or beginner's faith) does require images and
thought. But, the question comes up here: Is John of the
Cross speaking of this incipient faith? Is he not rather
speaking of mystical faith? We must leave the answer of
this question to another chapter.

[34] Cf. De Veritate, xiv,8, ad 11. Also 1 Cor. xiii,12

CHAPTER IX

Perfection of Faith

As THE READER followed the exposition of John of the Cross through the first nine chapters of this second Book of the "Ascent," he was perhaps struck by two things: first, that our author was speaking of ordinary Christian faith — supernatural, certain, lightsome and yet obscure; secondly, that there were indications that he was speaking of something extraordinary or at least unfamiliar to most Christians. Such was the assertion, for example, that the obscurity of faith demanded that the soul proceed to "unknowing." Then we came upon this significant statement: "For the soul that attains to this state has no longer any ways or methods." [1] Of what state is he speaking? What state is it that no longer has ways or methods? It will be well to clear up this question by a closer examination of these chapters, before we go further.

Let us first find the answer to this question: For whom was this book written? Or to whom may this Night of the Spirit apply? First, it should be noted that it is addressed to "the soul," by which is meant "souls" in general. Not all souls, however, but those who, as beginners, have passed through the night of senses. This is clear from the first chapter, where St. John speaks of the transition from the night of the senses to this night of the spirit. The soul of which he spoke in the first stanza of his poem is the same of which he now speaks in the second stanza, except that

[1] iv,5

there has been some progress. We must keep in mind that this doctrine is "as well suited to one kind of person as to another, if they desire to pass to the detachment of spirit which is here treated." [2] Then, too, this night of the soul is a *unity* which the soul must pass through if it is to reach the dawn of perfection.[3] The careful reader cannot help but conclude that St. John is treating of the *normal* way of the spiritual life. That certain dispositions are necessary at each stage of the journey, cannot be denied: note that he is addressing the "devout reader," and that things of great importance shall be said for "the person that is truly spiritual." [4] Whereas the soul was once a beginner, now, having been detached from temporal things in the first part of this night, it is a "spiritual person." [5] St. John wrote not only for souls seeking direction, but also for "those who teach them," [6] that is, the master and the disciple,[7] and confessors.[8]

Secondly, of what kind of faith is St. John speaking? Is he using the word "faith" in some sublimated or unchristian sense? Or perhaps, in a loose, poetic sense? Beginning to speak of faith (in chapter three), he treats of the obscurity of faith as being — poetically speaking — a dark night to the soul. He refers for authority to the theologians, to philosophers and to the Scripture; it is plain that he speaks here of the Christian virtue. If he refers to "pure

[2] Prologue, 8
[3] Cf. ii
[4] i,3
[5] vi,7; vii,4,8,13; xi,11; xii,6
[6] xvi,14
[7] xviii,1
[8] xxii,19

contemplation," it is merely that it may be clearly "understood that the soul must be in darkness in order to have
light for this road" of Christian contemplation. Because
of this obscurity of faith, it follows (cf. chapter four) the
soul must be willing to enter into this darkness, which
darkness pertains to the exterior and interior senses, the
understanding, the will, feelings, experience or any means
other than faith — such things as visions and revelations
not excepted. The title of this chapter four is not to be
overlooked. It proves that St. John is directing the soul
towards the highest contemplation, which can be reached
only in darkness — the necessary result of faith. This contemplation, then, proceeds from faith, and will participate
in its obscurity. So far, there has been nothing in John of
the Cross that should alarm us. But, now he speaks of
"unknowing"! How can there be faith or Christian contemplation without knowledge of the mysteries of our
redemption? Insofar as one proceeds towards *unknowing*,
does one not smother all possibility of spiritual life? The
answer is that "the soul that attains *to this state* has no
longer any ways or methods," [9] because it is united to God,
not through knowing, but through contemplation.

A little later, St. John tells us explicitly that he is primarily interested in contemplation, as the means of union.
"And it must be noted that I am now speaking *particularly*
to those who have begun to enter the state of contemplation . . ." [10] Notice that he is not speaking exclusively to
these; others who are spiritually-minded may also gain
much profit from his words. "But let us now address the
understanding of the spiritual man, and particularly that

[9] iv,5
[10] vi,8

of the man whom God has granted the favour of leading him into the state of contemplation (for, as I have said, I am now speaking to these in particular), and let us say how such a man must direct himself toward God in faith, and purify himself from contrary things, constraining himself that he may enter upon this narrow path of obscure contemplation." [11] From which it is clear that St. John wishes to lead souls, and particularly those souls who have already begun to be contemplative, into the state of contemplation. For this reason he describes the obscurity of faith, in which "obscure contemplation" is rooted, in order that the soul, directing itself towards God in faith, may avoid "contrary things." What are these contrary things? Evidently, the activity of the understanding, the desire to comprehend God by knowing Him.

> It is clear, then, that none of these kinds of knowledge can lead the understanding direct to God; and that, in order to reach Him, a soul must rather proceed by not understanding than by desiring to understand; and by blinding itself and setting itself in darkness rather than by opening its eyes, in order the more nearly to approach the ray Divine. And thus it is that contemplation, whereby the understanding has the loftiest knowledge of God, is called mystical theology, which signifies secret wisdom of God; for it is secret to the very understanding that receives it. For this reason S. Dionysius calls it a ray of darkness.[12]

To the question, of what kind of faith is St. John speaking, we answer, he is speaking of the theological virtue of

[11] vii,13
[12] viii,6

faith, because it is from this faith (together with the gifts of the Holy Ghost) that contemplation proceeds, and it is in the darkness characteristic of faith that the soul must travel in order to avoid the obstacles to contemplation. If the Carmelite friar seems to identify or mingle the concepts of faith and contemplation at times, that is because he thinks of faith as the stem on which contemplation flowers. With these principles in mind, these early chapters on faith should offer no insurmountable difficulty.

Let us summarize the nine chapters that we have covered so far. The Night of the Spirit is in the rational part of man's soul. It is a night of faith, which virtue by its very nature tends to darken the understanding. Because obscure contemplation is the flower of pure faith, it is necessary for the soul to proceed in darkness if it is to avoid the obstacles to contemplation. Faith, perfected in the obscurity of contemplation, is the proximate and proportionate means to the Divine union of love.[13] Later, we shall be in a better position to understand how St. John interchanges the terms "faith" and "contemplation" because of their close relationship, and how, therefore, there are elements of contemplation even in these early chapters.

[13] Cf. title of ix

CHAPTER X

Contemplation

ALTHOUGH ST. JOHN lingers lovingly on the subject of contemplation for a little while, here in the active Night of the Spirit, it is not with contemplation that he is immediately concerned, for contemplation belongs rather to the passive nights. He treats of it now only in passing, and several reasons may be given why he takes it up at all: first, because of its relation to faith [1]; secondly, because contemplation is the means of perfection and purification, and the kind of prayer he wishes the soul to attain; thirdly, because contemplation is one of the types of spiritual knowledge which the soul may encounter on the spiritual road [2]; but chiefly, because the subject of meditation, taken up in chapter twelve, requires the mention of contemplation for completion. Although some of this matter is by way of parenthesis or digression, it is not unrelated to the purpose of this Book, and not therefore without profit.[3]

[1] When the relation of faith and contemplation is fully appreciated, it may be better understood why frequent references are made to contemplation in these early chapters. Cf. iii,6; title of iv; vii,13; viii,6; ix,2.

[2] x,4

[3] xii,7 to xv may be said to be parenthetical, in that they deal with contemplation, which is properly the subject of D.N., I. Again, they may be said to be necessary, for no one should abandon meditation unless he is confident that he has something to take its place. I think no one would wish these chapters to be omitted.

Following the example of our author, we shall speak of contemplation only insofar as it is related to this night of faith. But first, it will help to give a descriptive definition of mystical contemplation. St. John is not speaking here of acquired contemplation, by which we mean that loving knowledge of God which is the fruit of personal activity aided by grace. He is speaking rather of a loving knowledge of God which is not the fruit of human activity, but the fruit of a special inspiration of the Holy Spirit. Acquired contemplation (as understood here) is not free from the imperfections of meditation, since it uses the concepts of the understanding ennobled by faith. Infused contemplation, however, is a simple and loving knowledge of God, *above reasoning* and in the *obscurity* of faith, demanding a higher illumination and inspiration of the Holy Ghost. The essential difference between the two (at least for practical purposes) is that infused contemplation is received in a superhuman mode, *i.e.*, independently of the use of sense images or the process of reasoning.

This contemplation, according to St. John, is mystical theology, that is, secret wisdom of God. Through this manner of prayer the understanding has the loftiest knowledge of God in a way which does not prevent it from being a secret to the very understanding that receives it.[4] It must not be confused with the contemplation of philosophers, for it is not an *act* of the understanding at all, being above the power of that faculty, but rather it is a *receiving*, and, as such, might be called "an inflowing of God in the soul," whereby God secretly instructs the

[4] viii,6

soul in the perfection of love [5] and "feeds and refreshes" the soul without its active help.[6] It is the science of love — an infused and loving knowledge of God, which enlightens the soul and at the same time enkindles it with love.[7] The reader who wishes further description of this celestial prayer should read elsewhere in our saint's writings.[8]

There are two elements in contemplation: first, knowledge, simple, direct, unclouded by images and reasonings (at least in its purest form); this takes place, of course, in the understanding and gives contemplation its name. The second element is love, and the more important of the two, for contemplation is a science of love. As regards the understanding, St. John speaks of it in such ways as these: "supernatural knowledge," [9] "Divine knowledge," [10] "pure intelligence," "heavenly intelligence," [11] and "general and confused knowledge." [12] If union with God "transcends all knowledge," [13] this is to be taken to mean that this knowledge of contemplation is above all the knowledge of the understanding when this faculty is not being moved by the Holy Spirit. As regards the second element, he speaks of "sweetness and love being communicated" to the will,[14] of "this loving or peaceful state

[5] D.N., II,v,1
[6] D.N.,I,xiv,1
[7] D.N.,II,xviii,5
[8] Especially D.N.,viii-x; L.F.,iii,32-67
[9] xiv,11
[10] xiv,14
[11] xiv,11
[12] xv,3
[13] xiv,4
[14] xiv,12

of waiting upon God." [15] We are assured that "Divine calm and peace will be infused into his soul, together with a wondrous and sublime knowledge of God, enfolded in Divine love." [16] More often St. John speaks of these two elements as a unity, as, for example, "a knowledge, general and loving," [17] "loving knowledge," [18] "general and loving attentiveness or knowledge of God." [19] Thus contemplation may be described "as an act of knowledge, confused, loving, passive and tranquil, wherein it [the soul] drinks of wisdom and love and delight." [20]

These two elements are communicated to the soul together, more often than not. However, it may happen that God will communicate Himself to the understanding only, which is the case when the soul cannot observe what is happening in it. But when God enriches the will also, which happens almost invariably, the soul is able to perceive, if it will reflect thereon, that it is occupied with God, for it experiences sweetness and love without particular knowledge of the object of its love. [21] For sake of completeness, it may be well to mention that the spiritual memory too is occupied by this contemplation: the three spiritual faculties are united, like an earthly trinity, in this loving knowledge; [22] the imagination, however, may wander. [23]

[15] xv,2
[16] xv,5
[17] xiii,4
[18] xiii,7
[19] xiv,6
[20] xiv,2
[21] xiv,12
[22] xiv,6
[23] xiii,3; xiv,5

In spite of the fact that contemplation is composed of two elements so familiar to human beings, namely, knowledge and love, the discussion of it is confusing, as St. John confesses, and in his day at least, was seldom treated as he treats it, because of its being extraordinary and obscure.[24] Although he professes to give merely practical hints on contemplation at present, nevertheless we may glimpse not a few revealing features of this manner of prayer. Let us examine some of these features and compare them with faith.

We said that faith, being supernatural, was infused into the soul. Contemplation, too, is supernatural and infused, but in a higher sense than faith. Besides calling it supernatural knowledge, it is clear that it is "received" into the soul, for "the faculties are at rest, and are working, not actively, but passively, by receiving that which God works in them" [25] "The soul, then, will frequently find itself in this loving or peaceful state of waiting upon God without in any way exercising its faculties — that is, with respect to particular acts — and without working actively at all, but only receiving." [26] God is working; the soul is passive; if the soul does anything at all, it is waiting upon God "with loving attentiveness." [27] Indeed, it seems doubtful if even this attentiveness to God is distinct from contemplation. St. John seems to identify them, for the third sign of contemplation is that the soul have an "attentiveness and knowledge, general and loving." [28] When

[24] xiv,14
[25] xii,8
[26] xv,2
[27] xiii,4
[28] xiii,4

the contemplative turns away from meditation, "he needs this general and loving attentiveness or knowledge of God." [29] Certainly this attentiveness to God is not an exercise of the faculties; rather the soul itself does not work at all, *"save only by waiting upon God and by loving Him without desiring to feel or to see anything."* [30] At any rate, it is a willingness, perhaps at times implicit, to wait for the action of God and to refrain from acting with one's natural faculties. To incipient contemplatives "the advice must be given to learn to *abide attentively* and *wait* lovingly upon God in that state of quiet, and to pay no heed either to the imagination or to its working." [31]

Can such a soul be said to be idle? The soul would certainly be idle if it were occupied with neither meditation nor the loving knowledge and attentiveness of which we have spoken.[32] But if the soul observes within itself the signs which St. John gives, it may be sure that, although it seem to be doing nothing, it is well occupied.[33]

If the soul seems to be doing nothing, that is because its natural faculties are at rest, and since the work is all on God's side, the soul enjoys "quiet and repose," "peace and rest of interior quiet, where it is filled with the refreshment of God," "peace, rest, pleasure and delight without labor." [34] The contemplative finds "tranquillity" in his proper kind of prayer, but "great weariness and distaste" in reasoning and meditation.[35] Hence contem-

[29] xiv,6
[30] xv,2
[31] xii,8
[32] xiv,7
[33] xiv,13
[34] xii,6,7; xiii,7
[35] xiv,3

plation is like a spiritual slumber in which the spiritual
faculties are no longer awake to their own human operations, but the soul is still very much alive, being lifted
up to a supernatural plane of wakefulness.[36] If, as may
happen in extraordinary cases, the imagination and the
senses should participate in this spiritual sleep, the soul
would enter into a great forgetfulness, so that it would
not know where it has been or what it has done, nor be
aware of the passage of time, passing many hours in this
forgetfulness, and, when the soul returns to itself, it would
believe that less than a moment had passed, or no time at
all. For contemplation lifts the soul into the land of
things eternal, and only the sense faculties keep it in
touch with (or chained to?) the things of time.[37] Before
leaving this consideration of the infused nature of contemplation, it may be well to say something of the term
"passive," which occurs frequently in St. John. "Passive"
does not necessarily mean "inactive," but rather it means
the potency or disposition to *receive*. Thus the wax is
passive in regard to the impression of the seal, because it
is ready to receive it. Our eyes are in *passivity* as regards
light, because they always receive the light when light
is present to it without an intervening obstacle; and it is
not possible for the eyes to *act* of themselves, that is, to
perform the action of vision unless light acts upon them
from without; yet, you would not say that the eyes are idle.
Rather, passivity in this sense is identical with activity;
and that which is passive in this sense merely requires the
action of an external agent to activate it. It is in this way
that the intellect and will are passive towards God, re-

[36] xiv, 11
[37] xiv, 10-12

ceiving from Him the excellent activity of supernatural
"loving knowledge" without any natural stimulus. Thus,
our first comparison of faith and contemplation has revealed that they are alike infused.

As we saw previously, faith is a spiritual light illuminating the truths of revelation. Contemplation, too, is a
light: "the Divine light of Divine union." [38] But whereas
the light of faith casts its glowing rays of eternal truth
upon articles of the creed to which the soul might not
have assented, this light of contemplation does not bring
into visibility any of the images of the imagination or the
concepts of the understanding, if it be perfectly pure. We
compared faith to the sun rising behind the hills and illuminating the clouds, the tops of trees and other high
objects. But the light of contemplation should be compared to light that has not been reflected by an earthly
object but is received directly from the source of light
without any intermediary. "Then God communicates
Himself to it passively; even as to one who has his eyes
open, so the light is communicated to him passively, without his doing more than keep them open. And this reception of light which is infused supernaturally is passive
understanding. We say that the soul works not at all, not
because it understands not, but because it understands
things not discovered by its own industry and receives
only that which is given to it, as comes to pass in the illuminations and enlightenments or inspirations of God."
The soul must be careful not to obstruct this "pure and
serene light" by interposing other lights which have no
comparison with this "Divine light," such as images, ideas
and reasonings. Any lights of the natural understanding

[38] xxvii,5

would be as clouds impeding the vision of this "pure and simple general light of the spirit." This marvelous light never fails as does the setting sun, but is ever present to the eyes of the soul; if the soul does not receive it, that is because the soul itself has covered itself with veils which keep it in the shade.[39] The soul ought to be like a window that is free of mists and stains. If a window is wholly pure and clean, the ray of sunlight will transform it and illumine it in such wise that it will seem to be a ray and will give the same light as the ray, but if the window is less free from dust and dirt, it will be illumined to a lesser degree. So also, the soul will participate in the nature of the supernatural light in proportion as it is free from the mists and stains of natural knowledge.[40] The difference, then, between the light of incipient faith and the light of that perfect faith which is contemplation is that the latter is independent of natural forms and images, and the more pure and simple as it is free from them.

In speaking of faith in a previous chapter, we said that it was not only light, but paradoxically, also darkness. Contemplation likewise is not only light but darkness, and the more pure the light, the more obscure is the darkness. The darkness of faith was threefold; so also the darkness of contemplation. First, faith and contemplation are dark or obscure because neither reveal God in clear vision. Secondly, they are dark because they blind the understanding to all that is merely natural and temporal. The third kind of darkness is one of both comparison and contrast between faith and contemplation. Both faith and contemplation blind the natural reason; more precisely,

[39] xv,2-4
[40] v,6-7

the act of either faith or contemplation cannnot coexist in the intellect with an act of merely natural reasoning. The point of contrast is this: faith blinds the purely natural reason: the act of faith is incompatible with an act of purely natural reasoning. But faith does employ and illumine the faculty of reason, since we speculate, meditate and draw conclusions from revealed truths. But contemplation is not only above reasoning, but it causes reasoning to cease. So, whereas faith darkened the intellect only as regards natural science, contemplation darkens the understanding even as regards its faculty of reasoning illumined by faith. Faith elevates reasoning; contemplation dispenses with it. Faith enlightens our natural way of thinking; contemplation lifts us above the human mode of thought. It is evident, then, that contemplation is a greater darkness than faith.

Earlier in this work we compared faith to a light which is reflected by the multiplicity of objects upon which it shines. Now John of the Cross uses the comparison of the ray of sunlight to show the purity of contemplation. If a ray of sunlight enters a dark room through a window (or better, through a small hole in the roof), it will appear more visible, bright and palpable to the eye in proportion as it is charged with specks of dust and particles of matter, since it is these that are visible to the eye, and it is by their reflection that the shaft of light seems to be something visible. It is not, however, the ray of sunlight that appears to the vision, but rather the impurities in it. The more impurities in this beam of intangible gold, the more brilliantly it seems to shine; while, on the contrary, the fewer foreign substances and the more free and pure it is in itself, the less apprehensible it is. If the shaft of light were completely pure and free of all motes of matter the ray of sunlight would be indistinguishable from darkness and nothing would be seen. Wherefore, if such a ray should enter without meeting anything that has material form, it would be as a ray of darkness; yet, notwithstanding, that ray of light would be purer and clearer in itself than when it was more clearly perceived through being full of visible forms.

The same thing happens in the realm of spiritual light with respect to the sight of the soul, which is the understanding. The faith of beginners is comparable to the shaft of sunlight glowing with myriad particles: faith itself seems to be apprehensible because of the images and forms of knowledge that it illumines. The eye of the understanding seizes upon these images of matter, for without them it remains in darkness; nevertheless, faith is not more clearly perceived by the multiplication of such motes; rather, faith is more pure and simple as it is free from these tangible forms. As it would be an error to identify the beam of light with the particles that make it perceptible to the natural eye, so it would be self-deception to think that the light of faith is one with the phantasms, ideas and judgments of the understanding. Although the natural understanding should perceive nothing and be in darkness, it is not therefore to be supposed that the light of faith is not present in all its intangible purity. There is a ray of Divine light which strikes so purely and simply on the eye of the soul that it remains indistinguishable from darkness, at any rate as far as the natural understanding is concerned: this is contemplation. Contemplation blinds the understanding to its accustomed lights, forms and fancies, and thus comes as darkness to it.

At times, when it is purest, this general, supernatural knowledge or light becomes darkness to the soul, even so far that the soul seems clearly to perceive darkness.[41] For this reason Dionysius calls this contemplation a ray of darkness, for it is secret and dark to the very understanding that receives it.[42] Let the spiritual person, then, learn to love such darkness, and let him beware of thinking that, if loving knowledge presents itself in a more comprehensible and palpable manner, it is purer, brighter and more sublime. The exact opposite is the case, for, as the theologians say and even the pagan Aristotle knew, the higher and more sublime the Divine light, the darker it is to our understanding.[43] The reader may now realize why St. John calls this infused loving knowledge "indistinct," "obscure," "confused, general and dark," [44] and why, when he speaks of it as a ray of light, it is "so subtle and delicate, particularly when it is most pure and simple and perfect, most spiritual and interior." [45] So also it is well to note that, though the soul is conscious of the love in its will, this love has not the vividness and clear-cut outlines of sensual love, but this sweetness and love is also received obscurely and confusedly, so that the soul cannot have a distinct knowledge of the object of its love.[46]

[41] xiv,9,10
[42] viii,6
[43] xiv,13
[44] x,4
[45] xiv,8
[46] xiv,12

CHAPTER XI

Signs of Contemplation

As CONTEMPLATION is the proper subject, not of this active night, but of the passive night, so also, if the strictest logic were to divide this work, the signs of contempla- would not be written here but in the "Dark Night," where, indeed, they are repeated.[1] However, St. John is not so much the speculative theologian whose words are written with the inflexible orderliness of a dictionary, but he is the spiritual practician who gives first consideration to the needs of the souls whom he is addressing. In the Prologue he lamented that there were many souls who remained in an elementary stage of communion with God because there was no one to teach them how to get away from the beginnings of spirituality. It is sad enough when souls fail to reach contemplation for want of will; St. John will not have it happen for want of knowledge.

The contemplation of which he speaks is infused contemplation. It is not necessary that he label it "infused"; the description, the signs, and the advice he gives, all prove this. Who are called to contemplation? In giving these signs, our mystical author does not mean to say that all souls are not called to contemplation, even remotely. These are the signs of the *proximate* call: the soul in whom these three signs are verified may and should enter into the practise of contemplation as the Holy Spirit moves it.

[1] D.N.,I,ix

The first sign is the soul's realization that it can no longer meditate, but rather finds aridity where before it found pleasure and sweetness. By meditation is meant, of course, the exercise of the imagination and reason. It matters not if reason predominates; indeed, the wandering of the understanding and reason is more of an obstacle than the indeliberate wandering of the imagination, for, since the imagination is a distinct faculty, it may wander even when the understanding is united to God. There are two reasons why one must leave the way of meditation and reasoning when one finds difficulty and repugnance rather than pleasure in it. First, the little pleasure that is now found in meditation is a sign that this method of prayer no longer profits it or, at least, has outgrown its usefulness. St. John evokes the principle: that which is palatable nourishes and fattens. This is not a principle to be applied universally and without discretion; nevertheless it is true that certain human operations do receive pleasure as an encouragement to rational exercise. For example, the pleasureable energy and activity of the growing child affords it the necessary exercise needed in the formation of its body. So, as a rule, whenever the soul receives some spiritual blessing, it receives it with pleasure, at least spiritual pleasure. The child, when first it receives an intricate toy, finds pleasure in examining and playing with it; afterwards when the toy is no longer a novelty (when it no longer learns from it), the pleasure evaporates. This first reason, then, is that the soul has received all the spiritual good which it could derive by means of meditation, and the aridity and difficulty now experienced means that this source of living water has dried up. The second reason amounts to the same thing:

the soul now has both the substance and habit of the spirit of meditation. In other words, the soul has formed a habit of spirituality through its practise of single acts of knowledge and love. A child at the breast takes its food in small amounts and the simplest food at that. With time its appetite and digestive powers grow stronger. It becomes able to take larger quantities and now becomes accustomed to the strong diet of meat. Without saying that St. Paul's words refer to contemplation, let us use them as means of illustration: "And I, brethren, could not speak to you as unto spiritual, but as unto carnal. As unto *little ones* in Christ. I gave you milk to drink, not meat; for you were not able as yet. But neither, indeed, are you now able; for you are yet carnal" [2] "But strong meat is for the perfect; for them who by custom have their senses exercised to the discerning of good and evil." [3] The little ones of Christ, striving to grow up into spiritual manhood, exercise themselves in meditation, which is like milk, and proportioned to their weakness. These are as yet carnal and must be weaned from the methods of spiritual infancy. By faithful meditation, they "gain some knowledge and love of God, and each time that the soul gains this through meditation, it is an act; and just as many acts, of whatever kind, end by forming a habit in the soul, just so, many of these acts of loving knowledge which the soul has been making, one after another from time to time, come through repetition to be so continuous in it that they become habitual. . . . And thus that which aforetime the soul was gaining gradually, through its labor of meditation upon particular facts, has now through practise, as we have been saying,

[2] 1 Cor. iii,1
[3] Hebrews v,14

become converted and changed into a habit and substance of loving knowledge, of a general kind, and not distinct or particular as before." [4] The appetite and digestive powers of the infant have grown so that now it may give up its milk-diet and take to eating meat. The soul with its spiritual faculties and senses has by custom become exercised to the discerning of good and evil; its capacity for spirituality has increased, so that now its food needs no longer to be diluted, but now it can receive the *substance* of nourishment. The substance of spirituality is contemplation, in which sense St. John often applies the adjective "substantial," not only to contemplation but even to its effects, as, for example, "substantial and loving quiet." [5]

I might take another illustration from the natural order. The young student just beginning his philosophy course, must have been exercised in such minor sciences as physics, chemistry or geometry, from which, by repeated examples, demonstrations or experiments, he learns universal principles detached from material things, and acquires the habit of logical and not too imaginative thinking. When he begins to study philosophy, he must recur to concrete illustrations. But at the end of his course, he has acquired a facility in understanding spiritual principles, and he is able to listen for a long time to the discussion of abstract principles of reality. Going a step farther, we might say, supposing that mental telepathy were practicable, that he would now be able to *receive passively* from the mind of his professor the spiritual knowledge which formerly was incomprehensible to him.

[4] xiv,2
[5] xiv,4

So it is with contemplation, but in a fuller and higher manner: the soul having accustomed both its mind and will to the reception of supernatural loving knowledge, God now proceeds to infuse this substance of loving knowledge into it without any labor of its own. (It remains true, however, as St. John says, that God could set a soul in the state of contemplation from the beginning.)

A student who could receive his lessons passively would be saved all the labor of imagination and reasoning, and would have merely to receive that which is prepared for him. So also, the contemplative receives substantial spirituality without any labor of his own. Our Carmelite mystic uses several examples to make this clear. A baby drinks its nourishment without any need to prepare it for itself; likewise the contemplative eats his fruit from which the rind has already been removed; one to whom water is brought has no need to labor in drawing it from an aqueduct or a well.[6] When, therefore, meditation becomes insipid because it no longer gives the nourishment required, when the soul is no longer able to meditate and no longer desires to do so, this is the first sign of the proximate call to a more substantial prayer. But this is not sufficient, since many souls might be deceived in this way, having lost the savour of meditation because of their sensual life. If meditation is difficult for those who are carnal, contemplation is no less impossible.

A second sign is therefore necessary. It is that one does not desire to fix his imagination or understanding on other particular objects, whether exterior or interior. The reason is that, if the spiritual soul has no pleasure in those images and thoughts in meditation which bear some re-

[6] xiv,2,3

semblance to God and which serve as at least a remote means of union with Him, much less will it take pleasure in things that draw the mind and will away from God For the soul that begins to enjoy contemplation must ordinarily have passed through the night of the senses, that is to say, have become detached from all natural and temporal things. This does not mean that the imagination will not go fluttering about, like a butterfly, touching upon this thing and that, for this faculty is in the habit of coming and going and varying of its own accord, even at times of great recollection. But this is not according to the good pleasure of the soul; rather it is troubled thereby, since its interior peace and joy are thus disturbed.[7] But not even these two signs together are enough, for it could happen that the soul cares to think neither of God nor created things, because of melancholy, ill-humor, fatigue or other, physical disturbance.

The third and surest sign is that the soul takes pleasure in being alone, waiting with loving attentiveness upon God, with no desire to labor with its imagination or understanding. In interior peace and rest of the faculties, that is, in the quiet of the understanding which makes no acts, at least, no exercise of the reason, and in the loving attentiveness of the will, the soul is occupied with God, although it may often not be conscious of the fact. This is the loving knowledge, confused and general, which we described in our last chapter. The reason why this loving knowledge which is contemplation must be present is obvious. For, if the soul turned away from meditation and had not contemplation to take its place, it would be spiritually idle. But so long as this infused contemplation is

[7] xiii,3; xiv,5

present, the soul is occupied in a way far more spiritual and substantial. So true is this, that even the soul who is habitually in the way of meditation ought to abandon meditation the moment that God leads it into this state of "peace and quietness." [8]

These three signs are strictly necessary if one is to abandon the way of meditation with security. The only difficulty is in the third sign. How can one be sure that one is enjoying contemplation? As St. John admits, in the beginning this loving knowledge is very subtle and delicate and almost imperceptible to the senses, so that a person hardly realizes what he is experiencing. Accustomed to the distinct forms of the fancy and the natural perspicuity of the understanding, the soul scarcely perceives this new and ineffable condition so purely spiritual — and only God knows how many turn away from this bottomless well of living water because they do not understand it! Even souls that are accustomed to it, if they are unusually pure and far removed from the coarse habits of sense and knowledge of particular things, may neither realize nor perceive this contemplation, if it be more delicate, interior and spiritual than usual, for when this general and confused knowledge is most simple and perfect, the understanding is least conscious of it, or regards it as most obscure. And, contrariwise, when this knowledge is in itself least pure and simple, it seems to the understanding to be clearest and of the greatest importance, since it is clothed in, or mingled with, that which the understanding or imagination may seize upon, like the ray of sunlight rendered visible by the impurity of dust particles. [9]

[8] xiii,2; xv
[9] xiii,7; xiv,8,9

How, then, can one be sure that this third sign is being verified in himself? The consciousness of attentiveness to God or forgetfulness of all that is less than God is ordinarily a sign that the will is occupied, if the person is one who is habitually solicitous about the things of God and not suffering from some physical disturbance. Sometimes this attentiveness is made more perceptible by the sweetness which the will feels in this holy exercise. Again the soul may be conscious of a void in itself — a nothingness so real, as it were, that the soul is at least vaguely aware of it. This void is more particularly in the understanding, for that faculty is withdrawn from all distinct knowledge and occupied only with general knowledge which is of God. The will, too, may seem to be unoccupied, but at least there is no desire to dwell on earthly things. If distractions in the imagination cause a disturbance of the soul's peace, this is a good sign that the soul was occupied. The principle invoked in all these negative signs is that the natural faculties are so inclined to busy themselves about temporal things, that some sufficient reason must be given for their unwonted detachment and seeming emptiness.

In order that beginners may see their way clearly toward the goal of contemplation, our mystic devotes a chapter to the period of transition.[10] As he called "beginners" those who were striving to detach themselves from worldly things, now he calls "progressives" those who are beginning to experience contemplation. "Proficients" or "progressives" are those who have acquired the habit of contemplation and no longer need the practise of meditation. How, then, ought the "progressive" conduct himself,

[10] xv

in order that he might become proficient in mystical prayer? At first, the experience of infused loving knowledge may not be frequent. It will be necessary for him to try to return to meditation, at least for a short time, that his will may be aroused to love. Loving knowledge is the substance of meditation; the work of the imagination and the understanding is merely the means by which we gain knowledge of Divine things and pile up logs for firing the will. By many acts of loving knowledge of God, depending both on the natural help of reasoning or meditation and the supernatural help of grace, a supernatural habit of loving knowledge is formed in the soul. Ordinarily (granting for the present that contemplation belongs to the normal order), when this loving knowledge has acquired a certain strength, meditation is no longer helpful. When water reaches the level from which it flowed, it can rise no higher, but requires rain from above to raise its level yet higher. So, in God's design, the soul must ordinarily form the habit of knowing and loving Him through human means. Afterwards, He nourishes and develops this habit without the need of meditation, simply by infusing the loving knowledge directly and in the darkness of the understanding. One wonders why many find this doctrine a hard saying. It must be recalled that all that is supernatural needs to be infused. There is nothing supernatural in meditation that we acquire by our own natural efforts; all that is natural in meditation cannot give of itself the least degree of grace to the soul; all that is supernatural in meditation is infused just as truly as contemplation. The only point of difference to be noted is that in meditation faith requires images and judgments to illuminate, whereas in contemplation the

light comes to the understanding without being reflected
in the earthly dust-particles of intelligible forms. In meditation, the natural is mingled with the supernatural, and
we call it the work of faith; in contemplation, the natural
understanding is darkened and the supernatural is infused
in its simple purity, wherefore St. John calls it *pure* faith.

 The gifts of the Holy Ghost are in the souls as habits
designed to stream-line our spirituality. By repeated acts,
of infused loving knowledge the habit of contemplation
is cultivated and strengthened. Although a new illumination and inspiration is required for every act of loving
knowledge, the soul becomes disposed for these anointings
of the Holy Spirit to such perfection that St. John can say
implicitly, that the soul acquires the habit of contemplation, and gains such proficiency in the science of contemplation that it can give itself to the act thereof
whenever it wishes.[11] The "progressive" must at times return to meditation: first, because, not having gained the
necessary proficiency in loving knowledge, the soul would
find itself in a state of idleness; secondly, because it has not
gone so far beyond meditation that this practise becomes
absolutely impossible to it or that it cannot find something
savoury and profitable therein. By faithfully withdrawing
itself from the things of sense, by giving itself to contemplation as often as the Holy Spirit invites it thereto, by
faithfully practising meditation when loving knowledge
is not otherwise forthcoming, the soul will in time perfect
itself in mystical prayer to such perfection that, as soon
as it turns to pray, it will, at least habitually, experience
the knowledge, love and peace of God, unable to meditate
and no longer desirous of doing so.

[11] xv, 1

The incipient contemplative ought, therefore, to remember the following points. Practise meditation quietly
and in moderation, peacefully musing upon some Divine
truth, whenever this is necessary to fire the will. When
you find yourself in the loving and peaceful state of waiting upon God, have no desire to feel or see or understand
any particular thing, for that would be to set a cloud in
the way of this pure and serene light of the spirit, even
as one might impede one's vision of the distant stars by
setting lighted candles before the eyes. Do not mistake
the peace and quiet of this state for idleness; learn to be
still in God, fixing your loving attention upon Him. Thus,
little by little and *very quickly*, the habit of Divine contemplation with its wondrous calm and peace will be infused into the soul; and the soul would only be disturbed
by the restlessness of the understanding, and experience
distaste and repugnance. If you have scruples about doing
nothing, reflect that you are doing no small thing by
pacifying your soul and voiding it of every natural desire,
which is an excellent preparation for the work of God.

CHAPTER XII

Natural and Supernatural Acquisition of Knowledge

THE PURPOSE of this second Book of the "Ascent," as we now know, is to lead the understanding to God through a means which is really proximate and proportionate, that is to say, a means which is really a means, and to guide the understanding away from things which may be a hindrance and a danger, or at the least, which fail to serve as anything but remote means to union. As we have seen so far, and as will become clearer as we go along, the true means to Divine union is faith understood in its fullest sense as infused contemplation. In these early chapters, St. John has been laying the groundwork of this book by showing how faith is the only direct means of uniting the understanding to God. Chapter five described the soil from which faith springs, namely, the soul supernaturally enriched with grace; chapter six proved the necessity of supernatural principles in all the faculties; the remaining chapters were concerned, directly or indirectly, with showing how faith and contemplation are the only road by which the intellect may journey toward the mount of perfection. So far, our Carmelite friar has been speaking only in general, preparing the way for what is to follow. For example, in stressing the darkness of faith, he spoke in a general way, but promised to describe more minutely, hereafter, the way in which the soul is to conduct itself.[1] A little later, speaking

[1] iv,1

of how the soul must be free and void of what may hinder it, either spiritually or sensually, he promises that he shall explain this presently in more detail.[2] In treating of the theological virtues, he said that he would describe a method whereby the spiritual faculties could be voided and purified of all that is not God, by setting them in the darkness of the virtues.[3] When proving how no creature and no natural knowledge could serve as a proximate means of union, he remarked that afterwards he would begin to speak in detail.[4] And now, in chapter nine, after enunciating what might be called the theme of this book, namely, the efficacy and necessity of faith, he says that it now remains to describe in detail all the types of knowledge that may hinder the understanding in its seeking after God, and the way in which the soul must conduct itself, in order that the apprehensions of the understanding may cause it no harm.

Chapter ten begins to fulfill these promises, by dividing and subdividing the types of knowledge possible to the mind. In doing this, St. John is digging down to the very root of the problem and preparing the foundations of spiritual life. For, since the intellect is the direct principle of our knowledge and the remote principle of our love (no one loves that of which he is entirely ignorant), and since the memory, too, depends on the intellect (in the practical way in which St. John considers it), it is clear that our whole spiritual life receives direction from the notions and apprehensions of the understanding. The proper thing to do, then, will be to guide the understand-

[2] iv,6
[3] vi,6
[4] viii,1

ing towards knowledge that is truly spiritual, and to protect it from the deceits of false or inadequate knowledge. Such is the purpose of this Book as we have already seen in general.

There are two channels or modes of receiving knowledge: the natural and the supernatural. By natural knowledge is meant all that the understanding can comprehend by means of the bodily senses and its own natural ability and capacity. For example, the eyes, ears, *etc.*, bring into our interior the sense-impressions of exterior objects, and from these the understanding conceives ideas. The understanding depends on this method for all its apprehensions; without the work of the senses it would remain a blank, so far as the natural method of attaining knowledge is concerned. The supernatural channel is that by which the understanding receives intelligence over and above this natural method. This does not necessarily mean that such knowledge is above the natural capacity of the understanding as a faculty; it means precisely that the natural method of knowing external and natural objects through the senses has been overreached. The genesis of knowledge is not the easiest study in the world, but, fortunately, it is not necessary that we know everything about it. It suffices that we remember that three things are required for natural knowledge: external reality, the ability of the senses to perceive that reality, and the power of the understanding to conceive an idea of it. If intelligence is obtained without either the external, natural object or the work of the senses, this intelligence must have been given to the understanding in a way above the natural, *i.e.*, in a supernatural mode.

With the natural mode, we are not concerned for the

present, for that is easy enough to understand. The supernatural knowledge may be confusing by reason of terminology. It will be necessary for the reader to put out of his mind any thought of grace and the theological virtues for the present, for the supernatural knowledge of which we speak is not necessarily identified with them. By supernatural, we mean here any intelligence that is received without an external, natural object, or without the use of the senses, whether exterior (eyes, ears, etc.) or interior (imagination and fancy).

Supernatural knowledge is of two kinds: corporeal and spiritual. The corporeal is that which is received by means of the body, whether exteriorly in the outward senses, or interiorly in the inward senses. For example, supernatural corporeal knowledge is that which is perceived in the eyes, ears, *etc.* either by a miraculous apparition or without any external reality at all. Or supernatural corporeal knowledge is that which is received in the imagination without any work of the five exterior senses. In either case there is something outside the natural mode of acquiring knowledge, and therefore, it is called here "supernatural." "Preternatural" would be a better term, for, though such knowledge is received *beside* the natural method, it is not *above* the ability and capacity of the corporeal faculties.

The spiritual supernatural knowledge is that which is received directly in the understanding without any corporeal aid whatsoever. It is called "spiritual" because it is received without any corporeal aid. Thus, if I should become conscious of the presence of some object near me without having perceived it through corporeal means, that would be spiritual knowledge, because received in a directly spiritual way. It is to be noticed that although

Chart of all apprehensions and types of knowledge which can be apprehended by the understanding. (A,II,x)

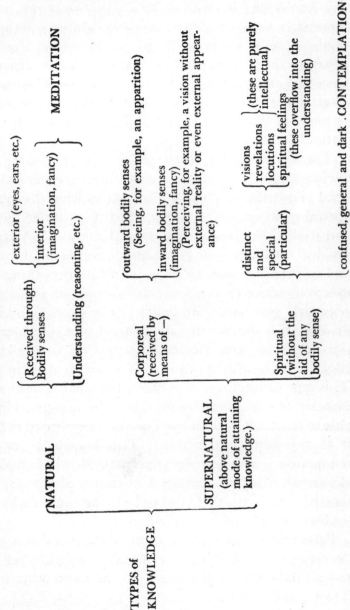

TYPES of KNOWLEDGE

NATURAL
- (Received through) Bodily senses
  - exterior (eyes, ears, etc.)
  - interior (imagination, fancy)
- Understanding (reasoning, etc.)

} MEDITATION

SUPERNATURAL (above natural mode of attaining knowledge.)
- Corporeal (received by means of —)
  - outward bodily senses (Seeing, for example, an apparition)
  - inward bodily senses (imagination, fancy) (Perceiving, for example, a vision without external reality or even external appearance)
- Spiritual (without the aid of any bodily sense)
  - distinct and special (particular)
    - visions
    - revelations
    - locutions
    - spiritual feelings (these overflow into the understanding)
    } (these are purely intellectual)
  - confused, general and dark . CONTEMPLATION

this knowledge is received in a way *beside* the natural method, it is not necessarily *above* the ability and capacity of the natural understanding, and therefore, would be better termed "preternatural" rather than supernatural, as we said of the corporeal knowledge above. This manner of attaining intelligence is "supernatural" in the manner or mode in which it is acquired, but not necessarily supernatural in substance.

The accompanying chart will be useful in getting these divisions clearly in mind. Notice that supernatural spiritual knowledge is of two kinds: that which is distinct and special in its nature, and that which is confused, general and dark. The distinct and special (or specific) kind is divided into four species: visions, revelations, locutions and spiritual feelings. Of these we shall say nothing now, except to notice that they are the uncommon phenomena popularly associated with sanctity. The second kind is not divided: it is the obscure and general type of contemplation which we have already described as "loving knowledge." This is infused contemplation and is given in faith. This type of intelligence is above the natural ability and capacity of the understanding, but the understanding is able to receive it, "when our Lord may be pleased to bring it to a supernatural action." This knowledge or contemplation is *substantially* supernatural, which makes it clearer why St. John can speak of contemplation as "substantial," and says that, through it, the soul reaches the "substance and purity of spiritual good." [5]

Particular notice must be taken of the fact that it is this "contemplation that is given in faith" to which "we have to lead the soul" by guiding it past all these other means

[5] xiv,4; xxiii,4; vi,7

of natural knowledge and "supernatural" knowledge which is not substantially supernatural. When a person begins to realize that the types of knowledge which are *supernatural in mode only* do not surpass its natural knowledge, being natural in substance like it, he will not be surprised at what St. John has to advise in their regard, but will be anxious to seek only the "contemplation that is given in faith."

This latter phrase does much to clear up the purpose of those frequent references to contemplation in earlier chapters, for the descriptions of faith had one principle object: to lead the soul to this "obscure and general type of knowledge," the infused contemplation that is given in faith. And it will be well for the reader to remember in the chapters to come, that this contemplation is the principle goal of this book, and that, therefore, any references to faith will probably mean contemplation.

Before concluding this chapter, let us dispose of the first type of knowledge, which is the natural knowledge received through the exterior and interior senses from an external object. For such knowledge does not come up as the proper subject of this book, but belongs rather to the Night of the Senses as treated in the first Book of the "Ascent." Considered in the light of what we said above, that first Book of the "Ascent" takes on a new importance, since the rejection of that first type of apprehensions is the first step on the road to contemplation. The things of the world are the first head of the beast of the Apocalypse, and it is greatly to be lamented that many souls who engage in spiritual battle against the beast do not even destroy its first head by denying themselves the sensual things of the world.[6] That such detachment is necessary is evident from the second sign of the proximate call to Contemplation, which is that the soul have no desire to meditate on worldly things.[7]

[6] xi,10
[7] xiii,3; xiv,5

CHAPTER XIII

Visions in the Outward Bodily Senses.

AMONG THE kinds of knowledge which may come to the soul in a supernatural (preternatural) way are the apprehensions of the understanding which proceed from something preternaturally represented in the outward bodily senses. We must notice that our chief concern is with the understanding, since it is in this faculty that contemplation takes place, insofar as the "knowledge" part of this "loving knowledge" is in question. Keeping in mind that it is St. John's purpose to bring the understanding into the spiritual night of mystical prayer, we ask, what relation with the understanding have these representations which are received in the outward senses in a supernatural mode? [1]

At the risk of being overcareful, let us repeat that these 'supernatural" representations in the exterior senses are supernatural only in this sense, that one of the three elements of the natural mode of human knowledge is missing, namely, the external and natural object. We say external and *natural* object, because by angelic or Divine power there could be something external which is above the natural order. If several hundred people, for example, witnessed a supernatural manifestation, it would seem that there must be something external there, if not substantial, at least in appearance. It is written of St. Cajetan that the devil appeared to him one evening in the form of

[1] Cf. title of xi

an ape and began to cut the most ridiculous monkey-capers for the purpose of distracting him from his reading and writing. For a time the Saint completely ignored the diabolic visitor, although the monkey jumped up on his desk, tumbled about the books there, pulled at the Saint's sleeve and made many grimaces to distract him from his work. At last, the ape became angry, snatched the candle and made towards the chimney to escape with it. By the power of God, the Saint commanded the monkey to return and hold the candle in his paw like a candlestick, while the Saint continued to write. The candle kept burning lower and lower while the ape held it perfectly still, unable to disobey. As the flame began to lick the monkey's hand, he began to make faces from pain. As the candle burnt out, the Saint allowed the monkey to escape, while he himself lit another candle and continued writing his book. Now, it would seem that a scene like this must surely have some objectivity since the Saint himself took part in it. Many other examples might be given.

Such a vision would be supernatural in this sense, that the external thing, whether substantial or only apparent would be something miraculous. So far as the corporeal senses are concerned, it would require no more than natural power to perceive it. St. Thomas thinks that neither Christ nor His Blessed Mother appear on the earth in person, for they can be seen in their own proper species only in heaven, and it seems unlikely that they can be seen also on earth except by way of a miraculous semblance.[2]

A second way in which an apparition may be seen is when the eyes of the beholder is affected so that he seems to see something outwardly; such species is Divinely

[2] S.T., III,q.76,a.8

formed in the eyes in order to represent some truth, as when someone sees flesh or blood in the Holy Eucharist.[3] St. Teresa tells us that these corporeal visions ought to receive the honors due to the person represented, even though the vision should be an illusion or a deceit of the devil, for, she reasons, the portrait or image of Christ would be deserving of honor even though painted by a wicked man.[4] If however, one thought that the devil wished to gain adoration for himself under the appearance of Christ's humanity, such adoration should be given only conditionally.

John of the Cross does not make any great effort to distinguish these two modes of vision, probably because it doesn't matter, from a spiritual point of view whether the apparition has objective reality or is impressed immediately on the senses. He says that there may come to spiritual persons "representations and objects of a supernatural kind," and that, with respect to sight, they are apt to *picture* figures and forms of persons belonging to the next life; and with the ears they hear extraordinary words, sometimes spoken by these figures, sometimes without seeing the person who speaks them; and as to the sense of smell, they sometimes perceive the sweetest perfumes, without knowing whence they proceed; as to the taste, they may become conscious of the sweetest savours; and as to the touch, experience great delight. All these could be produced immediately in the senses. But it really does not matter whether they are exterior or only interior. The important thing to notice is that they are of the sensible nature; if St. John calls them "representations

[3] S.T., III,q.76,a.8
[4] Interior Castle, sixth mansion, ch. ix

and objects of a supernatural kind," that is only because
they have been produced in a way that is outside the natural order. As regards the substance of the act of sensation,
it is no more than natural; St. John likens the delight felt
to that sensible sweetness of devotion which flows into the
lower nature from the spirit. Even though sensations are
produced in the bodily senses immediately by God Himself, they are no more than natural, for our sensible nature is not capable of the supernatural as are the spiritual
faculties. "Bodily sense judges and makes its estimate of
spiritual things by thinking that they are as it feels them
to be, whereas they are as different as is the body from the
soul and [sensibility] from reason. For the bodily sense is
as ignorant of spiritual things as is a beast of rational
things, and even more so." [5] This principle of the great
chasm between sense and spirit is frequent and fundamental in St. John.

Although extraordinary things of this kind are confused in the popular mind with sanctity, they do not
elevate either the senses or the understanding above their
natural power. They may, therefore, take place apart
from both sanctifying and actual grace.

What does our saint advise in the case of one who should
receive these visions? Does he say with Teresa that we
should give them the honor due to the persons represented? No, but he exhorts such a one never to rely upon
them nor be complacent in them; rather one should fly
from them, without trying to ascertain whether they be
true or false, good or evil. There are several reasons for
rejecting them. First, these corporeal visions may be of

[5] xi,2. The text has "sensuality" but with no meaning nor con-
notation of sin.

the devil, for it is the wish of the devil to insinuate into the soul a secret satisfaction with itself, a sin or even tendency to pride that is well worth his trouble, and therefore he represents these objects to some, setting before the eyes the figures of saints and most beautiful lights, and before the ears words well dissembled, and representing sweetest perfumes, delicious tastes and things delectable to the touch. By exciting desires for such things, he may lead the soul into much evil, causing trouble or aridity or vanity or presumption. The devil knows how to make his visions seem good, for, as the Apostle says, he can transform himself into an angel of light. And, if the soul be pleased with his morsels, he will increase them, trying to obtain root in the soul, as has happened to many ignorant and uncautious persons, who relied on such things to such an extent, that they found it impossible to return to God in purity of faith.

But, what if a vision should be from God? The signs by which it may be known that a vision is from God is that it penetrates the soul and moves the will to love and virtue. But the soul must never presume to desire to receive them, even though they be of God. God is not offended by their rejection, nor does He fail to produce in the soul the effect and fruit which He has attached to them. These corporeal visions produce their effect upon the spirit at the very moment when they come, so that the soul has neither time nor opportunity to deliberate whether it will accept or reject them. For, as God works these things without any effort on the part of the soul, independently of any initiative of its own, even so, God produces in the soul the supernatural effect that He desires by means of such things, without any respect to its efforts and independently of its capacity. These visions, it is true, although received passively, are not above the power of the soul to receive them; but the effect which accompanies them is truly supernatural, penetrating the depth of the soul and requiring the power of grace. Of the visions, the soul is conscious, for these are in its natural part; of the grace, the soul is not conscious except afterwards when it experiences the loving knowledge of God within it. The visions can be rejected in this sense, that the will is not afterwards complacent in them nor desires them to be repeated. But the grace is not rejected by this rejection of the external vision, because both the vision and the grace were wrought in the soul passively before it could make any act of its own, and thus their acceptance or non-acceptance consists not in the immediate acceptance or the rejection of it by the will. These things may be compared to fire: it would matter little whether a person wished to be burned or not; the fire would of necessity accomplish its work, if applied to one's body. So it is with the visions and representations that are good: even though the soul rejects them afterwards, they have worked their effect upon it. One cannot reject these works of God any more than a window can resist the sun's rays when they strike it.[6]

As has been pointed out, there is a double content in corporeal visions when they are from God: first, the representation in the senses, which is afterwards retained by the sense-memory and by the understanding or spiritual memory; secondly, the strictly supernatural content of grace, which afterwards may flower in acts of loving knowledge. But the after-effects depend upon the soul's attitude toward these visions. If it esteems the memory of

[6] xi,6. Compare the simile of the sun's rays in v, 6-8 and xiv,9.

them, it is esteeming the baser metal in them, for it can remember only that which was natural in them. If, on the contrary, it rejects the memory of them, it leaves its spiritual faculties free for the flowering of grace. The spiritual faculties being simple, they cannot be occupied with both aspects or contents at the same time; either the understanding, memory and will are to be occupied with what is remembered of the vision, or they may be left free for the loving knowledge, of which these visions plant the seed. Thus "they are a hindrance to the spirit, if they be not denied, for the soul rests in them and its spirit soars not to the invisible . . . it begins to lose the effect of them and the inward spirituality which they cause it, because it sets its eyes upon their sensual aspect, which is the least important. And thus it receives not so fully the spirituality which they cause, which is impressed and preserved more securely when all things of sense are rejected, since these are very different from pure spirit." [7]

From what has been said, it may be seen what harm can come to the understanding through these corporeal visions, for they are so palpable and material that they stir the senses greatly, and it appears to the judgment of the soul that they are of greater importance because they are more readily felt. Thus the soul goes after them, instead of remaining in the night of pure faith, which alone elevates the understanding, thinking that the light which it receives from them is the guide to its desired goal of union with God. But the more attention it pays to such things, the farther it strays from the true way and means, which is faith.[8] The things that are experienced in the senses

[7] xi,7
[8] xi,4

derogate from faith, since faith transcends every sense. Thus the spiritual person must deny himself all the apprehensions of the outward senses, preferring living faith.

If St. John does not mention contemplation here, it is not to be supposed that he has forgotten about it, but it lies in the back of his mind as he mentions "the purity of faith," "the guide and means" to the goal which is union with God, "Divine union and transformation." But of contemplation he shall have something explicity to say in the following chapter.

CHAPTER XIV

The Imagination

IT IS traditional to speak of the higher powers of the soul as being the more interior; and the highest power of all or that which is truly supernatural as the most interior. According to this point of view, which corresponds to the ordinary genesis of knowledge, the outward bodily senses are the most exterior, resembling the outward rooms in a castle or the outside wall of a citadel. All our knowledge of this world must come first through the exterior senses, the eyes, ears, *etc.* The first step towards the interior is the interior bodily senses of imagination and fancy; these are nearer the center of the castle and may be conceived as the second wall towards the citadel. The third suite of rooms approaching the center or the third wall approaching the citadel is the understanding (as natural). The inner room of the castle, or the citadel itself, is the supernatural power of the soul. This is the most interior, and as regards actual union with God, it is that most interior recollection of contemplation.

The little child, first beginning to use its powers of knowledge, delights in the use of the exterior senses. It is all eyes and ears, so to speak. But the outward senses pour their substance into the interior sense of the imagination; and the second period of growth is the age of imaginativeness. From a world of imagination, children pass to the world or age of understanding and reasoning, the period of natural spiritual life. The natural life of the spirit is one in which the outward windows and the screen of imagination still play a big part. The interior life truly begins when a person develops the supernatural organism within him, for this transcends all his other powers. Even in this center of the soul, however, there is room for division, for even here light enters through the outward windows of the senses and the screen of the imagination and the transparent wall of understanding and reasoning. The most interior point of the soul is that in which all exterior natural light is shut out, for only the serene, purely supernatural light of contemplation shines there. This is the night of faith, into which images and reasoning cannot enter. Happy the soul that finds its way into this inmost point of recollection!

We described above the way in which life may gradually draw within itself, until, becoming conscious of that truly interior and supernatural life, the soul loses interest in the outer rooms through which it traversed. We have now to describe another phenomenon which takes place in the matured spirit. It is this. The outside world, which at first was a necessary means to obtain material for the outward walls, now becomes the enemy of the spirit and lays siege to it, trying to draw it out again into the open, in order to destroy its interior life. The senses, the imagination and the natural understanding, which at first served as windows and transparencies for introducing light, are now changed into walls of stone to hold off the enemy from that inmost citadel of the spirit. The senses must be strong and firm against the incursions of the inimical world; if at times or in certain places the enemy hordes break through the outer defense, the wall of the imagination must withhold them. Higher and stronger yet is the inner rampart of the understanding. If the understanding should totter the citadel itself is in danger.

St. John begins by treating first of the outward senses. In the first Book of the "Ascent" he described the battle with the hostile world. In our last chapter, he proved that even preternatural apprehensions, if they should succeed in passing into the interior faculties are a danger to true spirituality. And now he comes to the second wall, and he will show how it is to be protected against those forces which might apprehend it.[1]

The interior bodily sense of which we now speak is the imagination and fancy. A slight distinction may be made between the two: the imagination being the power which receives and retains images derived from the eyes, ears, *etc.*; the fancy being the power of separating and re-forming the patterns in the imagination. For practical purposes they are the same. The imagination is the receiving room and storehouse of images, forms and figures imported from the world of material things. At birth the imagination is like a blank slate; and its files of material data must be built up by daily experiences and recordings, to which the understanding has free access.

Although the imagination is the principal object of discussion at this time, it is not as an isolated faculty, but as related to the spiritual faculties, particularly the understanding. The imagination is the handmaid of the intellect, furnishing it with the patterns for reasoning. In this way the soul may represent to itself external realities, and "these things can be actively produced in it through its operation, beneath the forms, figures and images. And thus to these two faculties" of imagination and fancy, "by

[1] xii,1-2

means of images, forms and figures that are produced and imagined by the said senses," belong the material of "meditation, which is a discursive action." [2] This discursive action is, of course, reasoning enlightened by faith, which serves as a *remote* means of union with God. But St. John does not delay over the theory of knowledge, for his purpose is to show that the imagination cannot lead the soul to Divine union, except in a remote way.

The reason is that the imagination cannot fashion or represent anything except what it has experienced through the exterior senses of sight, hearing, *etc*. It is true that the imagination can compose likenesses of those things that it has seen or heard or felt, can multiply them, divide them, reassemble their parts, diminishing or magnifying this or that aspect. But, of what profit is this, since all its work remains in the order of material things? Indeed, it is less than material, for though one may imagine palaces of pearls and mountains of gold, these are of less value than an ounce of real gold or one genuine pearl. But the kernel of the argument is this: no created thing can be an

[2] xii,3. For further understanding of St. John's psychology, notice: "meditations, forms and ideas" (xii,5); "consideration and meditation upon forms" (xii,6) ; "meditate and reason" (xii,7). It is evident from the following chapters that by "faculties" he means the understanding, spiritual memory and the will. "Form" may mean the activating principle or "idea" which gives a determinate reality to matter, as in A,I,vi,2. Or again it might mean a concept of the mind. "Figure" might be conceived as the material extension affecting the exterior senses; the "image," that which has affinity with the imagination; sometimes, however, it is difficult to say precisely how these terms are used. In any case, it is of no importance, because all these affect the understanding and its concepts, which is what St. John is principally concerned with, insofar as knowledge is in question.

133

adequate representation of God; therefore, no image or likeness of those things can serve as a proximate means to union with Him. Wherefore, those who imagine God beneath the likeness of anything created — for example, a great fire or brightness — and think that anything of this sort will be like Him, are very far from approaching Him. These are the ways of beginners, who delight in drawing pictures in their imagination, now representing Christ crucified, or bound to the column, or falling on the road to Calvary, now imagining God seated upon a throne with great majesty in a whirlwind of glory. All these imaginations, whether of human or Divine things, cannot serve the soul as a means of union with God. It is clear, then, that the imagination must be set in darkness, in order that the soul may find a more efficacious means of union.

Recalling that the understanding is the chief object of this Book, we see that this faculty cannot receive much help from the imagination, and, therefore, that discursive operations, known to spiritual persons as meditation, cannot lead to perfect union or transformation in God. We are now on ground where even angels fear to tread; we must be careful of what we say and why we say it. Why cannot meditation lead to perfection? The reason is that meditation deals with images, ideas and judgments, all of which have a certain natural deficiency because, as we have so often insisted, all our images and concepts are drawn from the created universe which bears no proportion to God. In stating that meditation cannot be a proximate and proportionate means of union, St. John is merely bringing his principles to their logical conclusion.

It would be well for the reader to review chapters three, four, eight and nine of "Ascent," Book Two.

It will help the reader to realize also, that by faith our author has in mind, not meditation but contemplation, particularly for those who discern in themselves the three signs of contemplation. For, it will be remembered, he has insisted all along that faith alone is the proximate means and the guide to Divine union. But now he tells us that meditation is only a remote means: we must conclude that by "faith," St. John means, at least principally, "contemplation." This is not the first place in which he pointed out the deficiency of meditation (cf. vii,8;xi,10). If it be objected that meditation itself partakes of faith, we answer that faith guarantees the Divine truth of its symbols or propositions, but it does not remove from them the deficiency proper to every analogical notion.

It is not to be denied that meditation is necessary to beginners: it increases their virtue and especially detaches them from the natural desires which would be an obstacle to contemplation; it also cultivates the habit of loving knowledge, which in contemplation is found in its purest state. But meditation itself will be a hindrance to those who persist in such "methods and manners." [8]

If formerly it was said that faith is the true guide to the goal of Divine union,[4] now it is clear that meditation is not the sufficient means to the goal.[5] But contemplation is

[8] Let the student examine the following in their contexts: "manner of its own" (iv,4); "ways or methods" (iv,5); "every way and manner" (v,5); "ways or methods," "other methods" (vii,8); "manners of meditation" (xii,5); "methods and manners" (xii,8).

[4] Cf. iv,1,3,4.

[5] xii,5

so excellent a means of union, that it may itself take the name of goal.[6]

It will be well to take notice here that St. John's discussion of contemplation, according to strictly logical division, is a digression. He speaks of it here only in its relation to meditation; meditation is discussed only because of its relation to the imagination, which is the proper subject of this chapter. If St. John wanders a little (for which we are not ungrateful), he will return to the subject of the imagination in his chapter sixteen. Of contemplation we have spoken in a previous chapter, and we say no more of it here, for that would take us away from the course of our theme, which is the types of knowledge which might be either an obstacle or a means of Divine union to the understanding.

[6] xii,6,7,9

CHAPTER XV

Supernatural Imaginary Visions

THE IMAGINATION is that interior sense which receives the apprehensions of exterior things through the medium of the five bodily senses. St. John speaks of these apprehensions of the imagination as coming within the category of images, forms, figures and species. In the mind of St. John, there was no doubt a clear distinction between these different terms, but he does not delay to dwell on it. The repetition of them often strikes the reader as a redundancy, but St. John's only purpose in using more than one of them seems to be to bring out the fact that such knowledge is well-defined and limited, clear and distinct in contrast to contemplation, which is general and confused. The point which he wishes to bring out is that the impressions of the imagination, like those of the outward senses, as also the concrete objects themselves, are necessarily limited and natural and, therefore, lacking the proportion necessary to serve as a means of union with God. The imagination is an archives and storehouse of the understanding to which ultimately are referred all these apprehensions; but, although the understanding is itself a spiritual faculty, it can find nothing that will serve as a proximate means of union, whenever it looks into the imagination as into a mirror of realities.

We treat here of the supernatural apprehensions called imaginary visions. What are these supernatural apprehensions? They are merely images in the imagination, like any that might come naturally, except that they can be much more beautiful and perfect. For example, Isaiah saw God in His glory beneath the smoke which covered the Temple, and beneath the Seraphim who covered their faces and their feet with their wings; Jeremiah saw the wand that was watching, and Daniel had many visions, *etc.* But why are they called supernatural? These visions are called supernatural because they come to the imagination in a way that is outside the natural method of acquiring knowledge. Naturally, the imagination should receive its phantasms through the five senses from the objects of this world. But these supernatural visions come to the imagination directly, without passing through the outer windows of the soul; they therefore demand a higher cause which impresses them immediately on the imaginative faculty. Although they are above the ordinary human method of apprehending, they are not above the natural capacity of the imagination to receive them, *i.e.*, the imagination itself requires no new power above its nature in order to apprehend them. As we remarked in the case of the visions of the outward senses, so here also, these visions are not supernatural in essence, but only in the mode of reception, and therefore are better termed "preternatural."

What does it matter if the imagination should receive its images without any assistance of the eyes, ears, *etc.*? So far as the imaginative faculty itself is concerned, there is no intrinsic change in power, no elevation of its natural ability. So far as the spiritual understanding is concerned, there is not necessarily any change in its natural operation, for it *never* finds anything in this archives and mirror of images, forms and figures that is intrinsically

supernatural. If the understanding is to be supernaturalized, it must happen *by a direct intervention of God,*
that is, through the theological virtues. Nothing in the
corporeal senses can possibly generate an act of faith,
which is the one true guide. From this it will be understood that nothing in the corporeal senses, whether exterior or interior, can serve the soul as a proportionate and
proximate means of progress in the spiritual life.

To what cause are these visions to be attributed? Either
God or the devil can represent these images and species in
the imagination. Certainly the devil can cause these phantasms, and this fact alone is sufficient proof of their deficiency, for, is it conceivable that the means of union with
God should be under the dominion of His eternal enemy?
But, since these phantasms are essentially natural and require the material cooperation of the body, they can be
caused by either the good or the evil spirits. It is not to be
wondered at, then, that St. John advises souls to reject
them. It is not merely because the devil comes with these
visions, as with jewels, to barter for the soul's attention
and desire; St. John rather insists upon their natural inadequacy which makes it possible for them to be, not only
unprofitable, but even a hindrance to steady progress, even
though they may come from God.

If God is their cause, He produces in the soul concomitantly supernatural intelligence, love or sweetness. Here
it is important to notice that if the supernatural effect
accompanies the vision, it is not therefore *produced* by it,
for God does not employ inadequate secondary causes.
Indeed, it may be better said that the vision accompanies
the supernatural effect as its outward sign. It is not necessary that God should employ such a sign: grace might

come unheralded, without the soul's being conscious of it and, therefore, without the soul being able to reject it. So great is the chasm between corporeal visions and their accompanying grace (when they come from God), that the soul may reject all that it imagines and understands, without thereby rejecting the grace.[1]

The soul must not, therefore, be desirous cf, or attached to, such visions, for that would be contrary to the purpose for which God gives them. It is the interior and true spirituality that God wishes the soul to possess. The images, forms and figures that come to the imagination are only, as it were, a cellophane wrapper. In using cellophane wrappers for His gifts, God does not for that reason deprive the devil of his power to make empty cellophane wrappers.

[1] xvi,10

CHAPTER XVI

Perils of Visions

ST. JOHN gave one chapter to the explanation of visions of the external senses and another chapter to those of the interior senses, but realizing the importance of a right understanding of their place in the spiritual life, he continues this subject of corporeal visions in chapters seventeen to twenty-two. These chapters contain much wisdom, but not all of it is concerned with the theme of this Book. Disgressing somewhat, St. John answers certain questions that press upon his mind, although, as he confesses, this impedes somewhat the speed of progress in what concerns the main current of this book.[1]

In this matter of corporeal visions, St. John's advice, as we know, is to reject them, and he adduces many reasons for this course of action. Some of these reasons, though strong in themselves, are not directly concerned with the purification of the understanding. These we treat of in this chapter, briefly; and in the following chapter we shall consider those reasons which are more closely related to the spiritual night of the understanding.

These corporeal visions, if desired and welcomed, are the source of much deception, labor, anxiety and peril.[2] To seek after them would be an offence against God,[3]

[1] xxii,1
[2] xviii,7; xxi,11
[3] xxii,5

amounting to at least a venial sin.[4] For, it must be known, this manner of communication between God and the soul is neither God's will nor pleasure, except in certain extraordinary cases.[5] Not only is God not pleased that we should use such methods, but He is oftentimes angry, notwithstanding the fact that He may answer our request.[6] The reason is that God, in His governance of man, has laid down certain rational and natural limits. There is no difficulty nor necessity that cannot be solved or remedied by reason or the principles of the Gospel. God desires that men make use of their reason and the Evangelical doctrine, and so He does not ordinarily make revelations. So true is this, that a person who receives a supernatural revelation ought to accept only that which is in conformity with the revelation of the Inspired Writings or the natural light of human knowledge. Indeed, one ought to follow the dictates of human counsel even more closely when there is question of a private revelation, since there is danger of diabolical intervention.[7]

The spiritual director is of great help in these matters. For God wishes that the government and direction of every man should be through another man. Therefore God gives, together with these extraordinary revelations, a kind of inclination to impart them to another who takes His place, as is evident in the Old Testament. The soul who receives extraordinary communications ought to give an account of them to the spiritual director, even though there seem to be no reason for doing so. The soul

[4] xxi,4
[5] xviii,8
[6] xxi,1
[7] xxi,4; xxii,13

may make no account of such things; nay, may even be embarrassed by them; nevertheless, it must ground itself in humility and reveal them to the director, even though it considers it of no importance. The director, on his side, should not make it difficult for his penitent to be frank in these things.[8]

But why must one be so wary of these visions? And why is it unlawful to desire these communications? It must be answered that, although in the Old Law it was fitting that the prophets and priests should seek visions and revelations from God, it is not so since the coming of Christ and the establishment of the New Law. For Christ is the Word of God and a sufficient revelation of Divine things. God has spoken to us, once and for all, in His Son, as St. Paul tells us. We must set our eyes on Him in Whom there is all grace and truth, all the treasures of wisdom and knowledge. In Christ dwells all the fulness of the Godhead corporally. To seek anything beside Him would be to find fault with God, as if He had not given us a complete sufficiency in His Son. In Christ and His Church we shall find the most secret mysteries and the superabundant source of sanctity.[9] Wherefore, in all our anxieties, trials and difficulties we can find no better and surer means than prayer and hope that God will provide for us by such means as He has ordained.[10]

There are certain dangers that accompany corporeal visions. First, there is pride, for, if the soul sets any value on them, it will begin to think that they are of some importance and productive of good, and that God must es-

[8] xxii,9-19
[9] xxii,2-8
[10] xxi,5

teem the soul to whom He sends such things, and then
the soul will begin to wonder if others enjoy such things.
In this way, visions become the root and foundation of
vainglory and the beginning of many evils. Foolishly becoming attached to vanities, the soul exposes itself to error
and blindness.[11]

Secondly, there is the devil, who seizes this opportunity
to enslave the soul through pride. Many locutions and
visions are from the devil; though it is God from Whom
the soul wishes to receive a communication, the devil may
be the one to answer. The devil will come and make
answer according to the desire and pleasure of a man,
who, being pleased thereat, since the answers and communications are according to his will, allows himself to be
deceived. The devil is crafty, and in his converse with the
soul, he habitually wears the same appearance as God assumes in His dealings with it. By setting before it things
that are very much like those preternatural effects of God,
the evil spirit is able to insinuate himself, like a wolf in
sheep's clothing, among the flock, with such skill that he
can scarcely be detected. It must be remembered that the
devil has a very clear natural intellect, by which he is able
to foretell future events, in a natural way that may resemble supernatural prophecy. With his great knowledge
of natural laws, he is able to reveal to the soul future
pestilences or earthquakes or things of this kind. He may
be able to foretell even the action of God, Whose Providence and dealings with men follow certain laws. After
baiting his hook with truth, the evil spirit, when he is sure
of his victim, begins to insinuate falsehood. And as the
soul departs from faith, God withdraws His light and

[11] xviii,3; xxi,11

favor, with this result, that the soul is deceived and blinded.[12]

What is perhaps more astonishing is that corporeal visions may be the source of deception, even when they come from God. This is certain from examples in the Old Testament. One reason is that God may not intend a vision to be understood properly until a certain time when it is fulfilled or some new light is shed upon it. Even the Apostles failed to understand everything that they heard from the lips of God's Son, until the Holy Spirit illumined them.[13] Another reason may be that God speaks conditionally. For example, God bade Jonas to preach in Ninive that this great city would be destroyed: "Yet forty days, and Ninive shall be destroyed." It would seem that this prophecy must have come to pass, and yet it did not, for the simple reason that the city of Ninive did penance for its wickedness. In God's mind there had been a condition attached to the threat, namely, that Ninive should be destroyed if it did not turn from its evil ways. Jonas was exceedingly troubled and filled with anger because he had been deceived by this communication from God. And yet it had been a true prophecy, because its fulfillment had depended on the aforesaid condition. In this way we may often be deceived by prophecies, even though they are true in themselves.[14]

Again, visions and locutions which are certainly from God may be a cause of deception because of our defective way of understanding them. We would naturally understand them in their strictly literal sense, but God some-

[12] xviii,3; xxi,2,7-13
[13] xx,3
[14] xx,1,2,4,5

times speaks mysteriously, using a spiritual or mystical sense above that which the words mean literally. The most famous example is that of the prophecies concerning Christ. To anyone who examines these prophecies today, it is clear that they were fulfilled perfectly in Christ. Thus, it was foretold of Him that He would be a king whose dominion would extend over the whole earth, that he would liberate the poor from the power of the mighty, that he would redeem enslaved Israel. Christ is now adored as the King of kings, before Whom every knee must bend in earth, heaven and hell; there is not a single soul over which His loving dominion does not exist; and He has certainly redeemed the spiritual Israel from the slavery of sin. But many of the Jews did not understand the prophecies in this way, and they would not believe in a Christ Who was born in a stable, Who lived in poverty and died like a criminal, Whose disciples were not freed from the power of the mighty, but were put to death like Himself, Who had failed to free Israel from the power of Roman tyranny. The Jews who were deceived by the prophecies concerning the Redeemer were those who could understand them only in a material sense, failing to see truth and beauty in them spiritually. Even when the prophecies had been fulfilled — Oh! the blindness of men! — the two disciples of Christ on the road to Emmaus were lamenting that their hopes had ended on a gibbet; and even when He was about to return to heaven, His mission having been gloriously fulfilled, His disciples asked Him, "Lord, wilt thou at this time restore again the kingdom to Israel?"

Many other examples might be given to show how men are deceived when they understand the communications of God in their natural sense, when they interpret literally what God means to be fulfilled spiritually.[15] And from all that has been said in this chapter of the evils or dangers connected with visions, it may be understood how sane is the advice given by St. John, to reject all that our faculties may grasp of them.

[15] xix

CHAPTER XVII

Corporeal Vision, A Hindrance to the Night of Understanding

THE FACULTY which principally concerns us is the intellect or understanding. The corporeal visions of which we have been speaking are impressed either on the bodily senses or in the imagination. We are interested in them, therefore, only insofar as they affect the understanding, since it is in this spiritual faculty that Divine union must take root, and not in the sensible faculties. It remains for us, therefore, to see what relation these corporeal visions have with the understanding.

The doctrine of preceding chapters must help us here. We proved that there is only one proximate and proportionate means to Divine union in the intellect, namely, supernatural faith. Whatever is less than faith is ineffective. But corporeal visions are not faith. Their very name betrays this, for faith, being the act of a spiritual power, cannot exist in a corporeal power. Then, too, faith is above nature. But corporeal visions are received by a capacity that is merely natural.

In regard to faith, St. John strikes familiar chords from earlier chapters. God communicated many visions in the Old Law but all these had reference to the mysteries of faith, at least indirectly; and now that faith is founded in Christ, there is no reason to enquire of God by extraordinary means, for that would be, as it were, to ask for more faith, which has already been given in Christ.[1] The form or figure of a vision is merely sensible; it is, as it were, the letter. But the letter killeth, whereas the spirit giveth life. This spirit which gives life is faith, and it cannot be comprehended by the senses.[2] Unless souls withdraw themselves from visions, they cannot grow in faith.[3] Sometimes directors set some value on such things, instead of edifying their penitents in faith; but to esteem such things is to avert the eyes of the soul from the "abyss of faith"; souls ought rather to be freed and empty of them, in order to "soar to the heights of dark faith"; otherwise they must remain without the "true spirit of faith."[4] One of the reasons why the soul should reveal these extraordinary types of knowledge to the director is that he might guide it in the spiritual poverty and detachment of the dark night (of faith); otherwise it will tend to the road of sense and leave the spiritual road, being allured by the distinct apprehensions of these things.[5] These visions are so little to be desired that if one were to retain naught but these, he would have no spirituality at all; therefore, the teacher ought to impress upon his disciple the necessity of dwelling in the liberty and darkness of faith, wherein are received spiritual liberty and abundance.[6] Souls must become accustomed to "purity of spirit in dark faith, which is the means of union."[7] We are to be guided by human counsel and industry in things

[1] xxii,3-5
[2] xix,5
[3] xviii,4
[4] xviii,2
[5] xxii,17
[6] xix,11
[7] xix,14

that fall within the limits of human judgment and reason; in higher things we have faith, which, although it is not contrary to judgment and reason, transcends them.[8]

We are now in a position to understand more clearly certain passages of St. John which occurred in the earlier chapters on faith, where, it is evident that he had in mind these communications of "supernatural" origin:

> [Since the Divine union of transformation cannot be comprehended] by human ability and sense, it must completely and voluntarily void itself of all that can enter into it, whether *from above* or from below, — I mean according to the affection and will — so far as this rests with itself. . . . But the soul must be voided of all such things as can enter its capacity, so that, however many *supernatural* things it may have, it will ever remain as it were detached from them and in darkness.[9]

The words italicized by me prove that he had in mind preternatural communications. The phrases "so far as this rests with itself" and "such things as can enter its capacity" are worthy of particular notice, for it does not rest with the soul to receive the truly supernatural content of such visions when they are from God, nor can it enter its natural capacity, as St. John teaches in chapter sixteen.

And is it not safe to say that St. John was thinking of corporeal visions as well as earthly things when he said that, in order to attain perfectly to union through grace and through love, a soul must be in darkness with respect to *all* that can enter through the eye, and to *all* that that can be received through the ear, and can be imagined

[8] xxii,13
[9] iv,2

with the fancy? How truly he wrote that the soul is greatly impeded from reaching the high estate of union with God when it clings to *any* understanding or feeling or imagination or appearance or will or manner of its own, or to *any* other act or to *anything* of its own, (by "of its own" meaning "of its own capacity") and cannot detach and strip itself of all these; since the goal which the soul seeks is beyond *all* these, yea, beyond even the *highest thing* that can be known or experienced.[10] Corporeal visions belong to the soul's own natural and proper lights, to which it must be as blind, if it desires to "see supernaturally" (*i.e.* in a truly supernatural manner).[11] Although its "communications may be as lofty as those of the angels," [12] the soul cannot progress except in faith.

The means of union with God must bear some proportion to the end; but among all the creatures "the highest or the lowest," "celestial or earthly," "angel" or "saint," there is none that bears any proportion to Him.[13] "Wherefore no supernatural apprehension or knowledge in this life can serve as a proximate means to the high union of love with God." [14]

For a brief and comprehensive understanding of St. John's estimate of these corporeal visions, it will be well to refer to what he says in the last lines of his treatment of them:

> Let confessors direct their penitents in faith, instructing them frankly to turn away their eyes from all such

[10] iv,4
[11] iv,7
[12] vii,8
[13] viii,3
[14] viii,5

things, teaching them how to void the desire and the
spirit [soul] of them, that they may make progress, and
giving them to understand how much more precious in
God's sight is one work or act of the will performed in
charity than are all the visions and communications that
they may receive from Heaven, since these imply neither
merit nor demerit. Let them point out, too, that many
souls who have known nothing of such things have
made incomparably greater progress than others who
have received many of them.[15]

[15] xxii,19

CHAPTER XVIII

From Sense to Spirit

"SENSE" AND "SPIRIT" are two words that frequently occur in the works of John of the Cross, sometimes separately, sometimes in conjunction. The word "spirit" he uses now and then to designate the soul, or the higher region of the soul; or again "spirit" may mean the Holy Spirit, but it is usually evident when thus employed, either because the word is capitalized or because of the context. In some few instances, it is not easy to distinguish whether the word applies to the soul or to the Holy Spirit.[1] Most frequently the two words are used, either in conjunction or, if only one of them is mentioned, in implicit contradistinction to the other.

Here we are interested in the meaning of "sense and spirit" as opposed to each other in the composite life of the soul, and we hope, by determining accurately their meaning in chapters eleven to twenty-two, that this explanation shall reflect light in those other places where they occur. First, what does he mean by "sense"? Does he mean merely the operation of the external senses, sight, hearing, smell, taste and touch? Does he mean also the operation of the interior senses, which, like archives, receive, store away, and bring forth again experiences of the natural world? This much would be easily understood as "sense." Does he mean also the visions repre-

[1] For example, Peers translates "Spirit" in spite of the reading "spirit" in the MSS and editions, in xiii,1. Not all agree with his interpretation.

sented to the outward bodily senses? and also those impressed on the inward bodily senses? By "sense" does he mean every operation of the corporeal senses, whether exterior or interior? We must remember that, according to the object of this second book of the "Ascent," St. John is not concerned with the senses chiefly, but only insofar as they affect the understanding. Could it be, then, that "sense" might also include the spiritual understanding insofar as it is dependent on the senses? Yes, a careful examination of these chapters on the natural and supernatural apprehensions of the understanding reveals that "sense" comprises all knowledge received through the corporeal faculties. A glance at the accompanying chart will make this clear. The understanding may receive intelligence either directly or indirectly. That which is received directly is spiritual; that received indirectly is corporeal, because it is received by means of the body. The corporeal can be either natural, as when the understanding comprehends a natural object through the corporeal senses; or supernatural (preternatural), as when the understanding receives knowledge through the exterior and interior senses in the absence of a natural object, or in the interior senses without the operation of the eyes, ears, *etc.* Now, what is important to notice is that in indirect or corporeal knowledge the understanding is always dependent on the senses, or at least the one sense of imagination. And because this knowledge is limited by the power of sense, it may be termed "sense" knowledge, even though afterwards the understanding may recall it in a purely spiritual way. "Sense" is, therefore, all the knowledge gained through sense, whether naturally or preternaturally.

Chart of SENSE and SPIRIT

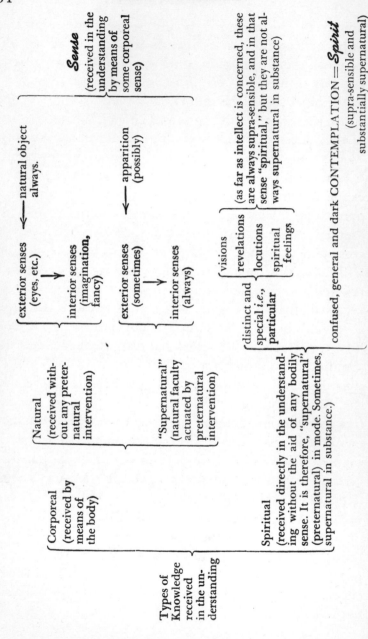

Types of Knowledge received in the understanding

Corporeal (received by means of the body)

Natural (received without any preternatural intervention)
→ exterior senses (eyes, etc.) → natural object always.
→ interior senses (imagination, fancy)

"Supernatural" (natural faculty actuated by preternatural intervention)
→ exterior senses (sometimes) → apparition (possibly)
→ interior senses (always)

Spiritual (received directly in the understanding without the aid of any bodily sense. It is therefore, "supernatural" (preternatural) in mode. Sometimes, supernatural in substance.)

distinct and special i.e., particular
visions
revelations
locutions
spiritual feelings
(as far as intellect is concerned, these are always supra-sensible, and in that sense "spiritual," but they are not always supernatural in substance)

confused, general and dark CONTEMPLATION = *Spirit* (supra-sensible and substantially supernatural)

Sense (received in the understanding by means of some corporeal sense)

"Spirit" is all the intelligence that the understanding may receive without the aid of sense (a materialist would deny this as being impossible). Is all "spirit" essentially supernatural? Not necessarily. For the understanding may receive directly knowledge either natural or supernatural. The knowledge that is received directly is called *supernatural in mode* but is not necessarily *supernatural in essence*. To illustrate: if God were to infuse ideas in your understanding as He does for the angels, that would be knowledge *supernatural in mode* for you, though natural for the angels. But when God infuses into the intellect of either angel or man the light of His grace, that is *supernatural in essence,* because that is absolutely above the nature of man or angel. The precise meaning of "spirit" in St. John we shall discuss later.

But, let us now discuss the method of progress. According to its nature, the soul must start from sense. The senses are the first to receive their perfection; the spiritual faculties lag behind. The light of day presents to the eyes the multifarious objects of the world, and, filtering into the interior, paints lasting pictures on the imagination. Later the natural light of the understanding illumines these images with a spiritual perspective, so to speak. Ideas and judgments are conceived in the understanding, which are the beginning of a life above matter, a supercorporeal life, a spiritual life of the natural order. Although spiritual, these ideas are yet circumscribed by sense, inasmuch as they are limited to the data of the senses, for no intelligence can come into the understanding in the natural order, except by way of the senses. However, man can reason and, from the borrowed beauty of created things, he can arrive at the knowledge of the

Creator. Following upon this natural knowledge may come a natural love for his God. So far all is sense, in that man's knowledge and love, though above sense, is yet dependent on the objects of sense. The God Whom he knows to transcend the objects of sense, he knows only by way of negation.

If the supernatural light of faith is shed upon man's intellect, an entirely new element enters into his being — a participation in the Divine life of truth. Now faith does not dispense with the materials gained through sense, but, illuminating them by eternal truth, it expresses higher realities through their symbolic or analogical meaning. For example, God is three Divine Persons in one Nature. Faith takes the idea of "person" and the idea of "nature" to express a Divine reality. If it seems naturally impossible to us, that three persons can be in one nature, that is because these words have a limited meaning for us, drawn from created things, whereas faith applies them to an Infinite Reality. Faith, therefore, departs from sense in a twofold way: first, as regards the primary object, which is infinitely above the objects of sense, being Divine Truth Itself; secondly, as regards the operation of the faculty, for the assent of faith is above the natural power, even of the spiritual understanding. Only in one way does the virtue of faith cling to sense, and that is its use of concepts gained through sense to express the hidden content of faith — but it employs such concepts merely as "veils" covering the Divine reality, or as "husks" covering the "substance" of things to come.

Let us suppose now that God gives a soul corporeal visions, either of the outward or inward bodily senses. As such, these are manifestly no more than sense, since they take place in the senses and cannot represent more than sensible objects. As operations of sense, they can have no more than a natural influence on the understanding, which will conceive ideas of them as *naturally* as it would of any worldly object. So also with the will, which can conceive only a *natural* love for the objects of the natural understanding. Although such knowledge is in a spiritual faculty, St. John terms it "sense" because of its origin in the sense powers, and its consequent limitation.

But what is to be said of meditation on the truths of faith? Meditation, too, is "sense," because the forms and figures of the imagination and the reasoning of the understanding derive from the senses. It is absolutely impossible for the imagination to attain that which is essentially supernatural; and, although our power of reasoning may partake of the certainty and merit of faith, there is nevertheless (as we have so frequently insisted) an inherent deficiency due to the fact that no image, form, figure or species can represent Light Inaccessible. Meditation is insufficient because its origin is in sense.

How, then, is the soul to approach God? Or, to be more precise, how can the soul purify its faith and love? Both faith and love are purified by removing from them that which is sense. Our first concern is with faith, because charity is pure according to the degree of purity of faith, even as natural love depends for its nobility on the loftiness of natural understanding. Now, faith is directed toward the super-sensible; any admixture of the sensible in faith is an impurity, even as lead when mixed with gold makes the latter impure. The purifying of faith, therefore, consists in removing from it any stain or mist of sense-knowledge. The understanding is like a window which

must be purified from all dust of sense if it is to be transformed by the sunlight of faith.[2] The sunlight of faith
may seem brighter when it strikes material particles, but
it is not therefore, more pure and enlightening. On the
contrary, the ray of sunlight is most pure when it is free
from the minutest specks of dust, and as a consequence
dark and invisible in itself.[3] This makes it clearer to
us why so much space was given to discussing the darkness
of faith.

Now, insofar as the soul soars above sense, it will enter
the atmosphere of "spirit," and when it becomes habitually aloof from sense, it has attained to "pure spirit."
What is "spirit"? When we speak of the soul as a spirit, we
mean that it is absolutely distinct and above matter, and
can exist apart from the material body which it vitalizes.
The understanding, too, is spirit, because its knowledge
is spiritual, even when it does not transcend the natural.
But when St. John speaks of "spirit," he is referring to
something that is essentially supernatural. This will become clearer as we go along.

Our author speaks of the progress of the soul as a journey toward a goal. The point of departure is sense, the
goal is spirit. God is a Pure Spirit, and must therefore communicate with the soul according to pure spirit.
But the soul begins from sense, and cannot ordinarily be
united with God in a purely spiritual way without some
preparation. God, who disposes all things sweetly, and
moves each being according to its nature, therefore condescends to the soul and treats with it according to its

[2] v,6-8
[3] cf, xiv,8-9
[4] xvii,2,3

own low methods of sense, in order that He may gradually raise it up to the other extreme of His wisdom, which belongs not to sense. God would give the soul spiritual wisdom all at once, if the two extremes of sense and spirit could concur and unite in one single act; but, as in the natural order, so in the spiritual order, many preparatory acts are necessary so that the soul may be disposed step by step for the higher degrees of Divine union. And thus God brings man to perfection according to the method of man's own nature, working from what is lowest and most exterior up to what is most interior and highest. As man begins with the exterior senses in the attaining of knowledge, so God perfects them first, by means of exterior things, for example, the hearing of sermons and Masses, looking on holy things, mortifying the palate at meals, chastening the sense of touch by penance and holy rigor. Sometimes he may send extraordinary favors, (though these do not belong to normal Christian life) such as visions of saints and holy things for the eyes, locutions for the ears, perfumes for the sense of smell, and delightful feelings for the sense of touch.

The next step is the interior senses of imagination and fancy, by which the spiritual person meditates on the mysteries of our salvation. God uses this method to increase faith and love in the soul by degrees; the spirit is being instructed for that which is higher. Here, too, extraordinary (and not strictly necessary gifts) may be sent to the imagination by means of visions. Though imaginary visions considered precisely as such may be the means of deception, pride, diabolical intervention, *etc.*, still when God uses them, they are accompanied by supernatural helps that will aid the soul to make progress, so long as it does not become attached to the visions themselves. Thus, by acts of faith, hope and love, the soul becomes habituated to the exercise of its spiritual part. After this manner God continues to lead the soul from the exterior to the interior, from sense to spirit. Needless to say, it is not necessary for God to bind Himself to this way in every case, for He is free to lead souls as He wills; nevertheless, His ordinary way agrees with what has been said.[5]

As a person makes progress towards pure spirit, he gradually becomes detached from the ways of sense on which he was formerly so dependent. The more closely a thing is attracted to one extreme, the farther it becomes removed from the other; and, when it attains perfectly to one, it will have completely withdrawn itself from the other. Likewise, the spiritual powers of man, in proportion as they attain to converse with God in pure spirit, are abstracted from the methods of sense, whether they be imaginations, reflections, formal methods of meditation or corporeal visions. Once the taste and sweetness of pure spirit has been experienced, the pleasures of the flesh, whether they have the world or God as object, become arid and insipid. Once the soul becomes perfect in the exercise of spirit, it pays no heed to sense, makes no important use of it in communicating with God, nor desires to receive anything through sense, for the things of sense and the knowledge that one may receive through them are the business of a child. When one is a child one thinks and

[5] xvii,4. In saying that God's ordinary way agrees with what has been said, St. John does not mean that corporeal visions belong to the ordinary way of Christian life, since he calls them "extraordinary" (xi,1; xxi,1,2), and says that one act of charity surpasses all such things (xxii,19). But he means that God's ordinary way is to lead the soul gradually from sense to spirit.

speaks as a child; but when one grows to manhood, one puts away childish things. So with the soul, if it never abstracted itself from sensible things, it would always remain a child in the sight of God. See, then, how important it is to give up sensible pleasures and operations.[6]

[6] In the light of this doctrine, it becomes easy to understand St. John's seeming severity in A,I,ix and xi.

CHAPTER XIX

Sense and Spirit

SCATTERED THROUGH chapters eleven to twenty-two, there are many references to "sense and spirit." It will be well for us to consider some of these, that we may receive clearer light on St. John's view of these two parts, or species of operation, of the soul.

First it is clear that the progress of souls must be from sense to spirit. The reason of this is that the soul has only two ways of increasing in knowledge; the soul can neither work nor receive save only by way of these two kinds of operation, that of sense and that of spirit. For by means of the faculties of sense it can reason and search out knowledge, and by means of the spiritual faculties it can have fruition of knowledge that is given to it.[1] It is God who raises the soul from sense to spirit, and if the soul be faithful and humble, He will not cease to raise it from the order of sense, which is in conformity with the smallness of its capacity, even to Divine union and transformation.[2] For God moves all things according to their nature, and therefore, "He begins to work from the lowest and extreme end of the senses of the soul, in order that He may gradually lead it, according to its own nature, to the other extreme of His spiritual wisdom, which belongs not to sense." [3] Following this natural order, St. John proceeds according

[1] xiv,6
[2] xi,9
[3] xvii,2,3

162

to a logical method, going from the more exterior to the more interior, until he reaches the most interior recollection in the night of the spirit.[4] But many who engage in this spiritual battle do not enter into purity of spirit, because they fail to abstract themselves from things of sense, namely, the world, visions and meditation.[5]

Meditation is sense, and contemplation is spirit. There are three signs by which the spiritual person may see that it is safe for him "to abandon the state of meditation and sense, and to enter that of contemplation and spirit."[6] There are many reasons why God wishes to lead us from sense to spirit. First, "it is more proper and habitual to God to communicate Himself to the spirit." For He dwells within the soul in substance; He can come to the soul and communicate to it, spiritually and substantially, being independent of sensible means.[7] The spiritual part of any communication is *infused* into the soul, for pure spirit cannot be apprehended by sense.[8] Consequently, when the soul first experiences pure spirit, it is hardly conscious of this new and imperceptible condition which is purely spiritual.[9]

Other reasons have to do with the nature of sense. Perhaps the most important is that sense is not the proximate and proportionate means to Divine union:

> ... bodily sense judges and makes its estimate of spiritual things by thinking that they are as it feels them to be, whereas they are as different as is the body from the

[4] xii,1
[5] xi,10
[6] xiii,5
[7] xvi,4,13
[8] xvi,11
[9] xiv,7

soul and sensuality from reason. For the bodily sense is as ignorant of spiritual things as is a beast of rational things, and even more so.[10]

... between spiritual things and all these bodily things there exists no kind of proportion whatever.[11]

And the more exterior are these corporeal forms and objects in themselves, the less do they profit the interior and spiritual nature, because of the great distance and the little proportion existing between the corporeal and the spiritual.[12]

... things that are experienced by the senses derogate from faith; since faith, as we have said, transcends every sense. And thus the soul withdraws itself from the means of union with God when it closes not its eyes to all these things of sense. . . . they are a hindrance to the spirit, if they [he is speaking of imaginary visions] be not denied, for the soul rests in them and its spirit soars not to the invisible. . . . it begins to lose the effect of them and the inward spirituality which they cause it, because it sets its eyes upon their sensual aspect, which is the least important. And thus it receives not so fully the spirituality which they cause, which is impressed and preserved more securely when all things of sense are rejected, since these are very different from pure spirit.[13]

The spiritual person, then, has to deny himself all the apprehensions, and the temporal delights, that belong to the outward senses, . . . desiring neither to lay hold upon, nor to be embarrassed by, that which is given to the senses, since it is this that derogates most from faith.[14] . . . these sensual apprehensions and visions can-

[10] xi,2
[11] xi,3
[12] xi,4
[13] xi,7
[14] xi,11

not be a means to union, since they bear no proportion to God; . . .[15]

For, although these considerations and forms and manners of meditation are necessary to beginners, in order that they may gradually feed and enkindle their souls with love by means of sense, as we shall say hereafter, and although they thus serve them as remote means to union with God, through which a soul has commonly to pass in order to reach the goal and abode of spiritual repose, yet they must merely pass through them, and not remain ever in them, for in such a manner they would never reach their goal, which does not resemble these remote means, neither has aught to do with them.[16]

. . . the eyes of the soul must ever be withdrawn from all these apprehensions which it can see and understand distinctly, which are communicated through sense and do not produce the sure foundation of faith, and must be set upon that which it sees not, and which belongs not to sense, but to spirit, which can be expressed by no figure of sense; and it is this which leads the soul to union in faith, which is the true medium, as has been said.[17]

. . . in this matter of sense the letter must be set aside, and the soul must remain in darkness, in faith, which is the spirit, and this cannot be comprehended by sense.[18]

[One of the dangers of visions is that the soul might] gradually, without realizing it, become callous as it treads the spiritual road, and draw near again to the road of sense; . . .[19]

[15] xi,12
[16] xii,5
[17] xvi,12
[18] xix,5
[19] xxii,17

From the above we are able to get some idea of what St. John means by "spirit." It is God who moves the soul from sense to spirit; spiritual communication is proper to God; spirit is *infused*; spirit is the proximate and proportionate means to union with God; spirit is sometimes termed "faith"; spirit is contemplation. From which we may conclude that "spirit" refers to something essentially supernatural.

CHAPTER XX

Characteristics of Sense and Spirit

THE NOTIONS of sense and spirit are so fundamental and important in John of the Cross that our time will be well spent in examining certain characteristics proper to each in opposition to the other. This study will not only clarify his doctrine further, but will serve the reader as a means of recognizing in his own soul what is of sense and what is of spirit. Of sense he says that it is "particular," it is an "act," a "morsel," it is a "journey," it is "labor," it is "human." On the contrary, spirit is "general and confused," it is a "habit," it is "substance," it is the "goal" and "rest," it is "Divine." We shall try to discover the reasons for such descriptive terminology.

By "sense" is meant, as we saw, all the knowledge of the senses, as terminating in, or as related to, the understanding. By "all the knowledge of the senses" we mean not only that which has its origin in this world, but even that which might be directly impressed on the corporeal senses by preternatural intervention. It is sense knowledge terminating in ideas. It is necessary here to recall briefly the natural mode of acquiring ideas. Our eyes, ears, *etc.* are in contact with the universe. Like delicate and precise instruments they re-act to the forces of matter, light, sound, *etc.* and convey their impressions to the interior senses of man, like the work of a lens on a motion picture film. The individual pictures are the images and figures of the imagination. The next step is rather mysterious, but nonetheless certain. The understanding, which is a faculty of the spiritual soul as distinct from the body, forms ideas from the contents or representations of the imagination (or phantasy). These ideas are the internal and spiritual means through which the understanding is united with the outside world; in other words, our knowledge of existing reality is through spiritual ideas formed from the data of the imagination received through the windows of the senses. The point of our consideration is that our knowledge is derived from *individual* objects; our knowledge is first *particular*; later we build up a science of general principles. We see a particular object, we hear a particular sound, taste a particular savor; in the imagination (or phantasy) there will be a particular image or figure corresponding to the individual object of the exterior senses; in the understanding there will be a particular, spiritual form (idea). Even when we attain to knowledge of a species or class of things; that species of reality is defined by particular characteristics, and so also, the interior species of our mind (the idea) will be particular in this, that it represents the particular and distinct properties of a certain class of objects.[1] In a word, our knowledge is particular because it represents something particular and not *being* in general. All our images, figures, forms and species are particular because derived from definite, concrete things

[1] St. John does not seem to distinguish between sensible and intelligible species, but it must be remembered that he is concerned with sense knowledge always in relation to the understanding. He is concerned only with the fact that our knowledge whether sensible or intellectual, is always of a limited nature limited by the imperfect being of created objects. Cf. A,II,xvi,3-4 where he seems to use "species" both of the imagination and the external object.

If our knowledge is particular, it must also be "distinct," that is, each object of our knowledge has the quality of being distinguished from all other objects. Every created thing is "particular and distinct" by reason of its limitation of being. Sense, too, is "particular and distinct," because it comprises all our sensible knowledge and the ideas drawn therefrom.

Opposed to these natural characteristics of sense are the terms "general and confused." By "general" is meant that knowledge which is in no way specific, or in no way reveals particular objects. "Confused" does not refer to enigmatic knowledge, but is that which is opposed to "distinct." Our knowledge of God is general and confused, not because God is not perfectly intelligible in Himself, but because in this life we have no clear and distinct vision of Him, not even in infused contemplation. In describing this contemplation as "confused, general and dark" St. John is able to distinguish it from all that is less than the purest faith.[2]

St. John points out that there are two ways of attaining knowledge of God: meditation and contemplation; sense or spirit. Meditation is of particular things; contemplation is "confused and general" knowledge. When the soul leaves the way of sense, it must have "this *general* and loving attentiveness," if it is not to be wasting its time in idleness.[3] The ways of meditation and contemplation are distinguished according to their mode of knowledge. The soul that is progressing beyond meditation takes pleasure in being alone, with an attentiveness and knowledge, *general* and loving, but without any *particular* understanding,

[2] x,4
[3] xiv,6

without any *particular* meditation, by which is meant, of
course, understanding or meditation on *particular* things.[4]
The reason for this change lies in the nature of contemplation, for this infused contemplation is "Divine light," "a
general and supernatural knowledge and light" far removed from all intelligble forms; it is "pure intelligence,"
"heavenly intelligence" withdrawn and abstracted from
all things, forms and figures.[5] Because this *general* knowledge is "far removed from other *particular* kinds of knowledge and intelligence," it is subtle and delicate and
obscure; the more pure and simple this spiritual ray of
light is in itself, the less palpable it is to the soul; if it were
to seem brighter or more palpable, that would be because
of particles of *particular* knowledge commingled with it.[6]
It is because of this obscurity of contemplation, wherein
the soul "understands nothing *clearly*," that many fail to
gain this spirituality. They think that the whole business
consists in understanding *"particular* things by means of
images and forms," but these are only the rind of spirituality. Souls must become lost to their first manner of perception, and try to realize that the less they understand, the
farther they will penetrate into the night of the spirit (the
subject of this book of the "Ascent"), through which night
they must pass in order to be united with God, in a union
that transcends all (particular and distinct) knowledge.[7]
When souls enter this state of contemplation, they feel
great weariness and distaste in making *"particular* acts of

[4] xiii,4
[5] xiv,10,11
[6] xiv,8,9
[7] xiv,4

knowledge." [8] This results from the fact that in this new state the soul does not exercise its natural faculties in "*particular* acts"; it acts not at all with its faculties.[9] In such prayer as this, it is true to say that the soul makes neither acts of *particular* knowledge nor *particular* acts of knowledge — it receives infused and passive understanding.

How important it is, therefore, that the soul which discerns in itself the signs of contemplation should refrain from desiring to understand and to consider "*particular* things, however spiritual they be," since this would obstruct the pure and simple "*general* light of the spirit," the "*general* and confused knowledge of God." [10] It is also important that the soul realize that this is not idleness. Divine calm and peace will be infused together with this sublime knowledge and love; but if the soul should "meddle with forms, meditations and imaginings" it would be disturbed; let it remember that it is doing no small thing by bringing itself into calm and peace, unaccompanied by any act or desire,[11] taking it for a sign that it is occupied if the understanding is withdrawn from all "*particular* knowledge, whether temporal or spiritual," and the will has no desire to dwell on either kind. However, if contemplation affects the will also, the soul becomes conscious of a sweetness and love therein, "without *particular* knowledge or understanding of that which it loves." "It is for this reason that this knowledge is described as *general* and loving; for, just as it is so in the understanding, being com-

[8] xiv,3
[9] xv,2
[10] xv,3
[11] xv,5

municated to it *obscurely*, even so is it in the will, sweetness and love being communicated to it "confusedly," so that it cannot have a *distinct* knowledge of the object of its love." [12]

All the knowledge of the senses, and all the knowledge which the understanding draws therefrom is "sense" and is therefore *particular* and *distinct*. Now this applies likewise to that knowledge of sense which is received outside the natural mode, namely, corporeal visions either external or imaginary. It will be noticed that St. John's teaching is the same here as in the sensible knowledge acquired in the natural way. I think it will be sufficient to set down a few quotations:

> I say, then, that with regard to all these imaginary visions and apprehensions and to all other forms and species whatsoever, which present themselves beneath some *particular* kind of knowledge or image or form, whether they be false and come from the devil or are recognized as true and coming from God, the understanding must not be embarrassed by them or feed upon them; neither must the soul desire to receive them or to have them, lest it should no longer be detached, free, pure and simple, without any mode or manner, as is required for union.[13]
>
> ... the Wisdom of God, wherein the understanding is to be united, has no mode or manner, neither is it contained within any *particular* or *distinct* kind of intelligence or limit, because it is wholly pure and simple. ... the soul must be pure and simple, neither bounded by, nor attached to, any *particular* kind of intelligence, nor modified by any limitation of form, species and image.

[12] xiv,12
[13] xvi,6

As God comes not within any image or form, neither is contained within any *particular* kind of intelligence, so the soul, in order to reach God, must likewise come within no *distinct* form or kind of intelligence.[14]

. . . clouds and thick darkness, which are the *confused* and *dark* knowledge whereof we have spoken, wherein the soul is united with God.[15]

Wherefore, in order to come to this essential union of love in God, the soul must have a care not to lean upon imaginary visions, nor upon forms or figures or *particular* objects of the understanding; for these cannot serve it as a proportionate and proximate means to such an end . . .[16]

Wherefore, if the soul at that time desires to receive these forms and to set store by them, it would be embarrassing itself, and contenting itself with the least important part of them — namely, all that it can apprehend and know of them, which is the form and image and *particular* object of the understanding in question. The most important part is . . . pure spirit.[17]

It is interesting to note that this sense knowledge, precisely because it is particular and distinct, acts as a veil and curtain over that which is spiritual. This may well be compared with what was said of meditation: that to understand and consider particular things, however spiritual they be, would be to obstruct the light of contemplation by clouds. ". . . creature forms are as veils which must be removed." [18]

14 xvi,7
15 xvi,8
16 xvi,10
17 xvi,11
18 xvi,11; compare xv,4

Wherefore the eyes of the soul must ever be withdrawn from all these apprehensions which it can see and understand *distinctly* . . .[19]

. . . it is not the will of God that souls should desire to receive anything *distinctly*, through visions, locutions, *etc*. . . .[20]

. . . if we desire to cling to these other bright lights — namely, to *distinct* objects of the understanding — we cease to cling to that dark light, which is faith . . . [In order to go forward in faith, souls must] close their eyes to all that is of *particular* and *clear* perception and sense.[21]

Speaking of "perceptions of some particular kind" and "particular perceptions," even though received in visions, St. John calls them "trifles" "narrow aqueducts" and "crumbs." [22]

We have a very spiritual letter of St. John's, written to one of his penitents, a Religious, from which we may extract something to our purpose:

Wherefore, in order to annihilate and mortify these affections for pleasures with respect to all that is not God, Your Reverence must note that all wherein the will can have a *distinct* joy is sweet and delectable, since this appears pleasant to it; and no sweet and delectable thing wherein it can rejoice and delight is God, for, as God cannot come within the apprehensions of the other faculties, so neither can He come within the desires and pleasures of the will; . . . all that the will can have pleasure in and desire as a *distinct* thing, it desires in so far as it knows it to be such or such an object. . . . And thus

[19] xvi,12
[20] xxii,2
[21] xvi,15
[22] xvii,7,8

it is clear that no *distinct* object from among all the objects that the will can enjoy is God. Wherefore, in order to become united with Him, a man must empty and strip himself of every inordinate affection of desire and pleasure for all that can be *distinctly* enjoyed, whether it be high or low, temporal or spiritual, . . .

. . . it is impossible that the will can rise to the sweetness and delight of Divine union, or embrace God or experience His sweet and loving embraces, save in detachment and emptying of desire with respect to every particular pleasure whether from above or from below; . . .[23]

We are now in a position to sum up this matter, and to formulate certain important principles regarding the types of knowledge so far considered, in answer to certain questions that will arise in the mind of the thoughtful reader: —

1. What is the importance of these terms "particular and distinct"?

Our knowledge is particular because directed to individual objects having, as it were, a *particle* of being; it is distinct because, through particularization (or limitation), one thing can be distinguished from another. "Particular kind of intelligence" is that which is "modified by any limitation of form, species and image." God alone does not come within any limitation of any image or form or any particular kind of intelligence, for two reasons: first, He cannot be seen clearly in this life (according to the opinion which St. John adopts); secondly, God, inasmuch as He is infinite, is said to be without image or form.[24] The force of these terms, then, is to af-

[23] Letter XI, Vol. III of Peer's translation.
[24] xvi,7-9

ford an easy and certain standard by which we may reject all that is less than God.

2. What is the meaning of "general, confused and dark"?

"General" is opposed to particular. St. John is not referring to general principles of philosophy or theology, since these also may refer to particular beings. But he is using "general" in negation of that particularization which is proper to things that only borrow and share existence. "Confused" is used in opposition to "distinct." "Dark" refers to a darkness of natural perception. "General, confused and dark" refers to a supernatural light which fails to illuminate or reveal any distinct particle of being, or, at least, its proper object is not to do so.

3. What types of knowledge (so far considered) are particular and distinct?

a) Purely natural knowledge of the world; b) Meditation, though enlightened by faith. c) Corporeal visions.

4. What type of knowledge is "general, confused and dark"?

Infused, obscure contemplation, which is given to the understanding apart from any figure, image, form and species.

5. Is particular and distinct knowledge always natural?

Considered merely as particular and distinct, it is always natural in essence, i.e., not above the natural capacity of the intellect as such. St. John calls some knowledge "supernatural" (modally) because it is impressed on a faculty in a way differing from our natural mode of knowing in this life. The knowledge of faith is supernatural in this, that we assent, by the grace of faith, to mysteries (dark and indistinct to our understanding) expressed in particular and distinct, but merely analogous concepts. In proportion as the knowledge of faith is particular and distinct it is commingled with the merely natural; as it becomes more purely supernatural, it becomes dark and indistinct. Contemplation is perfectly dark because it is the perfection of faith.

6. Is all particular and distinct knowledge identical with sense knowledge?

No, for the intellect can receive directly (preternaturally) infused ideas, which are always particular and distinct. Moreover, faith employs particular and distinct knowledge analogically.

7. Is all sense knowledge particular and distinct?

Yes, both in the senses and as terminating in the understanding. The reason is that such knowledge is proportioned to the objects themselves, which are always particular and distinct.

8. Why must the soul be detached from everything that can be *distinctly* enjoyed, whether from above or below, whether temporal or spiritual?

Because all that we can enjoy distinctly in this life is less than God. We have here a principle of paramount importance. For example, a soul might be harassed by doubts about a sweetness of delight that pervades even the body. If spiritual sweetness arises from clear and particular knowledge, it ought to be considered as natural; if, on the contrary, this sweetness or delight is experienced while the understanding is darkened, or when the soul is conscious of a confused knowledge or attentiveness to God (infused contemplation), it may be presumed to be from God. In this matter, the security of the soul lies in this, that its delight does not enslave it to any particular or distinct object.[25]

[25] Read Letter XI

9. Can these types of particular and distinct knowledge ever be essentially supernatural?

No. At most it can be symbolic or analogical, as in faith which employs natural concepts. St. John says that the clear and particular apprehensions of the understanding, in meditation as even in the corporeal visions sent by God Himself, are merely curtains and veils covering the essence of true spirituality.[26]

We said previously that spiritual progress must be from sense to spirit. Because sense is related to spirit as "particular and distinct" is related to "general and confused," we may now add that the progress of the soul is from particular and diversified acts to an act more general and confused, exercised habitually. "For, the farther the soul progresses in spirituality, the more it ceases from the operation of the faculties in *particular* acts, for it becomes more and more occupied in one act that is *general* and pure; . . ." [27] "And thus that which the soul was gaining gradually through its labor of meditation upon *particular* facts has now . . . changed into a habit and substance of loving knowledge, of a *general* kind, and not *distinct* or *particular* as before." [28]

How are we to explain this conversion from particular to general, from distinct to confused? Can this be progress? In the study of the natural sciences, is not confused knowledge a sign of stupidity, whereas particularization and distinctions are a characteristic of analytical proficiency? But of this more shall be said in the following chapter.

[26] xvi,11; xv,4
[27] xii,6
[28] xiv,2

CHAPTER XXI

From Act to Habit

THE SOUL or character of man grows and develops, or withers and decays, according to its habits. The life of the soul is in its acts, but these acts depend for their intensity and frequency upon habits. With good habits a character is strong and free; with bad habits the soul is weak and enslaved. It is to be expected, then, that in a spiritual treatise like the "Ascent of Mt. Carmel" we should find references, at least implicit, to acts and habits. In the first Book of the "Ascent," we found many such references in regard to the imperfection of the soul. For example, it was said that "some habits of voluntary imperfections, which are never completely conquered, prevent not only the attainment of Divine union, but also progress in perfection." [1] And we learned what such "habitual imperfections" were, and how great harm comes from any one of these, if the soul becomes "habituated" to it.[2] St. John insisted that one must mortify his desires "habitually," having an "habitual" desire to imitate Christ, and so enters the (active) night of sense "habitually." [3] When he speaks of "virtues of great loveliness," he has in mind supernatural habits.[4]

In this second Book of the "Ascent," we found that the

[1] A.,I,xi,3
[2] A.,I,xi,4
[3] A.,I,v,6,7; xiii,1,3
[4] A.,I,ix,4

Divine union consists of an "obscure habit" in the soul and its faculties.[5] In the faculties, these habits are the theological virtues.[6] In order to attain to union with God, the soul must rid itself of all that is repugnant to the Divine will, "not only in action, but likewise in habit, so that not only do the voluntary acts of imperfection cease, but the habits of those imperfections, whatever they be, are annihilated." [7]

Coming now to the obscure habit of faith, we find that progress is from repeated acts to the habit that is formed by them. Spiritual meditation is the remote means to true spirituality; it is the way of beginners and serves a twofold purpose. First, it helps to detach the affections from temporal, worldly and natural forms and images. Secondly, and with this we are now concerned, it helps to "dispose and *habituate*" the soul to spirituality.[8] How does a soul become *habituated* to spirituality? By many acts which are, at least partially, spiritual. Just as many acts, of whatever kind, end by forming a habit in the soul, so many acts of loving knowledge, which the soul has been making one after another from time to time, gradually perfect within it a habit of loving knowledge. These loving acts are made in meditation, which, though imperfect by reason of its images and forms that tend to lower God to the level of sense knowledge, is, nevertheless, the source of many acts of love of God. Thus, by practise and repetition, the virtue of charity is exercised and becomes so continuous a font of love, that the soul becomes gradually independent of med-

[5] v,2
[6] vi
[7] v,4
[8] xiii,1

itation upon *particular* facts, until its loving knowledge is changed into a habit of a *general* kind, and not *distinct* or *particular* as before.[9] The reason is that love has gained the ascendancy, and dispenses with the discursive process of the understanding. This causes us no wonder when we recall that charity is above reasoning, being infused both in habit and act from the beginning.

God treats with the soul according to its own nature. He, therefore, treats with the soul at first in the order of distinct and particular knowledge. As a painter combines certain elements to form paints, and then combines the paints, too, on a canvas, composing them in beautiful forms to radiate natural truths, so God condescends in the beginning to employ the materials of our natural life, combining certain concepts of our natural knowledge, so that under the illumination of Divine truth (the artistry of faith) they may reflect or symbolize, in shadow, the blinding realities of the supernatural order. But, though the painter cannot convey the spiritual element in his art without using material colors, God can. And God does; after exercising the soul in particular acts of love for some time so that the mind and heart may acquire strong habits of faith and charity, God dispenses with particular acts of knowledge (or acts of particular knowledge) and infuses the loving knowledge of Himself in a *general* mode, *i.e.*, without distinct images or forms, such as a natural painter must use. It is as if a teacher, condescending to the ignorance of his pupils, were to illustrate his doctrine by drawings and paintings pertaining to his science in the elementary stages, but afterwards, when his students had formed intellectual habits, would change his method and

[9] xiv,2

infuse learning into their minds directly by mental telepathy (supposing that to be practicable). With God it is not only practicable, but absolutely necessary that He infuse faith and charity, because these are above nature. Loving knowledge, insofar as it is a proximate means of union with God, is infused from the very beginning, though the *distinct* knowledge which is accidental to it, is of the natural order. It is not to be marvelled at, therefore, that God, should dispense with the *particular* acts of knowledge at a given time in the spiritual life, since He could infuse this contemplation without the preceding labor of the soul. "This end God is wont also to effect in many souls without the intervention of these acts (or at least without many such acts having preceded it), by setting them at once in contemplation." [10]

Let us illustrate this matter further by an example. Sunlight is something super-earthly. If the sun were suddenly to burn out, things would be dark indeed — like a world without faith. Now the health of our eyes and the facility of vision depend upon sunlight more than we realize. Strong, healthful eyes are able to glance, though momentarily, at the sun. A child, born in the mines and coming out into daylight for the first time, would find the vision of objects bathed in golden light, a bright experience indeed, and would, no doubt, be conscious of the super-earthly existence of the sun, without at first being able to receive its rays directly into his eyes. Although the things of this world break up the rays into a multiplicity of *particular* and *distinct* forms, the sunlight as such remains a super-earthly reality. The child's eyes become stronger, developing a keenness of vision, for which the

⁰ xiv,2

particular and *distinct* images in his vision are not so much responsible as the *formless* brilliance which exercises it. Just as in faith the primary object is Divine truth, in which the individual and distinct articles are illuminated, so in vision the primary object is sunlight, through which all other distinct things are seen. In earthly things, particularization and distinctness is not due to light primarily, but to their own limitation; in faith or meditation, clarity and distinctness is due, not to faith, but to the forms and species which are proper to natural things. This child, then, by particular acts of seeing, is forming a disposition or habit in his eyes for the reception of sunlight; after some time he will be able to abstract his gaze from the objects of sense, and looking up to that which is super-earthly in its essence, open his eyes and receive passively the light which shall be communicated to him in a *general* and *confused* manner.[11] Is that light any the less light for being without image or figure? Is it not more truly super-earthly for being indistinct and formless? So also "contemplation that is given in faith" is not less faith for being without images and ideas, but rather more truly supernatural for being general and confused. And, as this child's particular acts of considering the delicate tracery and intricate forms of earthly creatures were a preparation for the reception of the direct rays of the sun, so the soul's particular acts of meditation and multiple reflections are a preparation for reception of "the pure and simple general light of the spirit."

Here we may ask a very important question. Is this language of St. John merely rhetorical, designed only to show that contemplation, if perchance God should bestow

[11] Cf. xv,2 for this simile

this (extraordinary?) favor, should follow meditation only because meditation should precede as the lesser precedes the greater? Or does he mean that there is a causal connection between meditation and contemplation, and a normal transition from the discursive process to passive enlightenment? The answer cannot be except as follows. Contemplation is the normal outcome of meditation in those who have reaped the fruits of meditation and know how to pass onward. First, we must prove that St. John teaches the normal transition from meditation to contemplation. But what greater proof could we have than his assertion that the soul is prepared for the habit of the loving knowledge of contemplation through the single acts of loving knowledge in meditation? The sequence and connection between meditation and infused contempla tion is the same as between act and habit, always assuming that no contrary acts prevent this habit from being fully developed, which is the law for all habits.

Especially informative is that place where John of the Cross answers the question whether progressives (those who are beginning to practise contemplation) should never again exercise meditation. He replies that it will be necessary *at first* to return to meditation, since the soul will not always be conscious of that loving knowledge which is independent of the discursive method. His reasons are the focal point of our interest. When contemplatives are first gaining in proficiency, their "*habit* of contemplation is not yet so perfect, that whensoever they wish they can give themselves to the *act* thereof; nor, in the same way have they reached a point so far beyond meditation that they cannot occasionally meditate and reason" as they did formerly. For, until they reach proficiency in contempla tion, they use sometimes one kind of prayer, sometimes the other. When the soul sees that it is not occupied in contemplation — that loving attentiveness, in abstraction from the things of sense — it will frequently need to make use of meditation, quietly and in moderation, until it acquires the *habit of contemplation* with sufficient perfection. The soul will frequently find itself in this loving or peaceful state of waiting upon God, without any exercise of its faculties in particular acts; but, on the other hand, in order to reach this state, it will frequently need to make use of meditation. In the order of natural psychology, could there be any greater proof for the causality or relationship between an act and a habit than that, when the habit is not sufficiently perfect, souls must be further exercised in the acts that form it? Now, meditation is that which leads to, or disposes the soul for, contemplation, and if this latter "is not yet so perfect that, whensoever they wish, they can give themselves to the act thereof," souls must return to meditation, since they have not "reached a point so far beyond meditation" that they can no longer be helped by it.[12]

In speaking of God's manner of treating with the soul according to its nature, beginning with the exterior senses and working to that which is more and more interior, St. John says that God, in the case of the imagination and fancy, wishes "to perfect and *habituate* to that which is good, by means of considerations, meditations, and reflections of a sacred kind, in all of which He is instructing the spirit." [13] In other words, by means of the senses, God is instructing the spirit, perfecting it and *habituating* it to what is spiritual, namely, contemplation.

[12] xv,1-2
[13] xvii,4

Here, we may take notice of an objection. How can sense habituate to spirit? How can an act of the corporeal faculty form a habit of the spiritual faculty? How can the *activity* of the understanding form a habit of contemplation which is passive? The answer is that it is not meditation, considered precisely as such, which forms the habit of contemplation. But in meditation God communicates spirituality to the soul. Concomitant with the operation of sense, "the spirit [soul] may make particular acts and receive so many morsels of spiritual communication that it may form a habit in things spiritual, and may acquire actual and substantial spirituality, in complete abstraction from every sense." [14] The action of sense is one thing; the operation of spirit, or the supernatural action which must be infused by God, is another and entirely different thing, although they, taken together form a composite, as do also body and soul. Together with the acts of sense, then, the spirit makes particular acts of faith and charity, and receives morsels of spiritual communication (the infusions of faith and charity) by which it forms a habit in things spiritual, and acquires the actual substance of the spirit, in complete abstraction from every sense, *i.e.*, above all sensible operation. To this habit in things spiritual, "the soul cannot attain except very gradually, and in its own way — that is by means of sense — to which it has ever been attached." The soul passes from particular acts, or morsels of spirit to the habit and substance of the spirit, which might be also called the "substance and the habit of the spirit of meditation." [15]

In answer to the objection: How can sense habituate to

[14] xvii,5
[15] Compare xiv,2 with xvii,5

spirit? we answer that it is not precisely sense which habit-
uates to spirit, but rather the infusions of spirit (grace)
which are received concomitantly with the soul's own action. How can an act of the corporeal faculty form a habit
of the spiritual faculty? It does not: it is in the spiritual
understanding that both the act and the habit are formed.
How can the *activity* of the understanding form a habit of
contemplation which is *passive?* The activity of the understanding consists in its operations on sense knowledge; the
understanding is always passive in regard to the supernatural, whether in act or habit. The morsels of spirituality infused by God are received passively; so also the substance or habit which consists in an increase of grace or a
deeper rooting of grace in the soul and its faculties. The
terms "activity" and "passivity" are often misunderstood.
Some think of "passivity" as a kind of death to action, but
it is really more concerned with action than "activity."
We call that soul active which is acting by its own natural
powers; and that soul is passive which is in action or operation through the intervention of a force above nature.
Therefore, the soul is passive in every supernatural act.[16]
In meditation, of course, there are elements of both activity

[16] We are aware that authors usually speak of the soul's being
"active" in ordinary faith and charity, but "passive" in infused
contemplation. In thus using the term "active" they do not mean
to deny that grace is always infused; nor by terming contemplation "passive" do they mean to deny that the spiritual faculties
are supernaturally in operation. They speak of incipient Christian
life as "active" because there is so much of palpable and natural
action in it; while on the other hand, they term infused contemplation "passive" because natural activity is minimized, and the
soul seems inactive, because of the invisible nature of the supernatural. For further elucidation, see p. 353.

and passivity: the soul is active as regards images, forms and species; it is passive in regard to the light of faith and the fire of charity, which can only be infused; there is an element of passivity, therefore, even in meditation. It is this element in meditation, which by repeated and continuous acts forms the habit of contemplation. This is saying no more than that one grace prepares the soul for higher graces; St. John insists upon this principle in chapter seventeen.

The transition to contemplation consists of both a positive and a negative process. On the positive side, the soul must receive acts or morsels of spirit until it forms a habit of spirit. But, in order that this spirituality may be pure, it must become more and more abstracted from sense. "In proportion as the spirit attains more nearly to converse with God, it becomes more completely detached and emptied of the ways of sense, which are those of imaginary meditation and reflection." [17] When this negative process is completed together with the positive, the soul is habitually contemplative. There are acts contrary to the habit of contemplation, as is the case with every habit. These contrary habits, or "contrarieties," [18] are worldly desires, the desire for visions and meditation, for, since these are concerned with particular and distinct things, they are contrary to the acts of contemplation, which is general and confused.

[17] xvii,5
[18] v,4

CHAPTER XXII

Nutrition

WE HAVE been considering the characteristics of sense and spirit. So far we have ascertained that sense is particular and distinct, while spirit is general and confused; and in the spiritual exercises of sense, God infuses a morsel of spirituality, or an *act* of the spirit, by which, through constant repetition, the *habit* of spirit is formed. Let us now turn our attention to certain similes which St. John uses to describe spiritual progress.

The figure of nutrition is used frequently by him, and concerns both food and drink. He speaks of fruit, solid food, strong meat, of wine, milk and water, of morsels and crumbs (with the idea of insufficiency), of rind, husk, as opposed to substance. As the body is sustained and increased in life by food and drink in sufficient quantity and quality, so the soul is nourished in its supernatural life by faith and charity, according to the number and purity of its acts. In the natural order, it is a common occurrence for a child to choose food that is tasty rather than substantial, or for an infant to cling to the breast when it should seek stronger food. It is less conceivable that a person would desire the rind and the husk rather than the inner substance of food. In the supernatural order, we learn from St. John, such follies are of ordinary experience.

The food that God desires souls to eat is pure spirit or contemplation. But contemplation is not palpable or sweet to the soul that has not acquired a taste for it; many souls think that the only food is meditation, and when meditation becomes distasteful and unpalatable, they fail to realize that it no longer is able to nourish and fatten them. However, they still strive to find that earlier sweetness, not knowing that the soul no longer can enjoy that food of sense, since it needs not this, but another food, which is more delicate, more interior.[1]

The soul that strives to obtain all its nourishment from meditation, when the time has come for it to practise contemplation, is like a little child that is forced to feed itself by its own efforts instead of being allowed to be fed without labor from the breast; or such a person is like one who, after having removed the rind from a piece of fruit, refuses to eat and persists in peeling rind; or again he is like one who continually prepares a meal instead of partaking and tasting of that which is already cooked and served.[2] Such persons should be enjoying the substance of the fruit or of the meal, which is contemplation; instead they seek after images and forms, which, compared to spirit, are nothing but rind.[3] It is noteworthy that St. John applies these figures of speech not only to meditation but also to extraordinary things. If imaginings and reasonings are as rind, no less are imaginary visions; if the soul desires to feed on this outer rind of interior visions, it is clear that the understanding cannot receive the substance.[4] Therefore, "the soul must not allow its eyes to rest upon that outer husk — namely, figures and objects set before it supernaturally," (whether exteriorly or interiorly).[5]

[1] xii,6; xiv,1
[2] xiv,3,7
[3] xiv,4
[4] xvi,11
[5] xvii,9

The simile of water is also used of both ordinary and extraordinary practises. The soul that gives itself to contemplative prayer is like one to whom water has been brought, so that he drinks peacefully and without labor, and is no longer forced to draw the water laboriously and by small amounts through the aqueducts of meditation. On the contrary, the soul is now able, as soon as it comes to prayer, to *drink* of wisdom and love and delight.[6] As for corporeal visions, it is because God leads the soul according to its own weak nature, that He communicates to it "the abundance of His spirit by these aqueducts, which are so narrow — these forms and figures and particular perceptions . . ." [7] "For God is like a spring, whence everyone draws water according to the vessel which he carries. Sometimes a soul is allowed to draw it by these extraordinary channels; but it follows not from this that it is lawful to draw water by them, but only that God Himself can permit this, how and to whom He wills, and for what reason He wills, without any other party having any right in the matter." [8]

Taking up now the value of milk (and afterwards we shall take up wine), St. John no doubt was influenced by St. Paul's use of this figure. St. Paul was grieved by the lack of preparation and the incapability of men for receiving the Spirit. To the Corinthians he wrote, "I, brethren, when I came to you, could not speak to you as to spiritual persons, but as to carnal; for ye could not receive it, neither can ye now. I have given you milk to drink, as to infants in Christ, and not solid food to eat." To cling to

[6] xiv,2
[7] xvii,8
[8] xxi,2

the things of sense is to wish to be always an infant, and never to leave the breast. The soul must not desire to receive the knowledge of sense, even though it be through revelations sent by God, if it is to continue in growth, just as the child must leave the breast in order to accustom its palate to strong meat, which is more substantial. As regards meditation and reflection, one must not, of course, leave this breast of sense until God sets one in contemplation. But in regard to corporeal visions, one must never receive such nourishment, even though one be still an infant in the spiritual life.[9] The prophet Isaiah applied this simile to those who were atttached to the letter of prophecies rather than to their spirit, for the literal and material sense of prophecies is often like the milk of infants.[10] In the "Dark Night of the Soul" John of the Cross develops this figure beautifully. God is like a loving mother, who, as long as her child is an infant, warms it with the heat of her bosom, nurtures it with sweet milk and soft and pleasant food, and carries and caresses it in her arms. But, as her child grows bigger, she gradually ceases caressing it, and, hiding her tender love, puts bitter aloes upon her sweet breast, sets down the child from her arms and makes it walk upon its feet, so that it may lose the characteristics of a child and betake itself to greater and more substantial occupations. So God treats with the soul. As soon as it is regenerated by its new warmth and fervor in His service, He makes it find spiritual milk, sweet and delectable, in all the things of God, and great pleasure in spiritual exer-

[9] xvii,6-8. Though of no importance, it may be interesting to note that St. John uses this figure in an opposing signification in xiv,3

[10] xix,6

cises. These pleasures and sensible sweetness are the breast of His tender love. Little does such a soul realize how weak and imperfect it is, feeble like a child, in virtue. But the time must come when God takes this soul from its swaddling clothes, sets it down from His arms, makes it walk upon its feet, and likewise takes from it the milk of the breast and the soft and sweet food proper to children, and makes it eat bread with crust, that it may begin to enjoy the food of robust persons. This food is that which is dry and lacking the sweetness of sense — the food of infused contemplation.[11]

As for the wine, it is that which will inebriate the soul with love, when, after despising the milk and the morsels given for its strength and sustenance, and partaking of further and better food, it is led by the Spouse into the cellar of wine of His perfect charity.[12] Elsewhere the virtues of the soul are compared to a vineyard which yields to the soul a wine of sweet savor.[13] The wine of love is sweet, delectable and strong, and when spiced with the strong spices of virtue, inebriates souls in the Holy Spirit.[14] Again, new wine may be compared to beginners, and old wine to old and faithful lovers of God.[15]

The similes of "rind," "husk," "morsels," as opposed to "substance," brings out two principles with which we are already familiar. The "rind" or the "husk" pertains to sense, and indeed is identified with sense. There is, therefore, an irreconcilable opposition between the rind or

[11] D.N.,I,i,2-3; xii,1
[12] xi,9; Cf. also S.C., xxvi
[13] S.C.,xvi,4
[14] S.C.,xxv,7
[15] S.C., xxv,10,11

husk of spirituality and the substance of spirituality itself. By "substance" is meant pure spirit, spirituality in complete abstraction from the operations of sense, and contemplation, all of which are the same in the mind of St. John. Thus he speaks of the *substance* of general knowledge as being equivalent to the habit of contemplation; this *substance* of the spirit is acquired by particular acts of meditation. The soul has this substance when it is enjoying that "substantial and loving quiet" which means "the gain of that spirituality which is being given them." [16] Substance is "actual and substantial spirituality, in complete abstraction from every sense." It is the *actual substance* of the spirit as contrasted with the outer husk of sense. [17] It is that strong meat which nourishes the mature spiritual man. [18]

The rind or husk of spirituality must not be confused with pure spirit any more than the peeling of an orange may be mistaken for the fruit which is to be eaten. The reason for this is that "rind" and "husk" apply to sense operation which is of a lower order than spiritual operation. Thus, images and forms are as *rind* and are not found in that *substantial* quiet of contemplation. So also imaginings and reasonings are rind which must have been removed, for the soul to enjoy the spirit. [19] It does not matter whether the sensible operation be in the natural or preternatural manner, for, in the case of imaginary visions no less than in meditation, the soul must not be occupied with imaginary visions, with the *outer rind* of

[16] xiv,2,4
[17] xvii,5
[18] xvii,6
[19] xiv,4

sense, if it wishes to be free to receive the *substance* of pure spirit. But, if the soul casts aside the rind, these visions will profit the soul, *substantially*.[20] If only the soul will not cling to the sensible part of "supernatural" apprehensions, God will communicate a spiritual effect to it "much more substantially." [21] The soul must not allow its eyes to rest upon that *"outer husk"* of corporeal visions — it must set its eyes only upon the *"spirituality* which they produce," thus taking from them only the *"spirit"* of devotion, as God wills.[22] In all these places it is evident that the rind and husk of sense is but a covering for the substance of the spirit.

St. John is always careful to explain why God deals with rinds and husks in His commerce with the soul. It is because, when God adopts us, we are still children, at least as regards the spiritual life. He, therefore, gives the soul mere morsels of spirit which are in the order of sense, in conformity with the soul's capacity, in order that gradually He may grant it further and better food.[23] As before, we compared God to a mother, so now we may picture Him as a father. The father of a family procures many and different kinds of food for his table. Naturally, some foods are desirable for their nutrition, others allure the eye or tempt the palate. A child asks for a certain dish rather to satisfy his appetite than to increase his health. As the father sees that the child must have his own way, and will not eat of the better food, even though he should give that instead, he therefore gives the requested dish, though re-

[20] xvi,11,12
[21] xvii,7
[22] xvii,9
[23] xi,9

gretfully, lest his child become sulky and refuse to eat anything. So God, condescending to the nature and desires of souls, gives them that which is less good for them, planning in the meantime stronger and more solid food, such as the trials of the Cross of His Son.[24]

Men are as children, as St. Paul the Apostle well knew. Because of their lack of preparation, and their incapability for receiving the Holy Spirit, due to their bias towards sense, God must clothe his gifts in rind or husk. Because of their small degree of spirituality, he must feed them His wisdom in morsels — the crumbs of enlightenment to be gathered from forms and figures and particular perceptions.[25]

Here we must take notice of something important. Although St. John places "rind" and "husk" and "morsels" in opposition to "substance," it is not to be supposed that the term "morsels" has the same signification as its companion terms. "Rind" and "husk" are to be identified with sense; the "morsels," though associated with sense action, are higher. "Rind" and "husk" are related to "substance" as peeling to an orange: one is not of the same species as the other; no matter how much rind one accumulated, it would never equal the meat of an orange. St. John sometimes emphasizes the essential distance of one from the other by speaking of the *"outer* husk." On the contrary, a morsel of bread is of the same species as the substance of bread, the difference here being merely one of quantity. The term "morsels" applies to spirit, and is of the same essence as pure spirit, though sealed in the husk of sense. Thus, he speaks of "wisdom in morsels,"

[24] xxi,3
[25] xvii,8

"morsels of spiritual communication" and "crumbs of enlightenment." If perchance he uses the phrase "morsels of sense," his meaning is that a morsel of spirit is wrapt in sense.[26] Since a morsel of an orange is of the same substance as the whole orange, the term "husk" is related to both in the same way.[27] Moreover, it is to be noted that all the things of sense, whether meditation or corporeal visions, are husk; but that which truly nourishes the soul with supernatural food is morsels of spirit, and when the soul is perfect, the actual substance of the spirit without any husk. The outer husk of sense is characteristic of spiritual childhood; the substance of spirit is proper to spiritual manhood.

The transition from "act" to "habit" is the same as that from "morsel" to "substance." The morsel of spirituality fed to the soul by God is a spiritual and supernatural act (the loving knowledge acquired in meditation). By giving the soul morsels, God accustoms the palate and digestion of the soul to food whose substance is the soul's proper nourishment. By repeated acts, the soul attains to the habit of taking its proper substance, and leaves off the habit of taking child's food, the things of sense. Chapter seventeen is invaluable in this matter. After showing how God leads the soul from exterior to interior, from sense to spirit, St. John, *in a single sentence*, gives us the general principle of spiritual progress. Because of its importance, I wish to give it here, together with a diagram to show the symmetry of its structure and the simplicity of its meaning:

It is in this way, then, that God instructs the soul and makes it more spiritual, communicating spirituality to

[26] xvii,8
[27] xvii,5,6

it, first of all through outward and palpable things
adapted to sense, on account of the soul's feebleness and
incapacity, so that, by means of the outer husk of those
things of sense (which in themselves are good), the spirit
may make particular acts and receive so many morsels of
spiritual communication, (with this result) that it may
form a habit in things spiritual and may acquire actual
and substantial spirituality, in complete abstraction from
every sense (xvii,5).

God $\left\{\begin{array}{l}\text{instructs} \\ \text{communicates spirituality}\end{array}\right.$ by means of $\left\{\begin{array}{l}\text{outward and palpable things} \\ \text{outer husk of sensible things}\end{array}\right.$

The Soul $\left\{\begin{array}{l}\text{makes particular acts} \\ \text{receives morsels of spirit}\end{array}\right.$ that it may $\left\{\begin{array}{l}\text{form a habit of pure spirit} \\ \text{acquire the actual substance} \\ \text{of the spirit}\end{array}\right.$ in complete abstraction from every sense.

CHAPTER XXIII

Flesh and Spirit

WE HAVE been speaking of the characteristics of sense and spirit. In order to complete this matter, it will be useful to consider that St. John compares the way of sense to a journey or progress or climbing stairs. From the beginning of the "Ascent" the progress of the soul was depicted as a journey on the road to perfection — not an easy walk, but a climb, an ascent. Now he speaks of the soul as "journeying to pure spirit." [1] The work of the faculties may be compared to the labor of journeying, and arrival at the goal is the attaining to contemplation, which is pure spirit.[2] In a variation of this simile, the manner of progress is described as a stairs, by which one reaches the goal or peaceful room of the spirit.[3] Few souls know the goal of spiritual progress, and it oftens happens that souls think that they are going astray and wasting time, going backwards and losing themselves, at the very time that they are nearing their goal. They are indeed losing themselves, although not in the way they think, for they are becoming lost to the road of sense.[4] That soul is to be pitied which returns and retraces the ground that it has already traversed, abandoning the end and goal.[5]

[1] xiii,8
[2] xiv,7
[3] xii,5; xi,10
[4] xiv,4
[5] xii,7

It need hardly be remarked that to journey is to labor, whereas the end of the journey brings rest and peace.[6] Meditation or sense is the labor of journeying; contemplation is the rest and quiet of the journey's end.[7] Making particular acts of knowledge is labor and exercise of the faculties.[8] The difference between sense and spirit (or meditation and contemplation) is the difference between working and enjoying the fruit of work which has been done.[9]

Previously we asked the question: Is the term "spirit," as employed by St. John, supernatural? The answer is yes. Sense is human; spirit is Divine and supernatural, as is evident from the parallel phrases: "human and Divine, sense and spirit" in chapter seventeen. We can prove this in another way — by reviewing the characteristics of sense and spirit. The accompanying chart will prove useful. The progress of the soul, as we have seen, is from sense to spirit. Sense is the natural mode of our knowledge; it is particular and distinct; it is "act"; meditation and corporeal visions belong to sense; sense is the way of spiritual childhood, in which the soul, as it were, drinks milk and assimilates supernatural life in morsels covered with rind or husk; progress may be likened to a journey necessitating labor; finally sense is human. On the other hand, spirit is above the natural mode of our knowledge, and is therefore, darkness and a night of faith; it is general and confused; it is a habit; it is contemplation; it is the way of spiritual manhood, in which the soul is nourished with

[6] xii,7; xiii,7
[7] xiv,7
[8] xiv,3; xv,2
[9] xiv,7

substance or, figuratively speaking, strong meat, wine, the food and fruit of spirit; spirit is the goal of progress, bringing rest and peace to the laboring soul; finally spirit is Divine. Practically, contemplation and spirit and the night of faith are the same; but contemplation and faith are supernatural; therefore spirit is supernatural. Moreover, in a supernatural religion, the goal of union, the substance of its spirituality, the habit of the soul, *etc.* cannot be less than supernatural. And therefore, we may conclude that spiritual progress must always be from sense to spirit, *i.e.,* from natural to supernatural, from human to Divine.

I have treated this matter at some length because I think that it is important for souls to keep this principle before them. So many souls, I fear, mark time, fail to advance or even go backwards, because they wander in a labyrinth of methods, now going in this direction, now that, now progressing and now slipping back. The important principle to remember, even for the soul that has its first step still to take on the spiritual road, is that progress is in *one, definite, unchanging* direction — a straight line from sense to spirit, from human to Divine.

And now, considering the prominent place which this doctrine has in the writings of John of the Cross, we may well ask: Is this something new? Is this a departure from the teaching of the New Testament? No, there is nothing new in this doctrine, except the manner of presentation. It will be found implicitly in the common tradition of Christian life and perfection. But, nowhere, it seems to me, is it so clearly and succinctly expressed.

Is this teaching to be found in the New Testament? There is to be found in the Gospels, and particularly in the Epistles of St. Paul, an expression which in many in-

Chart of Spiritual Progress.

The Progress of the Soul is from . . .

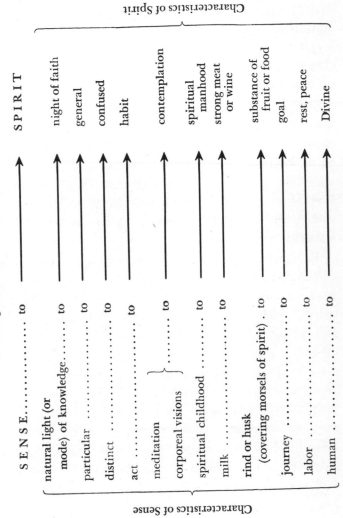

		Characteristics of Spirit
SENSE	to	SPIRIT
natural light (or mode) of knowledge	to	night of faith
particular	to	general
distinct	to	confused
act	to	habit
meditation	to	contemplation
corporeal visions		
spiritual childhood	to	spiritual manhood
milk	to	strong meat or wine
rind or husk (covering morsels of spirit)	to	substance of fruit or food
journey	to	goal
labor	to	rest, peace
human	to	Divine

Characteristics of Sense

stances is almost identical in meaning. This is the phrase
"flesh and spirit." Upon St. Peter's profession of faith in
His Divinity, Jesus Christ said to him, "Blessed art thou,
Simon Bar-Jona, because flesh and blood hath not revealed
it to thee, but my Father who is in heaven." [10] In the
Garden of Olives, our Lord warned His disciples: "Watch
ye, and pray that ye enter not into temptation. The spirit
indeed is willing but the flesh weak." [11] In these passages,
it seems evident that the flesh is not capable of attaining to
supernatural knowledge and strength; indeed the flesh is
weak even in less sublime things, and there is need of
spirit. It is not to be supposed that "flesh" or even "flesh
and blood" is to be taken in the strict sense. It means
rather the sensitive nature of man, or likely the whole
natural man.

Better for our purpose is that passage on the necessity
of Baptism, where Christ says, "That which is born of the
flesh, is flesh; and that which is born of the Spirit, is
spirit." [12] Here flesh means the natural man, human nature
left to itself. But that which is born of the Spirit, is spirit.
In other words, there is a supernatural element in man,
which is called "spirit," not only because it transcends the
powers of the flesh, but because it is the work of the Holy
Spirit. That this is the thought of the Mystical Doctor is
evident from that place where he treats of the Divine
union.[13] There the word "flesh" was used in opposition to
the work of the Holy Spirit; and though the phrase "sense
and spirit" is not employed there, the meaning is never-

[10] Matt. xvi,17
[11] Matt. xxvi,41
[12] John iii,6
[13] v,5

theless the same. It might well have been said that to attain
to pure spirit, is "to be born again in the Holy Spirit in
this life" and "to have a soul most like to God in purity,
having in itself no admixture of imperfection," such as
comes from the operation of sense.[14]

In our considerations of "sense and spirit," we noticed
that sense is of little or no value, that it is spirit which
quickens the soul with supernatural life. Now, take notice
of these words of our Divine Master: "It is the spirit that
quickeneth: the flesh profiteth nothing. The words that I
have spoken to you are spirit and life." [15] The flesh is of no
profit, *i.e.*, the works of the flesh are not the proximate
means of Divine union. The words of our Lord on the
insufficiency of the flesh are unusually striking in their
particular context, where the Saviour promises to give His
own Sacred Flesh and Blood. Whatever may be the precise
meaning of "flesh" in the above text, it certainly is dia-
metrically opposed to spirit, *i.e.*, supernatural life.

St. Paul frequently uses "flesh and spirit" as opposed to
each other. Usually, he uses the term "flesh" to designate
man vitiated by Original Sin, tending to evil. "Spirit," on
the contrary, is that element in human nature, by which
man is united to God, and this is the gift of the Holy Spirit.

> For they that are according to the flesh, mind the
> things that are of the flesh; but they that are according
> to the spirit, mind the things that are of the spirit.
> For the wisdom of the flesh is death; but the wisdom
> of the spirit is life and peace.
> Because the wisdom of the flesh is an enemy to God;
> for it is not subject to the law of God, neither can it be.

[14] v,5
[15] John vi,64

And they who are in the flesh [who live according to the flesh] cannot please God.

But you are not in the flesh, but in the spirit, if so be that the Spirit of God dwell in you.[16]

This evidence of the duality in our nature — the natural life of the soul versus the spirit or supernatural life — is everywhere to be found in St. Paul. John of the Cross knew the theology of St. Paul well, and quotes him again and again. Must we insist then, that the "flesh and spirit" of St. Paul are identical with the "sense and spirit" of the Mystical Doctor? The similarity is, without doubt, very close, particularly in two points: "flesh" or "sense" is not the proximate means of pleasing God or of attaining union with Him; "spirit" is the proximate means of Divine union, infused into our souls by the Holy Spirit.

What are the differences? First, St. Paul stresses the weakness of human nature because of Original Sin. St. John is not particularly concerned with Original Sin in this second Book of the "Ascent," although he did take account of its effects in the first Book, when he was treating of beginners.[17] Secondly, St. John is treating of our cognoscitive powers, and so far, he has written only of the corporeal senses in relation to the understanding. Whereas St. Paul thinks of man as existing in the flesh of a fallen nature, St. John's view is of man's power of knowing. It is merely a matter of point of view, but neither excludes the doctrine of the other. "Flesh" means fallen man, subject to death, darkened in understanding; "sense" is that part of the soul limited to the "particular and distinct" things of this puny world. Opposed to both of these is

[16] Romans viii,5-9
[17] A.,I,xv

spirit, that gift of the Holy Spirit which transforms the soul, making it Divine by participation, lifting it to the sphere of celestial light. Both St. Paul and St. John contrast that which is human in us with that which is Divine in us. "Sense and spirit," we may repeat, are opposed to each other, as human and Divine.

The particular value of the term "sense," as used by St. John of the Cross, lies in this, that it rests on the scholastic theory of knowledge. After all, Divine union demands knowledge. No one would maintain that we attain to Divine union according to the flesh, but there are many souls who fail to see that the senses profit nothing, and that they must journey towards pure spirit, if they are to reach perfection.

One advantage of our discussion in this chapter has been that we have proven that the doctrine of the Mystical Doctor, at least thus far, is the doctrine of the New Testament. St. John has interpreted for us the theology of Christ and St. Paul in the light of the scholastic theory of knowledge accepted in the Catholic Church.

CHAPTER XXIV

Supernatural Spiritual Knowledge

IN THE tenth chapter of Book Two of the "Ascent," John of the Cross distinguished all the kinds of knowledge that could come to the understanding. His purpose in classifying the modes of our knowledge was, we recall, to detach the soul from all those apprehensions which might hinder it on the road to God, or at least be of no profit. So far we have considered the kinds of apprehensions called "corporeal" because they come by means of the bodily senses. These corporeal perceptions were of two kinds: first, natural, *i.e.*, all those apprehensions which come to us from the outside world through our natural mode of knowing. To this class belongs meditation because it is an exercise of our natural faculties working on the materia of our senses. The second kind we considered was "supernatural," *i.e.*, corporeal visions, either in the external senses or in the imagination. Now we have to consider a new and superior mode of knowledge which is in the understanding alone, and is therefore spiritual. Here there is no longer question of material forms and figures as perceived by the senses, but only of spiritual truth, received directly in the understanding. Because such knowledge is received directly, and not through the *natural* channels of the sense faculties, it is called supernatural. But, it is important to note, such knowledge is not necessarily supernatural in essence, but only in the mode of our apprehension. As we spoke of "preternatural" knowledge in the senses, so also in the intellect we may speak of "supernatural" knowledge which is more precisely "preternatural," *i.e.*, outside the natural mode of knowing.

We are, then, about to study the "spiritual supernatural knowledge" of which mention was made in chapter ten; "spiritual" because it is a question of ideas and thoughts, "supernatural" because these were received without the aid of the senses.[1] This spiritual supernatural knowledge is also divided into two kinds: that which is distinct and particular, and that which is confused, general and dark, namely, contemplation. The distinct and particular knowledge is divided into four classes: visions, revelations, locutions, spiritual feelings. "The obscure and general type of knowledge is of one kind alone, which is contemplation that is given in faith. To this we have to lead the soul by bringing it thereto through all these other means, beginning with the first and detaching it from them."[2] It will be well to remember, then, that in the following chapters as in those that went before, St. John's purpose is to lead the soul into contemplation. This will help us to interpret other terms he may use, as for example, when he says that he wishes to "disencumber the understanding . . . and direct the soul into the night of faith."[3]

[1] We are now in a better position to understand the use of the term "spiritually" in iv,6. In the phrase "spiritually and naturally," "spiritually" refers to this knowledge received directly into the intellect; "naturally" refers to knowledge received in the natural mode by way of the senses. "Temporally and spiritually" seems to mean the same thing, and certainly "spiritually and sensually" does.

[2] x,4

[3] xxiii,1

CHART OF SUPERNATURAL KNOWLEDGE

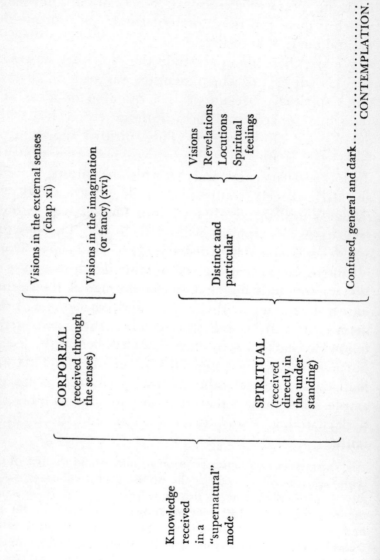

The first class of spiritual supernatural knowledge that presents itself to the understanding clearly and distinctly is visions. What is a vision? Strictly speaking, vision pertains to the eyes; both the operation and the object of sight is called vision. We have already spoken of visions of the eyes and of the imagination, in which was included all that could be represented by any image, form or figure. By analogy, we speak of understanding as seeing, in which sense, we say that we shall see God face to face. The Beatific Vision is intelligence formed in the understanding. And thus, all the apprehensions of the intellect may be called intellectual visions. For the soul, to understand is to see. All that falls within the limits of truth or falsehood, all the intelligible objects that come within the grasp of the understanding, cause within it spiritual vision, just as corporeal objects cause bodily vision in the eye. In this general sense, all the four classes of spiritual apprehensions could be called visions.[4]

However, there are just grounds for a fourfold division. Some objects of the understanding are corporeal like the objects of sight. Others, although incorporeal, are truly substances. Since in the natural order, the understanding grasps substances according to the faculty of vision, so in the supernatural (preternatural) order, when the understanding receives knowledge of substances, whether corporeal or incorporeal, we may speak of vision with greater propriety than if the object of the understanding was a naked truth. By spiritual visions, then, we mean the intellection of substances, whether corporeal or incorporeal, by an immediate apprehension. For example, St. Benedict

[4] xxiii,2

CHART OF PURELY SPIRITUAL, CLEAR AND DISTINCT APPREHENSIONS.

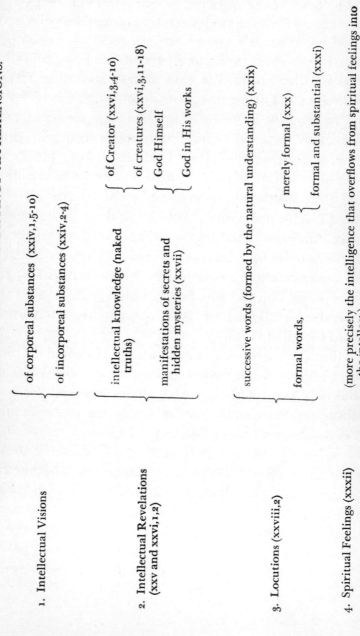

1. Intellectual Visions
   - of corporeal substances (xxiv,1,5-10)
   - of incorporeal substances (xxiv,2-4)

2. Intellectual Revelations (xxv and xxvi,1,2)
   - intellectual knowledge (naked truths)
     - of Creator (xxvi,3,4-10)
     - of creatures (xxvi,3,11-18)
   - manifestations of secrets and hidden mysteries (xxvii)
     - God Himself
     - God in His works

3. Locutions (xxviii,2)
   - successive words (formed by the natural understanding) (xxix)
   - formal words,
     - merely formal (xxx)
     - formal and substantial (xxxi)

4. Spiritual Feelings (xxxii)
   (more precisely the intelligence that overflows from spiritual feelings into the intellect.)

saw in a vision the whole world of corporeal substance, by the aid of a certain supernatural illumination from above. If one were to really see an angel, and not a mere representation of an angel, such would be an incorporeal vision.

Another kind of spiritual apprehension strikes the understanding, as it were, in the form of words, though the sense faculty of hearing has not intervened. This is called a locution, because the understanding is impressed as if a person were speaking.

The third kind of spiritual apprehensions is that called revelations. A revelation is the manifestation of a hidden mystery or secret. The difference between a vision and a revelation is this, that in a vision a substance is manifested to the intellect, but in a revelation it is a hidden truth concerning substances that is manifested. Since these three kinds of supernatural apprehensions are found abundantly in Scripture and in the lives of the saints, it was natural to divide them thus according to vision, locution and revelation.

But there is a fourth kind, less familiar, which St. John treats, namely, spiritual feelings. One is justly puzzled at the term "spiritual feelings" in regard to the intellect, but the matter is cleared up when it is understood that it is not spiritual feelings as such which enter the intellect, but rather the apprehensions or intelligence that overflows from the will or the substance of the soul when either of these experience the said spiritual feelings. In other words the understanding has a knowledge of what is passing within the soul, or perhaps it would be better to say that what the will enjoys by way of heat, the intellect enjoys by way of light, when the Divine fire approaches the soul. However, it is only with the intellect that the Mystic Doctor is concerned at present.

These classifications which we have noticed, are made for purpose of convenience; it is not to be supposed that we may judge the spiritual value of a supernatural apprehension merely by classifying it in this way. Other principles must enter in to determine this. Since the destiny of the soul is supernatural in essence, the journey also must be supernatural in essence; therefore, the progress of the soul can be ascertained only by examining whether a certain act of intelligence be essentially supernatural. Such was the purpose which our Saint set for himself. He himself insists upon this. After disencumbering the understanding of the things of sense, and directing the soul into the night of faith, he now wishes likewise to disencumber the understanding of all that is contrary to the night of faith, in order that he might lead it to the Divine and substantial union of God.[5] It was not his purpose to explain fully all that pertains to the matter in hand, but to point out how much of the instruction given in reference to corporeal apprehensions in previous chapters is also applicable here.[6] Aware that he is but briefly describing these things, since there remains so much to be said about them, he points out that sufficient instruction is being given for his purpose, and asks the reader to remember that the object of his book is to direct the soul through all its apprehensions, whether attained in a natural or supernatural mode, to Divine union with God, in purity of faith.[7] And, supposing that some case could not be

[5] xxiii,1,4
[6] xxvi,18; xxvii,7; xxx,7
[7] xxviii,1

fitted exactly into any of the sections of his writing, St. John nevertheless maintains that there is none that cannot be reduced to one of his classifications, and that he has given the instruction necessary for it.[8]

[8] xxxii,2

CHAPTER XXV

Intellectual Visions

THE FIRST of the four kinds of supernatural spiritual knowledge, which we are about to consider, is visions. Let it be clearly understood that we are not now speaking of apparitions, or the visions of bodily sight, or the images and forms which may be represented preternaturally in the imagination, but only of those visions which are spiritual and seen by the understanding alone. As the bodily eye, by means of physical light, sees natural, dimensional substances, so also the understanding may see (or "intue," if you prefer) these same substances, although absent. And since intellectual light is not confined by space or dependent upon matter, the understanding may see even incorporeal substances, when the soul has gone forth from the body, or perhaps in exceptional cases when the soul is temporarily abstracted from corporeal functions, as with Moses and St. Paul.[1] Visions are therefore defined as corporeal or incorporeal according to the substance known. (Previously, corporeal visions were defined as those which were seen by means of the corporeal senses, but not so here.)

As regards incorporeal substances, we need not be delayed long. St. John points out that the illumination necessary for the vision of them belongs to the order of glory, and consequently, angels and souls cannot be seen until the intellect is freed from the opaqueness of this

[1] xxiv,3

mortal flesh. Theologians are divided on the question
whether God can be seen in His Essence in this life under
any circumstances. St. Gregory the Great and St. Bernard
maintained that this is impossible. St. Augustine, and St.
Thomas under his influence, thought that Moses and St.
Paul had seen God face to face. The words of Scripture
are not easy to explain away. God said to Moses, "Thou
canst not see My face: for man shall not see Me and live." [2]
The Jews believed that the vision of God would cause
death. St. John, however, does not contradict St. Thomas,
but notice his reluctance: "... *it is thought* that St. Paul
saw these, (namely, the incorporeal substances in the
third heaven) ... Likewise, *it is believed* that God showed
His Essence to Moses ... "[3] He explains the possibility by
saying that these visions belong not to this life, save occasionally and fleetingly, by way of exception. But a kind
of death must intervene, which is to say that man's spirit
must be totally withdrawn from the natural functions of
the body, being wholly enraptured by the vision of the
Infinitely Attractive. Such miraculous exceptions can be
admitted only in the case of certain strong souls in the
favor of God.

This is not to deny the possibility of union between
God and the soul. God can be perceived or experienced
in the substance of the soul, by means of the sweetest
touches and unions. This is a union of a lofty and Divine
degree. The dark and loving knowledge of which we have
already spoken, serves as a means of being united with
God. Dark with the obscurity of faith, this infused contemplation serves in this life as an intermediary, even as

[2] Exodus, xxxiii,20
[3] Compare viii,4

in the next life the light of glory is the medium through which the understanding has a clear vision of God. But here we are only concerned with the fact that souls are not united with God face to face in vision.

As for the vision of corporeal substances, this is possible by means of intellectual light, derived from God outside the laws of nature. Thus St. John the Apostle saw the heavenly Jerusalem, whose description he was inspired to write in the twenty-first chapter of the Apocalypse. What is it like to have an intellectual vision? The Saint says that it is as though a door were opened, through which one sees light like a lightning flash, revealing clearly and distinctly a multitude of objects in the night. When the vision is completed, the objects disappear, leaving the impression of them clearly in the memory. This comes to pass much more perfectly in purely spiritual vision than in the sight of the eyes. What is seen through the eyes remains in form and figure in the imagination, but the vividness of the sensible memory is soon lost. But these spiritual visions, since they do not depend on a defectible bodily faculty, are retained in the soul with more fidelity, so that they may be seen again and again as in a mirror. For these intellectual visions are more clear and subtle than those of the senses, where matter plays a part. Here all is spiritual: God the agent, intellectual light the means, the intellect the subject. When God is pleased to communicate this favour, He does so by means of a supernatural light, wherein the soul sees the things that God wills it to see, whether they be absent or present, whether in Heaven or on the earth. What things does the soul see? Material and natural things. This is important to notice. For the vision of material and natural things, the light of glory is not necessary. A natural light suffices, that is to say, a light adapted to the operation of the natural intellect. If St. John speaks of a "supernatural light," it must not be thought that he has in mind anything in the order of grace. That light is supernatural only in this way, that it transcends the natural *mode* of spiritual knowledge derived from phantasms.[4] Since the natural windows of the soul have not introduced this light, it must be derived from a higher source. Such light is supernatural only in mode and manner. "For, just as the eyes see bodily visions by means of *natural* light, even so does the soul, through the understanding, by means of *supernaturally derived* light, as we have said, see those same *natural* things inwardly, . . . the difference between the two kinds of vision is only in the *mode* and *manner* of them."[4] The devil is able to imitate these visions "by means of a certain *natural* light,"[5] which he could scarcely do if they were supernatural in essence like contemplation.

It is not difficult to see why these visions, spiritual as they are, cannot unite the soul to God. First, because the derived illumination is not to be compared with the light of glory, nor even with the light of faith. Secondly, because

[4] xxiv,5

[5] xxiv,7. It is not to be supposed that St. John means that the devil can duplicate these spiritual visions in the understanding, for it is his teaching elsewhere that the devil cannot reach the understanding except through the senses. Scripture scholars cannot agree whether the devil, in this temptation of Christ, merely pointed in the actual direction of the kingdoms, or whether he conjured up an apparition before the eyes of Christ. St. Cyril thought that the devil caused a vision in the imagination of the Son of God, but others will not admit this, as being contrary to His dignity.

these visions are of created, material things, which have no proportion with God, and therefore cannot be a proportionate means of union with Him. It does not matter that these corporeal things exist in Heaven. Let us recall what the saint said in a previous chapter, namely, that "it is impossible for the understanding to attain to God by means of the creatures, whether these be *celestial* or earthly; inasmuch as there is no proportion of resemblance between them." God sees that "the celestial creatures" are very far from His Being.[6] Wherefore the soul must not treasure the spiritual forms and images of such visions, for to be encumbered by them would prevent it from making progress. A soul that is detached from them, however, even though the memory of them remains within it, will not be hindered. It is even true that the remembrance of these visions, when they are truly from God, exalts the soul to Divine love. Yet detachment is more profitable, for the soul is exalted much more by the pure faith and infused contemplation of which we spoke previously.

[6] viii,3

CHAPTER XXVI

Spiritual Revelations

ACCORDING TO the order outlined, we now come to spiritual revelations, by which is meant the impression of some hidden truth or secret or mystery upon the understanding. The difference between a vision and a revelation is taken from the difference in their objects. We speak of substances not so much as being "revealed" as being "seen"; on the other hand, a hidden truth is more properly "revealed." Therefore, the understanding obtains knowledge of substances through "vision"; but it comes to know hidden truths, secrets or mysteries through "revelations."

St. John makes a twofold division of revelations. But the casual reader may with difficulty find the principle of his division. These two kinds of revelation are not distinguished by reason of their objects, but according to the manner in which the revelation is made. Both the first and second kind may have to do with either God or creatures. While the second kind is described as the manifestation of secrets and hidden mysteries, the reader finds that the first kind also reveals secret and hidden mysteries. The real principle of division comes from the *manner* of revelation, or the *process* by which the intellect discovers the hidden and secret truths. Thus the first kind of revelation is of *naked truths* [1] or intelligence, revealed to the

[1] "nudam contemplationem ipsius veritatis", St. Thomas, S.T., II II, q.174, a.2

soul clearly and openly; it is the *intuition* of *naked truths*. The second kind is a *manifestation* in which truth is clothed in sensible garments. "... revelations of this nature come ordinarily through words, figures and similitudes, *etc.*" whereas the first kind of revelation is "in spirit alone." [2]

CHART OF INTELLECTUAL REVELATIONS

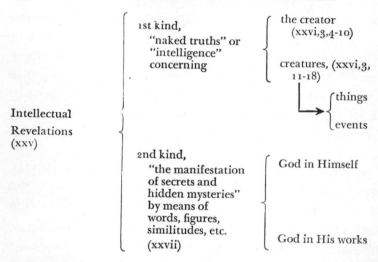

Here we may ask: if this second kind of revelations are clothed in sensible forms, why did not St. John treat of these in that place where he describes corporeal visions? The answer is that he did speak of revelations in those earlier chapters (to which he refers us repeatedly), but there he was concerned primarily with the detachment of the senses and imagination, whereas here he is concerned chiefly with the understanding and those truths which come to it by prophetic revelation. In those earlier chap-

[2] xxvii,3

ters he wished to show how sensible images and figures could not unite the soul to God; now he wishes to show that even the intelligible truths drawn from those images and figures, by means of prophetic light, are not necessarily the proximate means to Divine union. It is true, as we said there, that St. John in this book regards the lower faculties only insofar as they are related to the understanding, but there is a difference between those sensible apprehensions and these. For prophetic revelations are chiefly the work of the intellect: an intellectual light derived from God gives a new meaning to the similitudes that are grasped by the senses. An example will illustrate this. The chief butler and the chief baker of Pharao, the king of Egypt, each had a dream one night which they were unable to interpret. A dream is an imaginary vision such as St. John described in chapter sixteen. The chief butler saw in his imagination a vine on which grew three branches, each of which gradually budded, blossomed, and brought forth ripe grapes. He saw himself press the grapes into Pharao's cup and give them to him. What could one make of such a dream except that the butler was rendering a service to his king? Such was the only meaning that the intellect of itself could draw from it. But Joseph, to whom the vision was related, was illuminated with prophetic light by which a higher interpretation was possible. So also he interpreted in the case of the chief baker and even the king himself. Joseph interpreted the visions which their very beholders could not rightly understand.[3] This is convincing proof that the spirit of prophecy or interpretation is something distinct and more noble than the visions themselves. More often

[3] Genesis, xl and xli

the same person has both the vision and the prophetic instinct, but nevertheless the distinction between the two remains clear. What St. John is about to tell us is that even this prophetic light is not to be mistaken for the light of faith.

Here another question may be asked. Why does our saint make a distinction between these two kinds of revelation, namely, *naked truths,* and the manifestation of secrets and mysteries through signs, words, figures, etc.? And granting the distinction, why does he treat them in such close relation? The answer is because both belong to the spirit of prophecy. Thomas Aquinas treats this matter very lucidly, and notes the same distinction. Pure intellectual knowledge, St. Thomas says, is called prophecy with less propriety than those revelations which are manifested by means of the senses. Nevertheless, strictly intelligible truths without any imaginary vision are the more excellent.[4] St. John uses the word "revelation" instead of "prophecy," and says that the *manifestation* of revelations (through sensible means) is more properly called revelation. "The first is the revealing to the understanding of truths which are properly called intellectual knowledge or intelligence; the second is the manifestation of secrets, which are called revelations with more propriety than the others."[5] That St. John agrees with St. Thomas on the excellence of pure intelligence will be seen when we consider this kind of revelation.

The reason that these two classes of spiritual knowledge are treated in close relation is because the intellect plays the principal part in both. In either case there is an in-

[4] S.T.,II II, Q.174, a.3
[5] xxv,2

tellectual light that is above the natural dynamism of the active intellect.[6] In one case both the ideas and the light of judgment are infused; in the other case, as when Joseph knew the mysterious dreams and received from God the prophetic instinct to grasp their meaning, the light of judgment alone is infused. Both these kinds of revelation are correctly classed, therefore, with the spiritual and supernatural apprehensions of the intellect.

This matter will become clearer as we consider each in turn. I propose, in the following chapter, to consider the second kind of revelations, *i.e.*, the manifestation of hidden secrets and mysteries, and afterwards we shall come to pure intellectual knowledge or naked truths. My reason for thus reversing the order of our Saint is that, because of their similarity with the preceding matter, the manifestation of hidden truths by signs, words, figures, *etc.* will be more readily understood, and will prepare the way for a clear understanding of the other.

[6] The active intellect (intellectus agens) is that power of the mind which conceives a purely spiritual idea from a material phantasm.

CHAPTER XXVII

Manifestation of Hidden Truths

THE MYSTICAL DOCTOR does not delay long on this kind of revelations, namely, the manifestation of secrets and mysteries by means of signs, words, figures, images, or similitudes. The reason is, as we said, that these are very similar to corporeal visions. Indeed, they might be called corporeal visions that reveal a secret or mystery. Corporeal visions happen in different ways, we know. Sometimes there is an external apparition formed in the air by good or evil spirits. Again the representation may be impressed upon the external senses, in such a way that they perceive what really does not exist. Finally, visions may be stamped directly on the imagination. All of these, of course, convey ideas to the understanding according to the natural process of knowledge, in the same way as we daily store up spiritual knowledge of the world around us. In prophetic vision, however, there is besides all this, an intellectual light, derived from God, which we call prophetic light. This light reveals a deeper meaning which the understanding of itself could not obtain from the matter of the senses, as when, by a comparison in the physical order, fluorescent substances becomes luminous under the action of X-rays. Prophetic rays are not concerned with future happenings only, but reveal secrets or mysteries of the past and present as well.

These revelations may have for their object either God or creatures. First, as regards creatures, it might be revealed to someone that a certain person has not long to live, or that certain trials await him, or that a certain family is to fall into misfortune, that wars will ravage this kingdom or that, or that such and such is to take place in the whole universe. The existence of such genuine revelations is certain from the Divine writings which describe many instances: indeed, the Old Testament is divided into three groups of books, one of which is called the "prophetic" books. For example, to Jeremias, the prophet, the destruction of Jerusalem and the captivity of the Jews was revealed with such clearness and certainty, that he appeared before the people with chains around his neck to illustrate their future misfortune, and he himself refused to marry and have a family, lest he raise up children who should become victims of the sword or slaves of the Babylonians.[1] Also since the coming of Christ there have been many prophecies. St. Paul of the Cross foresaw the conversion of England by his own missionaries.

There is a type of revelation with which almost all are familiar, *i.e.*, a further manifestation or explanation of what has been revealed already, for example, the devotion to the Sacred Heart of Jesus revealed to St. Margaret Mary. As regards the mysteries of our faith, God may reveal more explicitly the truths hidden in them like ancient treasures. Nothing, however, can be added to the substance of Divine revelation. If anything novel, any absolutely new 'article were to be proposed, it must be necessarily rejected as false. Even if (to suppose the impossible) an angel from heaven were to communicate some new doctrine, we could in no way give our consent to it, as St. Paul tells us: "But though we, or an angel from

[1] Jeremias, xvi and xxvii

heaven, preach a gospel to you besides that which we have preached to you, let him be anathema." [2]

If even an angel from heaven were to be repulsed on such conditions, much more an angel from hell. Without doubt, the devil may meddle considerably in this kind of revelation. It matters nothing that the doctrine have reference to the Unity and Trinity of the Divine Nature: the devil may enter in wherever the pure nature of an angel does not fear to tread. By this I mean that the devils, retaining the purely natural powers of an angel, can transform themselves into angels of light. It belongs to the nature of an angel to move matter in space. This is to attribute to him not a little power, since all the wonderful effects which men have caused in the world from the beginning of time (speaking only of the natural order) have been accomplished through local motion. Great bridges span our rivers because men moved the iron beams outward from each shore. Each cozy home, every lofty building, the colosseum and the cathedral, were constructed in their symmetrical massiveness, piece by piece through movement in space. What painting, what statue, what symphony, no matter how sublime or spiritual, could have been realized without movement in matter? This is not to deny the reality of human thought, but only to indicate its dependence on matter for communication. All that man is able to achieve in this way, the angels likewise can do, and more, since their intellect surpasses man's, and their action on matter is ubiquitous, reaching more delicately and freely than a surgeon's fingers into the interior of the human organism, altering its emotions and passions,

[2] Galatians, i,8

affecting its senses, tracing in its imagination the phantasms in which human ideas are clothed. The devil, with his natural angelic knowledge unimpaired, can counterfeit any revelation that depends on the senses. (We took notice of this in corporeal visions.) But these manifestations of secrets and mysteries, of which we are speaking, depend on words, signs, images, figures, similitudes. Therefore, the devil can counterfeit these, "much more so than when the revelations are in spirit alone." [3] It is not a question here of pure, infused intelligence concerning the attributes of God, but a matter of images and figures either external or internal. Consequently, the soul may be deceived by them.

The devil habitually meddles in these things to such an extent that our Carmelite friar believes it impossible for one not to be deceived by them, except by rejecting them. For the devil first feeds men with truthful, or at least probable things, in order to give the soul that assurance which will afterwards blind it to diabolical snares. So many appearances and probabilities may be weaved together and firmly planted in the senses and imagination, that the person affected can scarcely be persuaded to disbelieve them. "Wherefore, the soul that is pure, cautious, simple and humble, must resist revelations and other visions with as much effort and care as though they were very perilous temptations." [4]

From the fact that these secrets and mysteries are manifested by means of images, figures and similitudes of the senses, the same conclusion may be drawn as in the work

[3] xxvii,3
[4] xxvii,6

of meditation and corporeal visions, namely, that no image or figure is proportionate to God, and therefore these cannot be the proximate means of Divine union. When sent by God, they are accompanied by prophetic light or instinct; but one cannot be sure that he has this instinct. Many have attempted to prophesy without it; others have prophesied without being conscious of the fact, as for example Caiphas, who thought he was speaking merely from his own reason when he said that it was expedient that Christ should be put to death.[5] Besides, this prophetic light itself is not to be compared with the light of faith. It is not necessarily supernatural in essence, for, as Benedict XIV says, "The recipients of prophecy may be angels, *devils*, men, women, children, *heathens* or *gentiles*." [6] Even the heathen sibyls prophesied concerning the Blessed Trinity and other mysteries of our faith. St. Thomas teaches that prophecy can be in those who are without God's grace, for prophecy is not directly intended to unite man's affections to God.[7] But, our faith is in the supernatural order of grace. The obscurity of faith surpasses, therefore, the clarity of these manifestations of secrets and mysteries. Even though there were no danger of deception from the devil, the soul ought not to desire to understand *clearly* the mysteries of Catholic doctrine, so that it may preserve the merit of faith, in its purity and entirety, because faith is night to the understanding, and because it is through the darkness of faith that the soul may come to the "Divine light of Divine

[5] xix,9; John xi,50

[6] Cf. the article on "Prophecy," Cath. Encyclopedia

[7] S.T., II II, q.172, a.4

union." [8] Let the soul, then, keep itself from these revelations, so that it may journey in the dark night of contemplation to the union of love.[9]

[8] xxvii,5
[9] xxvii,6,7

CHAPTER XXVIII

Purely Intellectual Revelations

PURELY INTELLECTUAL revelations, which the Saint describes in chapter twenty-seven are of a greater excellence than those which are manifested in words, signs, images, etc., because as St. Thomas says, this intellectual knowledge is an end to which the sensible species are ordered as means.[1] In speaking of "naked truths" we do not mean to say that such knowledge is absolutely bare of any phantasms whatsoever, but that the truths themselves are infused into the mind alone, and that whatever phantasms may be found in the mind with them, are the effect of the mind itself, following after the reception of spiritual knowledge rather than going before.[2] These revelations take place, then, without any predisposition of the mind by the action of the senses, either exterior or interior. This intellectual knowledge is more exalted than any that we have heretofore considered. St. John confesses his need of God's guidance in speaking of it.

This intelligence may have to do with God or with creatures. Let us speak first of that which has to do with creatures, thus going from the lower to the higher, as has been our manner of procedure so far. We divide creatures into things and events. In regard to the knowledge of "things," St. John takes notice that it is not always neces-

[1] S.T., II II, q.174, a.2
[2] S.T., II II, q.174, a.2, ad.4

sary to postulate an intervention of preternatural causes, for certain men have a keen instinct or natural talent for discerning what is in the hearts of others, what desires, inclinations, fears, sorrows, etc. are dwelling in their souls. The means by which they do this is merely natural, *i.e.*, words, movements and other signs. For a man is known by his conduct; the close connection between body and soul makes the former mirror the interior life within it; perhaps nothing has proved so well the relationship of the flesh and the spirit as a new device called the "lie-detector" which reveals invisible reactions of the material organism caused by inward falsehood and fear. The devil, having that subtle vision of matter which is proper to a spirit, can interpret man's interior life by means of outward indications, however slight, and a spiritual man, by his greater affinity for truth and good, ought also to have power in this matter above that of the ordinary person. The spiritual man judges all things, because his spirit is purified, and is therefore in harmony with the spiritual nature of truth.

Above this purely natural power, there is the possibility of supernatral enlightenment through the spirit of prophecy, or a gift of discernment of spirits. In treating of the manifestation of secrets and hidden mysteries, we saw that a prophet could read signs, similitudes, *etc.*, not by a natural power or insight, as above, but with the assistance of prophetic light. Now, we take notice of the fact that those signs and figures are not absolutely necessary, but by means of infused truth, a person may come to know hidden secrets and mysteries. The lives of the saints abound in examples of these things.

Again, a person may receive a gift of knowledge in a supernatural way. Certain favored persons may receive without effort, the natural habits of knowledge regarding natural things, which it took others many years to acquire. Such habits may be so general that the normal span of life and opportunities would be insufficient for their attainment. Solomon is the classical example, as we find in the book of Wisdom:

> For He hath given me the true knowledge of the things that are :
>
> to know the disposition of the whole world, and the virtues of the elements,
>
> the beginning, and ending, and midst of the times, the alterations of their courses, and the changes of seasons,
>
> the revolutions of the year, and the dispositions of the stars,
>
> the natures of living creatures, and rage of wild beasts, the force of winds, and reasonings of men, the diversities of plants, and the virtues of roots,
>
> and all such things as are hid and not foreseen, I have learned.[3]

The world knew only one Solomon, but there have been and will be many men possessing lesser gifts of knowledge, whose range of intellection extends only to certain classes of things or perhaps to one particular science. God imparts such gifts supernaturally to whom He wills. For God is a Divine Schoolmaster who can dispense with blackboards, pencils, books, and all usual instruments of pedagogy, by simply infusing pure intelligence into the mind, with the ease of one pouring ink into an inkwell.

[3] Wisdom, vii,17

In the early Church there were manifested special gifts for the good of the body of the faithful, which St. Paul enumerates: "The word of wisdom, the word of knowledge, faith [distinct from the theological virtue], grace of healing, working of miracles, prophecy, discerning of spirits, diverse kinds of tongues, interpretation of speeches." [4] These are "graces freely bestowed" or in theological language *"gratiae gratis datae"* or "gratuitous graces." Such gifts are more excellent in that they are ordered for the welfare and increase of God's kingdom on earth.

Worthy of distinct consideration is the knowledge of the events, the deeds and happenings of men taking place at a distance and secretly. One example of this is the case of Eliseus, the prophet, whose servant practised a deception in the matter of receiving gifts. Eliseus saw the event, though he was absent. "Was not my heart present, when the man turned back from his chariot to meet thee?" This, it seems, took place by means of an intellectual vision. Again, Eliseus, by the same means, knew what was taking place in the secret counsel of the King of Syria and his princes, and the prophet warned his own king of the danger.[5]

What are we to think of such gifts? Can these be the means toward Divine union? It is true that purely spiritual knowledge is delectable to the soul. It is likewise true that the intellect, in which this purely spiritual knowledge takes place, is the highest cognoscitive faculty of the soul. Nevertheless, the soul must be cautious. First, in regard to the devil, we must notice that he is not altogether

[4] 1 Corinth., xii,8
[5] xxvi,15

powerless here. Spirit though he is, he cannot see this knowledge of naked truths of which we speak. But he can detect it indirectly, by means of those corporeal things which accompany them, *i.e.*, phantasms, speech, outward signs, *etc.* The devil's wits are now tried to the utmost, and he meddles in these revelations as much as he can, for he sees the soul slipping beyond his grasp. But if he does succeed in deceiving a soul, such deception is very difficult to unmask. The only way for him to deceive a soul is to work on the imagination in a subtle way, and to insinuate that it is not by way of the imagination at all that the deluded soul is receiving knowledge. Such a method may be called "suggestion," since by the work of the imagination it is suggested to the soul that it is proceeding according to its own power of reasoning or that God is enlightening it. (It is by such suggestion to man's spirit — "spiritual suggestion," it might be called — that the devil is able to deceive the soul in regard to spiritual visions of material substances.[6]) Such deception is the more probable when one has neither speculative nor experimental knowledge of the distinction between corporeal and intellectual knowledge. The devil may then reveal to the soul such things as the moral weakness and guilt of others, and the soul may believe that it is God Who reveals this in order that prayers may be offered. But the damage that can ultimately result is very great.

Supposing, however, that a man of learning and experience knew how to outwit the devil, would it be profitable to him to traffic in this type of revelation? The whole problem always resolves itself into this: Is this knowledge truly supernatural? This is to say, is it supernatural in

[6] Compare xxiv,7 and xxvi,17

essence, so that it elevates man's faculties to the order of Divine things? For we must always distinguish between that which is merely outside the natural process (super-natural in mode), and that which is a participation of the Divine (supernatural in essence). Now, Friar John of the Cross calls this knowledge supernatural. And, indeed, this spiritual intelligence must be in some way superna-tural, for it cannot be acquired by the natural process of human knowledge, nor can it be imparted by the devil, nor even by a good angel, since spirits communicate with souls through the senses and imagination only. Therefore, there remains only God; but all that God gives outside the natural order of things, is called supernatural.

However, God may give things that are not above the capacity of a certain faculty: thus, we know that He can represent in the outward senses things that have no real existence among worldly objects; again He may infuse into the imagination images that did not filter through the windows of the senses; and here we see that He can place in the harbor of the intellect vessels of knowledge that did not voyage through the narrow channels of the senses. We have been calling such knowledge "superna-tural," and rightly so, for it is outside the procedure of nature. But it is easy to understand that such knowledge is not above the *capacity* of these faculties. I take the word capacity to mean that which a faculty is able to *receive*. For example, let us say that a certain scientist, wishing to play a trick on his friends, places in his camera a film that is sensitive to all kinds of light. With this camera he pre-tends to take a picture of a distant landscape, but does not expose the film in the usual way. Instead, he excuses him-self from their presence, and takes the camera into his laboratory, where by means of a special projector using X-rays, he casts a picture of a bird *through the top of the camera,* on to the film. Then he gives the camera to one of his friends, and allows him to remove and develop the film. Thus he makes them believe that he took a long-distance picture with an ordinary camera. Observe what has happened. The *natural* mode of taking a picture is through the lens of the camera in which the film is placed. We may compare the lens to man's senses and imagination, and the film to his intellect. When the scientist disregarded the lens of the camera, and projected an image upon the film from above and without regard to the nature of the camera, he took a picture that might be termed "supernatural" because it was the result of a process outside the natural mode of taking pictures. He did not, however, imprint on the film anything that was strictly "supernatural" to it, for it was "natural" to the film to receive the light. Neither the image nor the light was above the "capacity" of the film. By the "capacity" of the film, I mean its intrinsic power to receive that which was given to it, without any change being necessary in the nature of the film itself. If we call that image "supernatural" in relation to the film, it is only because the film received the image in a mode above the nature of the camera.

Now apply this to the cognoscitive faculties of man. Similar to the camera, the natural mode of receiving is through the lens of the senses: from the outward senses to the imagination, and from the imagination to the intellect. If the intellect receives any image (intelligible species) outside of this ordinary mode of procedure, that act of intellection, and even the idea thus received, may be called "supernatural" (or better, "preternatural"), because the natural mode was superseded. But the natural capacity of the intellect was not superseded: I mean that the nature of the intellect itself was not changed in order that it might receive the idea. Only the mode is supernatural. We rightly, therefore, call the intellection of naked truths "supernatural in mode," since they cannot come through the lens of the senses, but must be infused from above by the Omnipotent Scientist.

The point to be emphasized is that the capacity of the intellect is not altered by this type of spiritual apprehension. Its capacity and operation remain natural. That is why the devil can deceive it by "a certain *natural* light." [7] And, considering the objects of this type of intelligence, we see that no more than a natural light and a natural operation are required on the part of the intellect. For the essence of the intellectual light and the essence of the intellectual operation are always of the same order as their object.[8] A natural object requires only a natural light to illumine it. For example, only a natural illumination is necessary for the mind to understand the essence of a tiger, a tree or a star, according to the ordinary mode of knowing through the senses. But why should a higher than natural light be necessary if such knowledge is to come to the intellect directly? The mode of knowing would, of course, demand a cause that could impress the intellect directly, but the idea or spiritual apprehension would be the same in either case.

The first class of objects which St. John mentions is not

[7] xxiv,7
[8] Cf. S.T., II II, q.171, a.2

beyond human reason, but demands only that kind of knowledge which could be *acquired, i.e.,* granting the means of arriving at this knowledge, the natural intellect could *acquire* it.[9] Although the Mystical Doctor says that such knowledge, "God infuses into souls, by supernatural means," this is to be taken in the same sense as we described in the illustration of the scientist who impresses an image on a film in an extraordinary manner.

As regards the gifts which St. Paul enumerates, these are the "gratuitous graces" which comprehend the examples given by St. John a little further on. What are we to think of the "gratuitous graces"? It might be thought that, since they are termed gratuitous, that therefore they are very exalted, and exceeding all our merits. But the truth of the matter is that the term "gratuitous" is opposed to the term "sanctifying." Sanctifying grace is that which transforms the soul and makes it pleasing to God, and is therefore the nobler of the two. All grace is gratuitous, but not all grace is sanctifying. In other words, sanctifying grace (with the virtues and gifts that accompany it) is not only gratuitous — freely bestowed — but it raises up the soul and makes it capable of meriting.[10] St. John seems to emphasize the gratuitousness of non-sanctifying grace, for he says that God gives it *"freely to whom He will,* whether naturally or supernaturally; naturally, as to Balaam, to other idolatrous prophets and to many sybils, to whom He gave the spirit of prophecy; and super-

[9] I take this to be the meaning of the text: "For with respect to the spiritual knowledge of things that may be acquired..." xxvi,12

[10] Cf. S.T., I II, q.111, a.1

naturally, as to the holy prophets and apostles and other saints." [11]

The above passage is right to the point. There can be no doubt that prophecy is supernatural in mode — above the natural process of acquiring knowledge — whether given to Balaam, idolatrous prophets and sybils or to the holy prophets and apostles and other saints. But, as St. John points out, it may be given *naturally* to those not in the state of grace; this means that the spirit of prophecy does not necessarily transform the soul supernaturally. It may have only a natural effect on the soul as in the case of Balaam and the sybils; if it is to be of profit *supernaturally*, that is because of something added, namely, sanctifying grace.

The reason that this gift of prophecy may be given *naturally* is because its object (as we are now considering it) is creatures, things and events of this world; if sometimes it has to do with the revelation of heavenly things, it is only by means of analogous ideas which do not reveal those things as they really are. Since natural things require no more than a natural light that they might be known, it is not difficult to understand how they may be given *naturally*, as to pagan sybils, and perhaps even the devils. [12] Prophecy, and other gratuitous graces are not directly intended to unite man's affections to God, but this is the function of charity, as St. Thomas says. [13]

But let us see what St. Paul the Apostle teaches in this matter. In his First Epistle to the Corinthians, the Apostle

[11] xxvi,12. St. John's use of "natural" and "supernatural" sometimes requires careful interpretation.

[12] But see St. Thomas' explanation of diabolical prophecy, S.T., II II, q.172, a.5 and 6

[13] S.T., II II, q.172, a.4

of Christ compares the gratuitous graces with the virtues of faith, hope and charity. I will give his doctrine in substance:

Now there are diversities of graces, diversities of ministries, and diversities of operations, but all are from the same Spirit, and for the service of the one Lord. (1 Cor., xii,4-6)

All these things are the work of one and the same Spirit, Who divides His gifts to men as He wills. (xii,11)

These manifestations of the Spirit are for the profit of *all*. (xii,7) Not for one member of the Church only, but for all the members who make up the one body of Christ. (xii,11-27)

God has put a hierarchy of powers in His Church: 1st, apostles; 2nd, prophets; 3rd, doctors; after that, miracles, graces of healing, helps, governments, kinds of tongues, interpretations of speeches. Not everyone is an apostle, a prophet or a doctor, but these offices are divided. So neither do all work miracles, heal, speak with tongues, or interpret. Such offices and gifts are ordered for the good of the Church as a whole, and therefore, not necessary for the sanctification of the individual. (xii,28-30)

To one, the Spirit may give the gift of wisdom; to another, the gift of knowledge; to another, faith [a gift distinct from the theological virtue]; to others, the grace of healing or the working of miracles or prophecy or the discerning of spirits or diverse kinds of tongues or interpretation of speeches. All these are for the body of Christ, in order that the members might be mutually careful, one for another. (xii,8-10,25)

Not all these gratuitous graces are of equal value. Some are more desirable than others. If, therefore, you are desirous for such a gratuitous grace, be zealous for the *better* gifts. (xii,31;xiv)

But these gifts so freely bestowed by the Spirit, are not necessarily profitable to the individual. But I will show you a far more excellent way — the way of the theological virtues, especially charity. (xii,31)

If I should speak with the gift of tongues, or even with the tongue of an angel, and have not charity, I am become as sounding brass or a tinkling cymbal.

And if I should have the gift of prophecy, the gift of knowledge, or the gift of faith by which to remove mountains [an "extraordinary" gift, indeed!], and have not charity, I am nothing.

Even though I had such natural virtues which would inspire me to distribute all my goods to feed the poor, or to deliver my body to be burned, if I had not charity, it would profit me nothing. (xiii,1-3)

There is also this difference between charity and the gratuitous gifts: charity is immortal, even death cannot annihilate it. But the gifts of prophecy, tongues or knowledge shall pass away; even in this life they are transitory. (xiii,8)

All the said gifts can and do fail in this life, but the virtues of faith, hope and charity abide as long as we live. Indeed, charity, which is the greatest of these, *never* falls away (except through serious sin). (xiii,8,13)

By the gift of knowledge, we cannot know all that is knowable, but we know in part only; by the gift of prophecy we cannot reveal all that is hidden, but we prophecy in part only; even faith does not reveal its object clearly, but we see now as through a mirror, in reflected images, but in the next life, we shall see face to face. Now we know in part, but then we shall know God even as He knows us. When that which is perfect is come, then these imperfect things shall vanish away, for these are childish things which we shall lay aside when we reach spiritual manhood in heaven, through charity. (xiii,9-13)

St. John was very familiar with this doctrine of St. Paul, and quotes frequently from this thirteenth chapter of First Corinthians.[14] The reader will find this doctrine again in Book Three.[15]

Since, then, there is such a tremendous difference between the theological virtues and those other gifts which do not in themselves sanctify, we may readily agree with the Carmelite friar that it is best for the soul to reject purely spiritual apprehensions which have regard to creatures, lest it be hindered on the road to union. For these revelations are of no importance on the road to union; whatever profit God desires the soul to have through them, He will not fail to give it, so long as it does not become attached to them. Let the soul relate such experiences to the confessor, who must be careful to guide it past them.

What, then, is the road to union? It is faith. The soul is to be "directed in faith to Divine union," for this a journey to be made "by believing rather than by understanding." [16] We see here that the theme of this book has been faithfully retained. This is the dark night of faith: faith is an operation of truly supernatural light to which the clear vision of the natural understanding is opposed. Therefore, the understanding must remain in darkness, and "seek to journey to God by the way of unknowing." Where did we hear this before? Back in that fourth chap-

[14] See the Scriptural Indices, Peers, Vol. III, p.466; and in particular A,III,xxx.

[15] A.,III, xxx-xxxii

[16] xxvi,11

ter, where St. John was first telling us that the soul must travel in darkness in order to attain the highest contemplation, he said: "... and thus a soul must pass beyond everything to unknowing." [17]

[17] Compare xxvi, 18 with iv,4

CHAPTER XXIX

Spiritual Revelations of the Divine Attributes

HAVING SPOKEN of purely intellectual revelations insofar as they concern creatures, we now come to treat of that same type of revelation inasmuch as it pertains to the Creator. This type of knowledge has a direct relation to God, when the soul in a most lofty manner, has a perception of some attribute of God, such as His omnipotence, His goodness, sweetness, justice, mercy, *etc.* This is not to be mistaken for the knowledge which beginners acquire in meditation, for that was by means of images and figures of the imagination, whereas here there is question only of naked truths received passively in the intellect. Such knowledge as this is not easy for the reader to understand unless he has had experience of it. Two extremes are to be avoided: first, this is not a knowledge of God by means of sense knowledge or even of intelligible species that have been acquired from things of the world; secondly, this is not to be mistaken for the vision of the Divine Essence as happens by means of the light of glory.

It is interesting to note that St. John had used previously certain passages of Scripture with the interpretation that Moses and St. Paul had glimpsed the Divine Essence, but now using the same texts, he interprets them as merely a manifestation of knowledge, which would seem to be something less than the direct vision of God.[1] St. John makes it clear, nevertheless, that these revelations of which

[1] Compare xxvi,4 with xxiv,3

he now treats, although very exalted, do not reveal God clearly to the soul as He is in Himself. If God can infuse into the human intellect the intelligible species of creatures, and on the other hand is also able to infuse that light of glory which reveals Him as He is, it is not to be thought impossible for Him to infuse intelligible species (or naked truths) which have for their object something higher than created good and yet lower than the Uncreated Good as He exists in His indivisible unity. Although the attributes of God, His omnipotence, sweetness, *etc.*, are not really distinct in the flawless simplicity of the Divine Nature, still the human mind, whose weakness compels it to make a mosaic pattern of the most simple things, is forced to filter the glowing rays of the Divinity into the various colors of attributes. This is so especially in the order of reason, where the mind rises to the knowledge of the Supreme Being, through a knowledge of those Divine properties which are reflected meagerly in created things. The same is true in the supernatural order, when God infuses directly into the intellect certain truths about Himself. By the prism of His power, God refracts the blinding rays of His simple Essence into the various soft colors congenial to the blinking eyes of the understanding. Just as in the imagination God might imprint a vision whose imagery surpassed in beauty and brightness anything that the imagination had ever seen or could ever see on this earth, and which, nevertheless, fell far short of that Divine Beauty which it represented, so also in the intellect God is able to infuse pure intelligence, to whose loftiness nothing less than God could correspond, and which nonetheless could not equal that Beatific Vision revealed by the irrefrangible light of glory.

Lofty, indeed, are these spiritual apprehensions of the Creator. Not only are these spiritual rays supernatural in the sense that they could not be conveyed by phantasms, according to the ordinary mode of knowing, since they are too spiritual and exalted for that; but they are super-natural in essence, for they have no other source or object than Him Whose Substance is thus partially and obscurely perceived. We call that natural which has its source in natural things, or which, though infused from above, can be represented adequately by the natural imagery of the figures and forms of earth. But this type of knowledge is above words and figures, and can be described only analogously. Thus David, perceiving in a lofty manner the judgments or attributes of God, could express him self only by adding, one to another, an abundance of in adequate terms: "The judgments of God are true, justi fied, more to be desired than gold, and very much more than precious stones, and sweeter than the honeycomb and the honey." Likewise Moses, after God had passed before Him in some manner of revelation, could only say prostrate on the ground, "Ruler, Lord, God, merciful and clement, patient, and of great compassion, and true that keepest mercy promised unto thousands." The utter ance of so many words was necessary to reflect in some way the blinding vision he had seen. St. Paul, many year after his ecstatic experience, refused so much as to a tempt a description, merely saying that it was impossibl for a man to utter such secret words as would suffice t describe it.[2]

Such spiritual apprehensions of the Creator cannot b attained by the soul's own activity, for they are so loft

[2] xxvi,4

that meditation on the works and creatures of God, or any comparison or imagination that it might make, remain far below them. True, these may come at times of prayer or when one hears some thought from Scripture or remembers some holy sentiment, but such occasions are not the *cause*. For God alone sends them, and when the soul is least expecting or least desiring this, it may suddenly experience these recollections from above, sometimes faintly with serene spiritual refreshment, sometimes so forcefully and suddenly that the body will share in the experience with a certain trembling. This element of violence and surprise is due to the passivity of the soul, which cannot foresee nor efficaciously desire these free gifts of God.

The delight which the soul receives at these times corresponds to the sublimity and profundity of the knowledge, savoring of the Divine Essence and of eternal life. So delectable are such experiences, and so intimately delightful, that the soul would consider itself well rewarded for a lifetime of trials and sufferings, though innumerable, by even one such favor. Perhaps the surest test of a genuine favor of this kind is the courage and energy and desire which the soul extracts, as a bee from the flower, from its cup of joy. Such delight is in God Himself, and as the intelligence of the goodness of God was inexpressibly "sweeter than the honeycomb and the honey," so the spiritual pleasure flowing therefrom is "comparable to nothing whatsoever, and there are no words or terms wherein it can be described." The soul clearly understands that there is no way by which it may express what it has felt, except to speak in vague and general terms which cannot convey what it has apprehended.[3]

It should be noted here, that these revelations of the Divine attributes are, in one sense, distinct and particular, but in another way they resemble that general and confused knowledge of infused contemplation of which we spoke in previous chapters. St. John has, of course, placed them among the kinds of distinct and particular knowledge, according to his division in chapter ten. There remains, therefore, a distinction between this type of knowledge and that "contemplation that is given in faith." These spiritual apprehensions are distinct and particular in this, that they are perceptions of some attribute of God. Now the Divine attributes are known to us with a certain degree of distinctness, because of their reflection in the world about us. We know the Divine attributes through the corresponding virtues in created things. Thus, I come to apprehend the justice of God, though in a limited way, from the justice written in His works; I glimpse something of His beauty in the delineations of His creative hand. I see in creatures a reflected and mosaic pattern of Divine perfection. The attributes of God are comprehended by me, therefore, with a particularization and distinctness, which, though not really found in themselves as they exist in the Divine Unity, are given to them by my mind through the finite mirror of particular and distinct powers and virtues of creation. Thus, Moses, though realizing how inadequate his words were, nevertheless was able to attribute to God particular and distinct qualities, for example, mercy, which he stressed in many words: "O the Lord, the Lord God, merciful and gracious

[3] xxvi,3

patient and of much compassion . . . Who keepest mercy
unto thousands . . ."

On the other hand, because of the transcendence of
this knowledge, it may seem somewhat general and indistinct in comparison with natural knowledge. The
reason for this is that the farther any intelligence is removed from the senses and imagination, the more indistinct and general it becomes, for the sense faculties
have for their object *a particular thing*. In human knowledge that which is more distinct seems more real, because
we start from phantasms; but among the angels, those are
the higher who know by more general and comprehensive
forms. Now this purely intellectual knowledge of the
Divine attributes resembles the angelic mode of knowing.
It is, moreover, so far removed from the apprehensions
that we mortals daily experience, that distinct concepts
or words are powerless to express it adequately. "These
Divine manifestations of knowledge which have respect
to God never relate to *particular* matters, inasmuch as
they concern the Chief Beginning, and therefore can have
no *particular reference* . . . He cannot be experienced
manifestly and *clearly*, as in glory . . ." Thus David "used
only common and *general* terms," for a soul who experiences this, knows "that there is no fit name by which it
is able to name it." [4] It becomes apparent, therefore, that
as knowledge rises in the supernatural order, it transcends
the distinct and particular and becomes more general and
obscure, in relation to our natural process of knowing.

What power has the devil in this type of revelation?
The devil, we recall, can communicate with the soul only
through local motion of matter, *i.e.*, by apparitions, signs,

[4] xxvi,4,5

imaginations. It follows that this spiritual knowledge, which is above the significations of signs, words or phantasms, is beyond the devil's reach, and he cannot counterfeit anything so lofty. All along we were perhaps surprised to know how much power the devil has. We are glad to hear at last that he cannot meddle with this, for both the knowledge and the delight which follows are so lofty, that he cannot produce anything like it. Nevertheless, the malicious spirit does what he is able, making some pretence of imitating it, by representing to the soul through the senses great and important matters which might distract it from God. But the revelations from God may always be known by the love they inspire and the virtues and blessings they bring.

Are these spiritual apprehensions of the Creator the means to Divine union? Here, the reader may be puzzled by the twofold answer given by the Saint. For, first of all, he affirms that "this kind of knowledge is of God Himself, and the delight is of God Himself . . ."; that this is "pure contemplation," [5] although not to be confused with that type which is dark and general. "And these lofty manifestations of knowledge can only come to the soul that attains to union with God, for they are themselves that union; and to receive them is equivalent to a certain contact with the Divinity, which the soul experiences, and thus it is God Himself Who is perceived and tasted therein." ". . . such kinds of knowledge savour of the Divine Essence and of eternal life . . ." [6] ". . . they are a part of the union, towards which we are directing the soul . . . they are granted through a very special love of God

[5] xxvi,3
[6] xxvi,5

toward the soul which loves Him likewise with great detachment." [7] What may puzzle the reader is that such lofty experiences should not be desired. The Mystical Doctor is kindlier towards these than towards previous types of revelation. "And I say not that the soul should behave in the same negative manner with regard to these apprehensions as with regard to the rest." But, the soul must neither desire to have them, nor desire not to have them. The reason why the soul must not reject them is because they further it towards ultimate union with God, by enkindling it with love, with virtues and blessings, with courage and love of suffering. Add to this the fact, that they are God's favors to those who love Him in great detachment, as promised in the Gospel. But, why then must the soul not desire to have them? Notice the reasoning of St. John: "And since these manifestations of knowledge come to the soul suddenly and independently of its own free will, it must neither desire to have them, nor desire not to have them; but must merely be humble and resigned concerning them, and God will perform His work how and when He wills." [8] The reasons seem to be: 1st, because the soul has no power over them, since they come suddenly and independently of its own free will; 2nd, because they depend on God's will alone; 3rd, in order that the soul may remain detached from these apprehensions, "for these favours are not granted to the soul which still cherishes attachments," and it must be remembered that, however lofty these revelations may be, they are less than God Himself, they are merely manifestations or infused ideas which retain that particularization and distinctness

[7] xxvi,10
[8] xxvi,9

which is proper to whatever is less than the Divine Unity. There is always danger that the soul may become attached to something less than God Himself; such loss is an infinite loss, for that which is less than God is always *infinitely less.*

It is interesting, and perhaps important, to notice that another manuscript varies from the above reading in this way: "it must neither strive to have them nor strive not to have them." According to this, it is not the occasional or the implicit desire for this type of revelation that is inadvisable, but rather the *striving* after them or attachment to them, which would be a merely natural activity of the soul. In speaking of the memory in the following book of the "Ascent," St. John does not forbid, but even advises that the soul recall such intelligence as often as possible, that it may revivify love for God. Such remembrance must not be through the images of the imagination, however.[9]

The following passage from the "Spiritual Canticle" is a good account of our author's attitude:

Hence it is to be noted that, however lofty are the communications of a soul with God in this life, and the revelations of His presence, and however high and exalted is its knowledge of Him, they are not God in His Essence, nor have aught to do with Him. For in truth He is still hidden from the soul, and therefore it ever beseems the soul, amid all these grandeurs, to consider Him as hidden, and to seek Him as One hidden, saying: "Whither hast Thou hidden Thyself?" For neither is a sublime communication of Him or a sensible revelation of His presence a sure testimony of His gracious presence; nor

[9] Cf. A.,III,xiv,2. A.,III,xiii and xiv are good reading in this connection.

is aridity or the want of all these things in the soul a testimony of His absence from it. . . . If the soul should experience any great communication or spiritual knowledge or feeling, it must not for that reason persuade itself that that feeling is to possess or see God clearly and essentially, or that it is to possess God more completely or be more deeply in God, however profound it may be; and that if all these sensible and spiritual communications fail, and it remains in aridity, darkness and desolation, it must not think that for that reason God is failing it in one estate more than in another. For in reality the one estate can give no assurance to a soul that it is in His grace, neither can the other, that it is without it. As the Wise Man says: No man can know if he be worthy of grace or abomination before God.[10]

In the "Living Flame of Love," the attributes of God are compared to lamps or flames which cast their shadows on the soul. Thus, while the shadows are proportionate to the flames or lamps which cast them, they remain shadows, mere semblances of the reality. So also the perceptions of the soul have some proportion with the Divine virtues and attributes, giving a distinct idea of each as it differs from the rest, but nevertheless they remain *in shadow*, for here on earth they cannot be comprehended as they are in the ·infinite simplicity of the Divine Nature.[11]

But let us not delay here any longer, for we shall come to understand this matter better as we continue.

[10] S.C., i,3,4. See also xiv and xv,15.
[11] L.F., iii,13-17

CHAPTER XXX

Successive Words

WE ARE speaking in general of supernatural spiritual knowledge, the purely intellectual knowledge which comes directly to the understanding outside (or above) the natural order. In particular, we have spoken of visions and revelations, a division depending on the objects of such knowledge. Visions, as we saw, were the spiritual knowledge of substances; revelations, the knowledge of hidden truths; and now, we come to speak of locutions whose object is words — spiritual ideas of words. Locutions may be auricular, imaginary,[1] or spiritual. At present we are concerned only with spiritual locutions, of which there are three kinds, according to their source or effect.[2]

The first kind are called "successive," because they follow in succession like the parts of a conversation or an argumentation. These are not locutions in the strict sense, since they are not heard by the understanding, but rather it is the understanding itself that forms them. Because of the close relation of the intellect with the imagination, it is natural to reason, as it were, in words. Thus one may find himself answering one's own questions, or solving the difficulties and objections raised in one's own mind, and that sometimes with such vividness that the answers seem to come from without. So also in

[1] Cf. xvii
[2] xxviii,2

recollection or meditation, when the Holy Spirit enlightens the soul, as the understanding proceeds in its reflections and reasonings, drawing one truth from another, proceeding from image to image, forming words and arguments, a person may come upon a new fact of truth in such a way that he is deluded into believing that another person is communicating with it, supplying it with reasons and answering its questions and teaching it.

It is not to be denied that the Divine Spirit does enlighten the mind in times of recollection, both as regards the truths of faith and the conclusions to be drawn from them. And it is not unnatural for the soul to translate into words the inspirations which it receives. Though truly from the Holy Spirit, such illuminations are not to be mistaken for locutions, for in a locution the wording itself is from the Holy Spirit.

Further deception enters in, followed by danger and the devil, when a person, being unable to discern what is from God and what is from his own nature, goes on to reason of his own accord, forming more words and believing them to come from another. The illumination of the Holy Spirit is wont to be spiritual and subtle, so that the understanding can scarcely grasp it, being accustomed to clear and coarser apprehensions. Bringing into play the skillfulness or clumsiness of its own lowly views and method of discoursing, it is natural that it should change its way of thinking, in accordance with its intellectual capacity, and continue all the time to speak to itself, without detecting the moment when the voice of the Divine Spirit faded away. The experience of John of the Cross as a spiritual director serves him in this matter, as no doubt in many other chapters. He writes that he knew a person who had successive locutions, some of which were true, but others were sheer heresy. We get a glimpse of his times in the following sentence: "And I am appalled at what happens in these days — namely, when some soul with the very smallest experience of meditation, if it be conscious of certain locutions of this kind in some state of recollection, at once christens them all as coming from God, and assumes that this is the case, saying: "God said to me . . ."; "God answered me . . ."; whereas it is not so at all, but as we have said, it is for the most part they who are saying it to themselves." [3]

The dangers of such deception are easily understood, if not always avoided. First, this is a delightful playground for the devil, who likes nothing better than to have his words mistaken for the words of the Holy Spirit. By means of the imagination, he is able to *suggest*[4] to the understanding words that have the appearance of truth. In this way he may fill the mind with heresy, as he is accustomed to communicate with heresiarchs, filling their minds with heretical teaching. Secondly, there is the danger of attributing to God the work of one's own understanding. This is a very great danger, we believe, and it would be difficult to say how much time of meditation is thus wasted in mere natural speculation. There are certain types of understanding, says St. John, which are so quick and responsive that, during time of meditation, they begin to reason naturally, forming their conceptions into words and arguments with such facility and pleasure that they do not doubt that their own cerebrations come

[3] xxix,4

[4] This use of "suggestion" is another clue for the proper understanding of xxvi,17 and xxiv,7. Cf. also xxxi,2.

from God. This happens very commonly, he says and such persons are greatly deceived, thinking that they are receiving communications from God, which they write down for posterity, and they think that they have attained to a high degree of prayer, but it all turns out to be nothing, like an exploded bubble. When the thoughts or words of one's meditation come from a mere natural illumination of the understanding, without any supernatural aid, the will is not inflamed with charity, nor zeal for the virtues, but all is but natural brilliance and the will is moved to love with only a *natural* love. A terrifying thought! It is to be lamented that many religious, perhaps, spend many long years in good works and outward religious observance with little profit because it all has its source in the acts of the natural understanding and the natural love of the will. Is this not the reason that some do not make progress? They traffic and barter in spiritual things, but never penetrate beneath the husk or rind; like wholesale merchants they buy and sell foods and fruits without so much as tasting their substance. What need our spirit has of darkness!

Added to the above dangers is the fact that a soul deceived either by its own spirit or the evil spirit fails to attain the purity of faith. For the clear perception of words is contrary to the obscurity of that faith which is contemplation. Being quite clear and of little importance, these successive locutions are quite sufficient to hinder contemplation, "wherein God supernaturally and secretly instructs the soul, and exalts it in virtues and gifts in a way that it knows not." [5] This chapter reminds us of previous

[5] xxix,7. This is one of those infrequent passages where "supernaturally" refers to sanctifying grace.

instruction on the insufficiency of meditation and the value of infused contemplation as the proximate means of Divine union. If the images and figures of the imagination and the reasonings of the understanding were shown to be disproportionate as a road to God (chap. xii), the same reasoning holds here, and the words by which the understanding expresses itself must be likewise inadequate, even though such meditation be enlightened by the Holy Spirit. For with the Divine Spirit there are different modes of illumination, and He treats with the soul according to its habitual state of recollection; but the Spirit cannot illuminate it in a better way than in that refined faith and infused charity which is infused contemplation.[6]

As we conclude this chapter in order to hasten onward on our journey, we note that this is one of those chapters in which lovers of John of the Cross are willing to overlook his characteristic fault of rambling. He is like a little child who wanders now and then from the straight road, in spite of his own anxiety to get onward, and leisurely picks flowers in the bypaths of theology. But we love him for it, for although flowers are not usually found amongst the impediments of hasty travellers, their perfume is such that we are impelled by desire to return to the road and quicken our steps in the ascent of our spirits toward the summit of the Divine transformation. However, we shall not stop here to speak of those ramblings, but perhaps later they will be of use to us, as we look back over the paths traversed.

[6] xxix,6

CHAPTER XXXI

Formal Locutions

A LOCUTION properly speaking is the impressions of words from an outside force upon the ears, upon the imagination without any outward sound, or on the intellect by means of ideas. The successive words of which we spoke in the previous chapter were not really or formally locutions, but only the work of the understanding itself. St. John, therefore, distinguishes between successive words and formal locutions. The latter are called "formal" because they are communicated to the spirit (or soul) formally by a third person, *i.e.*, having the form of a true locution. Since such locutions are spoken to the soul by an agent outside or above the nature of the soul, they are called supernatural, differing in this from the speech formed within the understanding at time of meditation.

These supernatural locutions are of two kinds: those which are merely formal and those which are formal and substantial. The first kind is called "formal" to distinguish it from the second kind which is called merely "substantial." Because formal locutions are received supernaturally, it is not necessary for the soul to be meditating upon the matter which they convey, but they may come suddenly, unexpectedly, like the greeting of a stranger. Though purely spiritual, they may be accompanied by an apparition or imaginary vision. These locutions have for their object either instruction or a command, as happened to the prophets of old. Sometimes the command is difficult, and God does not remove the repugnance of the soul, in order that it might remain humble and gain the merit of pure obedience. In the mind of one who has heard a formal locution, there can be no doubt that the words came from without, especially if it had not been thinking of the matter spoken to it.

But a person cannot be too certain as to the identity of the speaker. For the devil may meddle in these locutions, imitating spiritual words by means of words that are auricular or imaginary. One way in which Divine spiritual locutions may be distinguished from the diabolical is by their effects. When God commands a person to accomplish things of a high order in which fame may result, the spirit feels repugnance, a lack of courage, its own lowliness; and if God command things of a low order, which are more safe for its humility, it responds with ease and alacrity. On the other hand, when the devil asks for great accomplishments, he presents them in such a way that the natural inclinations and desires for glory may be glutted, and therefore imperfect souls will be very powerfully solicited in this way; or if the devil should ask some deed that will not command great attention from others, the soul naturally conceives repugnance, because the attraction and assistance that God could give to the will is lacking. These formal words, when they proceed from God, may be distinguished from the successive words of one's own cerebellum, in much the same way, for God commonly inspires the soul with readiness to do His will; but in the case of marvellous performances He is pleased that the soul should feel aversion and mistrust of self.

We wish to point out here two thought-provoking sentences very important for spiritual persons:

> Nevertheless successive words [uttered by one's own spirit] may sometimes produce a greater effect [than formal words] by reason of the close communication that there is at times between the Divine spirit and the human.

> ... sometimes words which come from the devil have more efficacy with imperfect souls than have these others, which come from a good spirit, with souls that are spiritual.[1]

In substance, St. John says above that the Holy Spirit sometimes produces *lesser* effects by His formal words than either the soul or the devil by their own methods. What is to be thought of this? The meaning is clear, if not from the immediate context, then certainly from the doctrine of St. John in general. The greater effects or efficacy, of which there is question, is not purely spiritual, but of the sensible order, things that make a "splash," as they say. As the early training of the human heart is through sensible methods, so also the tendencies of that heart are toward the sensible, with more or less impetuosity, until the state of perfection is reached. The characteristic quality of human zeal and ambition (yes, even in spiritual matters), is that outward display which the world mistakes for true success. Therefore, if in some instances the commands and instructions of the Holy Spirit happen to fit in with the soul's own preferences, the soul will, in all probability, add its own natural strength and impulsiveness to the deep and secret forces of the Spirit, with the result that *more sensible* effects will follow. It is in this way that *sensibly* greater effects may follow "by

[1] xxx,4,5

reason of the close communication that there is at times between the Divine and the human." This is not to be understood as if the Divine and the human ever become identical in mode of operation, but only that the will of the Divine Spirit and the sense energies of the imperfect soul may often terminate in the same object. Needless to say that such an object or such a work is not genuinely greater because of the lowly mode and sensible attraction of the human spirit.

As regards the devil, since he also operates in the material and sensible order, his works are usually agreeable to imperfect souls, who, it is to be regretted, often mistake his suggestions for the inspirations of God. The devil hates the interior life, and knows how to tempt proficient souls, such as Religious, to outward deeds of theatrical dimensions, and to this purpose may speak to them auricular or imaginary words that describe in glowing colors some colossal project. The Holy Spirit, on the contrary, when He uses these purely spiritual words (or even in other inspirations) attracts the soul to things that make no noise, things having no sensible allure because they are genuinely supernatural and spiritual, as for example, dark and general contemplation. That is why, according to our Carmelite Religious, words which come from the devil have more efficacy sometimes than these others which come from the Divine Voice. It is only reasonable, then, that one ought never to trust one's own preferences in so difficult and dangerous a matter, but should reveal spiritual locutions to a skillful director, and rely upon his advice.

Most important of all, let the soul remember that these locutions are neither the proximate means to union with

God, nor the legitimate means — taking "legitimate" to
mean according to the ordinary and normal principles of
the spiritual life; for that which is outside these normal
principles (*i.e.*, "supernatural" in mode) is unlawful.[2]
Thus we return to the notion of faith, which, in the
tapestry of this doctrine on the understanding, is like a
silver thread, appearing and disappearing and reappear-
ing, weaving in and out, binding the whole in proportion
and harmony. Faith is the legitimate and proximate
means to union with God, which cannot be practised except in the silence of every successive and formal word.

Coming now to "substantial" words, we define them as
words coming to the understanding in a supernatural
(*i.e.*, preternatural manner) and signifying the effect which
they work in the soul passively. Merely formal words do
not impress on the soul that which they signify, but substantial words implant in the soul that substance of which
they are the verbal sign. These locutions might be compared to a Sacrament, which has the power of operating
in the soul that grace which the external sign signifies.
For example, when the priest says: "I baptize thee . . ."
or "I absolve thee . . ." the grace signified by those words
is immediately infused into the soul by the instrumental
efficacy of the words, the signs that accompany them, and
the power of the one who administers the sacrament. But,
what God can effect through instruments, He certainly
can effect directly. "Are not My words perchance as fire,
and as a hammer that breaketh the rock in pieces"?[3]
Therefore, when God wills to speak in this efficacious

2 xxx,5. Also xxi,1 and xxii
3 xxxi,2

manner, using only these spiritual locutions as a means, the effect of those words is wrought passively in the soul. For example, if God should say to you, "Love thou Me," immediately you would have the substance of Divine love infused in your soul, or if He should say, "Fear thou not," courage and tranquility would at once drive out all trepidation.

These substantial words, when truly from God, are invaluable, for they bring incomparable blessings with them. One such word might make the soul more virtuous than all the active works of preceding years. How ought the soul to conduct itself? By simply doing nothing, for God does all. One ought neither to desire them nor fear and reject them.[4] It is not necessary to desire them, for God gives these as He wills, and without the desire of the soul. It should not reject them because of their good effects, or because the devil cannot duplicate these. Nothing need be feared in this matter so long as the locutions are spiritual and work a spiritual effect in the soul, for neither one's own spirit nor the devil is able to effect this. As previously asserted, the devil's communications must always be through the senses and passions.

[4] According to Peers' translation (xxxi,2) the soul "should neither desire them, nor refrain from desiring them." But let not the reader be discouraged by the apparent impossibility of such counsel. The true meaning is that they should neither be desired nor positively rejected. The reader may try his skill on this one also: "nor is it sufficient for the soul to refrain from desiring, in order for the said effect not to be produced." Juggle these ideas until you get something like this: "To refrain from desiring them (or to reject them) is not sufficient for the said effect not to be produced." In other words, it avails nothing for the soul to reject substantial words, because God works His effects simultaneously with the words, and the devil cannot work thus.

St. John dismisses the subject of substantial locutions rather quickly, and says nothing of faith in this chapter, but it must be remembered that his purpose is to guide the soul past all the particular and distinct apprehensions of the understanding, which, of course, applies to the matter in hand.

CHAPTER XXXII

Spiritual Feelings

IN CHAPTER TEN, our author divided supernatural spiritual apprehensions of a distinct and particular kind into four types. Three of these types we have already considered, and only one remains, namely "spiritual feelings." To be precise, it is not spiritual feelings that interest us here, but only the intellectual apprehensions which overflow from them into the understanding. Spiritual feelings, says the Saint, are of two classes: those which move the will, and those which are in the substance of the soul. Let it suffice here, merely to explain that some mystics attribute to the substance of the soul what in reality is an unusually profound or sublime feeling or movement in the will. The substance of the soul itself is of the order of *being*; all the *action* of the soul is in its faculties; in other words, the soul acts, not through its substance, but through its powers or faculties. Since, however, the powers of a being are rooted in its very nature or substance, it is not unnatural to attribute operations to substance. For example, we attribute to a person what he does by means of his powers; thus we say, "Frank went to the store," and not, "Frank's body went to the store." Moreover, some actions, because of their sublimity or depth are said to be more interior. These more interior operations are often described by the mystics as being in the summit or the center or the substance of the soul. Thus, St. John, when speaking of the purely intellectual apprehensions of the Creator, speaks of them as a certain contact of the Divinity, as a certain touch of knowledge and delight so sublime and profound that it penetrates the substance of the soul; on the contrary, those exterior perceptions of the senses, by which the devil works, are not in the substance of the soul.[1] In this connection, the Mystical Doctor habitually uses the term "touches." For, since the purely spiritual and truly supernatural knowledge and love of God are above the powers of sense and even above the natural powers of intellect and will, they are, as we said, described as being in the soul's substance; and when God infuses such intelligence and love, He is said to *touch* the soul, since contact with a substance is, humanly speaking, by means of the sense of touch. Let this suffice for the present.

As in the natural order the intellect and will have a mutual influence and interrelation, so in the supernatural order of grace, we find that the mind solicits the will, and the will in turn can guide or restrain the mind, it always being necessary, however, that God give the necessary grace to each faculty separately, in order that it be able to function. The spiritual feelings in question have their proper place in the will, and as such are not the proper subject of this book, but frequently, and even in the majority of cases, apprehensions or knowledge or intelligence (which, if not identical, are much the same) overflow from them into the understanding, and so the question comes up: What relation have such apprehensions to Divine union?

The answer is that these touches are all *touches of union*, and these kinds of knowledge help the soul greatly in its progress toward Divine union. St. John shows that,

[1] xxvi,5,6

in these touches, both the experience of the will (called feeling) and the knowledge overflowing into the understanding are caused by God in the soul passively. Whether the said feelings are faint or distinct, whether they are of short or long duration, whether they are more or less lofty, is not the point of importance here. The point to be stressed is that we are here concerned with passive knowledge, that which is received in the understanding without any effort of its own. In regard to such knowledge, there is always danger that the natural understanding will disturb such communications, by interfering, as it were, with its natural power. The intellect with its natural impetuosity towards concrete reality, its inborn preference for that which is most particular and distinct, is in danger of disturbing and ruining the effect of these *delicate* manifestations of knowledge. It is not by anxiety, activity and striving that the soul will experience these touches, "which are a delectable supernatural intelligence that human nature cannot reach or apprehend by its own efforts, but only by an attitude of receptivity." The soul must do nothing, and God must do all. "And thus the soul must not strive to attain them or desire to receive them, lest the understanding should itself form other manifestations," lest the understanding should substitute for these truly supernatural touches, the merely natural works proper to itself.[2]

What can the devil do here? Nothing, except, in his usual way, to substitute sensible knowledge for this spiritual knowledge; that is, by tempting the soul to think with its own natural understanding aided by the senses. He

[2] xxxii,4

might also stir up the *sensible* feelings, tempting the soul to believe that these are touches of God.

The intelligence of which we are now speaking is very similar to those spiritual revelations of the Creator; many identical terms are noticeable there as here.[3] The chief difference seems to be that spiritual revelations are first in the intellect, and then influence the will to love, whereas spiritual feelings are first in the will, and then overflow into the understanding. God is able to observe whatever order pleases Him, since, as we observed, both faculties require separate grace in order to function supernaturally. Since these spiritual feelings are in the will and at times are faint and indistinct, it may happen that the soul will be unaware of them; and yet they serve nonetheless as means to Divine union. How important it is, therefore, that we keep our understanding in restraint, and discipline our desires, so that we may not disturb or ruin, by our own spirit, the work of God.

In this, the last chapter of the second Book of the "Ascent," dealing with the last type of the apprehensions of the understanding, let us notice that St. John gives but one sentence to faith. But his doctrine is clearly stated, to wit, the necessity of "directing the understanding, through these manifestations of knowledge, in faith, to union with God."[4] Thus we see how faithful the Carmelite priest has been to his purpose, as laid down in chapter ten, where he divided and subdivided the types of natural and supernatural knowledge, "so that then, with regard to each of them in order, we may direct the understanding with greater clearness [conviction] into the night and obscurity

[3] Compare xxvi,3-10 and xxxii
[4] xxxii,4

of faith. . . . The obscure and general type of knowledge is of one kind alone, which is contemplation that is given in faith. To this we have to lead the soul by bringing it thereto through all these other means, beginning with the first and detaching it from them." [5]

We have thought the Saint too brief at times or too carefree in his ramblings, but never, we must admit, did he entirely forget the symphony of spirituality resounding and inspiring him in his heart. For faith has been like a mysterious musical refrain, that was repeated ever and again. If not heard for the moment amid the swelling and voluminous cadences that wandered through melodic bypaths, it returned again, soft, yet true and insistent. Each variant phrase found its way back, for faith, pitched in a note of Divine transcendence, is the proportionate means of Divine union in the understanding. Various, multifarious notes severally strive for recognition, striking the ear or the imagination clearly and distinctly like carefully chiselled words, but faith, like a melodic undertone gives movement and proportion to each accidental part. Never wholly lost amongst extraordinary modes, never drowned by striking measures or bombastic beats, but always recurring as the burden of a song, always sustained like the rythmic flow of passionate poetry, faith is the refrain. Dark is faith, vague is faith, passive is faith, but, serene as the remembrance of spiritual light, it grows, living and throbbing, when the drumming of noisy passions and desires is past, when the crashing of the meaningless cymbals of language is forgotten, when the stridence of instrumental forms and symbols has ceased. Subordinating all, stilling the ears, hushing the imagina-

[5] x,1,4

tion, silencing even spiritual words, heard only by an ethereal sense, this strange, mystic strain, in the quiet of soul-stirring peace, is faintly perceived among the fading sounds receding in darkest night. Non-sensible, yet more real than sound, faith contrives a harmony that subdues every lesser grace, enchants a sunless solitude with its beauty, casts a spell upon the senses, and binds the understanding in mystic darkness and silence. Faith is the theme and refrain.

CHAPTER XXXIII

The Essential Elements of this Night

Now THAT we have studied the second Book of the "Ascent" chapter by chapter, looking closely at the proximate means of union which is faith, as a merchant would gaze intently and admiringly at a most precious pearl; and since we also considered momentarily those other experiences of the cognoscitive faculties which do or might enter into the spiritual life, only to cast them aside as gems not to be associated with the pearl of great price, or at least not to be striven after, it will be well for us to look back over the ground we have traversed, in order that we might survey the matter covered, see the unity of the parts of this Book, and get a definite idea of the direction in which this road takes us. It is very important that we have a clear comprehension of what this night of the understanding consists, and that for two reasons: first, a clear comprehension of this night of faith will serve to clarify many other obscure places in St. John's works, and to bring out the hidden beauty and profundity of passages that otherwise might seem common and trite; secondly, this second Book is a key to the chapters that follow, and its rays shine even as far as the passive night — "The Dark Night of the Soul" — where faith reaches its perfection. As regards the following book of the "Ascent," which treats of the night of the memory and will, there is and must be a close relation of doctrine because of the interrelation of the faculties and the virtues. In the order of spiritual faculties the understanding is first, the memory follows as the archives of the understanding, and the will completes and perfects these as the power which can choose and embrace that which seems best of their objects. According to the nobility and perfection of the understanding, the memory and will also will be able to reach perfection; if the understanding be led astray, the memory can only record the error, the will can only blindly embrace it. But if the eye of the understanding will be lightsome, the will shall be guided and urged to the highest good, the memory will become a storehouse of the excellent stock of truth and love. Now the virtues of faith, hope and charity have much the same interdependence. Faith is first among the theological virtues, as sense-activity precedes the movement of the body. As the hand does not reach for that which is not seen, so hope could not operate without faith. Faith is the eye which perceives, though darkly, the truly supernatural goods of eternal life. Hope is the hand that reaches out for them as something good to be possessed. Charity is the arms which embrace the well-beloved object. The better appreciation faith has of the existence and goodness of God, and the purer its estimation of the transcendence of such a Good (like the pure gaze of eyes undimmed by motes of dust, and not misted by cataractous veils), the farther-reaching will be the soul's hope, the more loyal and disinterested will be its love. Hope knows not for what to strive, Love is as blind as a hand that gropes; therefore, it is above all things necessary that faith be strong and pure.

The accompanying chart will show this interrelation of the faculties and the theological virtues according to which St. John has divided the parts of the "Ascent."

OUTLINE OF THE "ASCENT."

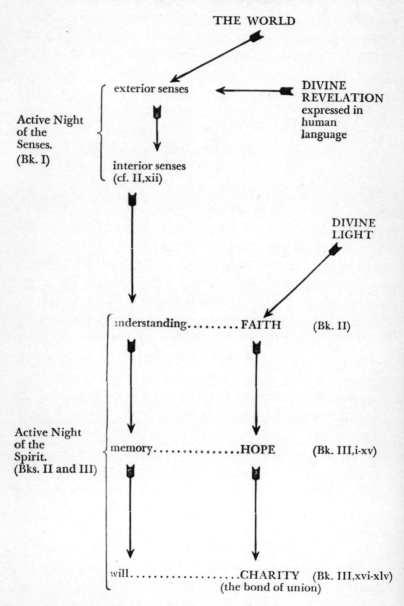

THE WORLD

exterior senses

DIVINE
REVELATION
expressed in
human
language

Active Night
of the
Senses.
(Bk. I)

interior senses
(cf. II,xii)

DIVINE
LIGHT

understanding.........FAITH   (Bk. II)

Active Night
of the
Spirit.
(Bks. II and III)

memory...............HOPE   (Bk. III,i-xv)

will..................CHARITY   (Bk. III,xvi-xlv)
(the bond of union)

First in order are the senses, interior and exterior. These bring the soul into touch not only with the world of good and evil, but also with the language and imagery of Divine revelation, the articles of our faith. In Book One St. John wrote of the Active Night of the Senses which is the purification and detachment of the soul from the desires of worldly satisfactions. As the senses are deprived of natural pleasures, they must be fed with the food of eternal life, the truths of our faith. The imagination, and to be sure, even the spiritual faculties, must journey in this night, because of their mutual relations. (The arrows on the chart show this relation of all the faculties in regard to both the world and the external expression of Divine revelation.) Having purified the soul in regard to worldly things — "from the natural apprehension of objects, and in consequence, from the natural power of the desires" — in Book One,[1] he goes on, in this second Book, to purify the understanding, by means of this spiritual night, (and concomitantly the senses, since they are the windows of the understanding) of all the natural forms in which Divine revelation was expressed. If, then, the understanding is to be made dark and void as to all images and figures and signs and similitudes, the dependent powers of memory and will must likewise be affected by such darkness and emptiness. Is this to deprive the faculties of *everything*? No. As the time comes for the soul to enter upon this new way, God infuses the pure and serene light of contemplation which has nothing to do with the imagery of this world. Consequently faith, which came to the soul disguised in the vestments and symbols of this life, casts off these garments and conceals itself in this night of the

[1] Cf. xii,1

spirit to which the senses and natural intellect have no entrance.

The point I am emphasizing is that hope which is related to the memory, and charity which inheres in the will, must share with the intellect this new purity of the Divine light passively received. It is evident, then, that the following Book, which treats of hope and charity in this spiritual night, will borrow from the doctrine of our present work. Clearly then, the time and efforts spent on our present work shall be profitable for the comprehending of other parts of the Mystical Doctor.

In our review of the night of the understanding, we shall begin with these two questions: What is the negative aspect of this night? (For night implies a negation.) What is the positive element of this night? Or must we wait till later on, until we have pieced together all the parts of this *one* night of the soul? [2] Let us go over the ground again, but briefly and in haste. In the first chapter, explaining the first stanza of his poem, the Saint says that this spiritual night is a spiritual detachment from all things, that the soul must remain in darkness "as to all light of sense and understanding, going forth beyond all limits of nature and reason," [3] "going forth from all phantasms of nature and reasonings of the spirit." Its "spiritual and rational part" must be put to rest.[4] It is different in this night of spirit than in the night of sense where "the

[2] It should not be forgotten that, because of the simplicity of the soul, this night is *one*, though composed of different aspects and elements. Cf. A,I,ii,5 and II,ii,1. It is because of this unity that the "Ascent of Mt. Carmel" and the "Dark Night of the Soul" constitute but one work.

[3] i,1

[4] i,2

understanding and reason remain, and are not blinded."
But this night deprives the soul of both understanding
and sense.[5] So we see that from the very beginning, St.
John says that this night causes darkness in the spiritual
part, the understanding and its power of reasoning. The
positive element, in that same place, is "pure faith," explained in later chapters as infused contemplation, which
indeed is the only manner of faith which can explain this
complete darkness of the understanding. It is contemplation, moreover, and not the mere virtue of faith which
has the power to lead the soul to a union of "simplicity
and purity and love and similitude," which terms occur
frequently in relation to contemplation.

In the second chapter we read that this second part of
the night of the soul belongs to "the rational part" and
deprives the soul of "the light of reason" and indeed
"blinds" reason, which can be verified only in contemplation.[6] The third chapter begins to describe the obscurity
caused by the positive element of faith. Without doubt,
faith is first discussed as merely the virtue, as is evident
from the definition and examples given. But there are
principles here that cannot be followed to their logical
conclusion, unless faith reaches the sublimity of contemplation. For example:

> And faith greatly surpasses even that which is suggested
> by the examples given above. For not only does it give
> no knowledge and science, but, as we have said, it de-
> prives us of all other knowledge and science, and blinds
> us to them, so that they cannot judge it well. For other
> science can be acquired by the light of the understand-

[5] i,3
[6] ii,2

ing; but the science that is of faith is acquired without the illumination of the understanding, which is rejected for faith ...[7]

If taken in reference to the theological virtue, the above means that faith darkens the understanding to every other motive except the Divine veracity. Any truth which is accepted because of science or inherent evidence is not *believed*; it is understood. In the simple act of belief, the understanding adheres to Divine truth alone, remaining in darkness to the evidence of the senses or the demonstrations of science. However, the intellect still retains its concepts insofar as these are necessary to express the articles of faith.

But in that perfect faith which is contemplation, the Divine light shines upon the passive intellect, wholly absorbing it and darkening it to its natural light of knowledge and science. Contemplatives, it seems, experience darkness: the rational part of the soul is blinded for the time, and, because of the relationship of the imagination to the intellect, the former seems, at least sometimes, to be entirely enveloped in a darkness that is almost palpable. "It is clear then, that faith is a dark night for the soul, and it is in this way that it gives light; and the more it is darkened, the greater light comes to it." In complete darkness, the purest light of contemplation comes to it. "In the delights of my pure contemplation and union with God, the night of faith shall be my guide. Wherein He gives it clearly to be understood that the soul must be in darkness in order to have light for this road." [8]

Chapter three, begun with the notion of incipient faith,

[7] iii,4
[8] iii,6

ends on the note of contemplation, which is sustained in
the title of the next chapter. Chapter four —

> Treats in general of how the soul likewise must be in
> darkness, in so far as this rests with itself, to the end that
> it may be effectively guided by faith to the highest
> contemplation.

Faith is the guide to the *highest* contemplation, be it
noticed. It is nothing less, therefore, than infused contemplation which is the positive element of this night.
We call it an "active" night, because the soul, "in so far as
this rests with itself," is content to remain in darkness
rather than in the light of its rational part. Is it not sufficiently clear (at least to us who have some knowledge of
the chapters to come), that the negative aspect is nothing
else than the necessary concomitant of the positive element, just as the shadow is the necessary result of the
light shining on an object?

The essential distinction between faith as a virtue and
faith as contemplation is that the first employs concepts,
judgments and reasonings, while the second transcends
these natural modes of human knowledge. Now the faith
which is to guide the soul to the goal of union is of such
kind that it casts a shadow of darkness, not merely "with
respect to that part that concerns the creatures and
temporal things, which is the sensual and the lower part,"
but likewise "according to the part which has respect to
God and spiritual things, which is the rational and higher
part, whereof we are now treating." One must be carried
away "from all that is contained in his nature, which is
sensual and rational." The soul must be emptied of all
that "can enter its capacity," that is, all that it "understands, experiences, feels and imagines," for faith is above

all that it "understands and experiences and feels and imagines." ⁹ Such phrases are repeated frequently in the fourth chapter. For the goal of contemplation is beyond all this, beyond even the highest thing which the soul can know or experience, and thus the soul must pass beyond everything to a state, which may characterized by its negative element as "unknowing." ¹⁰ "Wherefore, passing beyond all that can be known and understood, both spiritually and naturally, the soul will desire with all desire to come to that which in this life cannot be known, neither can enter into its heart." ¹¹ Although the true guide is said to be "faith," this cannot be understood merely as the virtue, for such darkness as this chapter requires must extinguish all but that invisible light of contemplation.

In chapter five, the subject is the union of the soul with God by means of the habit of sanctifying grace, which is called an obscure habit because of the obscurity of faith. The positive elements here are grace in the soul, love in the will, and Divine light in the understanding. With the first two, this book of the "Ascent" is not immediately concerned, but only with the illumination of the understanding. The soul is like a window transformed by sunlight, so that it participates in the nature of the sun's rays. But there can be no perfect transformation unless there be perfect purity, and the enlightenment of the understanding will be according to the proportion of its purity.¹²
Again, the faculty of understanding may be compared to

⁹ iv,2
¹⁰ iv,4
¹¹ iv,6. This paragraph has reference to all the kinds of knowledge received in a supernatural mode, whether corporeally or spiritually, of which the saint treats in later chapters.
¹² v,6,8

the power of vision. The delicacy and excellence of, say a fine painting, will be perceived in proportion to the strength and delicacy of vision. He whose vision is more refined will be able to see greater beauty and perfection. That person will be able to see the greatest art and beauty of a painting whose vision is most clear and adapted to the delicacies of the masterpiece.[13] But how can the understanding attain to such perfection, except by means of a knowledge that is subtle and delicate, pure and simple and perfect? But such is contemplation.[14]

On the negative side, it is required that the soul be stripped of all things created, and of its own actions and abilities, its understanding, liking and feeling, every way and manner of judging and comprehending with the understanding.[15] For such is the night of the rational part, in which contemplation may flourish.

The obscure habit in the soul, that is to say, the grace, virtues and gifts, is as a root which blossoms in the acts of intellect, memory and will, by means of faith, hope and charity.[16] The positive elements here are the theological virtues, among which we are concerned with faith alone at present. Faith brings obscurity to the understanding, for the "soul is not united with God in this life through understanding, nor through enjoyment, nor through the imagination, nor through any sense whatsoever . . ." [17]

Few souls can enter, and desire to enter, into this com-

[13] v,9
[14] Cf. xiv,8
[15] v,4,5
[16] We do not say that hope inheres in the memory in the same way as faith in the intellect, and charity in the will. This is not the place to study the memory and hope.
[17] vi,1

plete detachment and emptiness of spirit. The road to life is indeed narrow, and it is to be understood as emptiness of spirit, *i.e.*, "the spiritual and rational part."[18] The cup which Christ offers to his disciples is death to the natural self, detachment and annihilation of understanding, enjoyment and feeling.[19] The abandonment of Christ on the cross is our model in the annihilation of our natural spirit. St. John is addressing particularly those whom God is leading into the state of contemplation. The man who would enter upon the narrow path of obscure contemplation must purify himself of those things that are contrary to it, and such is the purpose of this night of faith.[20]

The reason that this negative element of the spiritual night is so necessary is because "all that the imagination can imagine and the understanding can receive in this life is not, nor can it be, a proximate means of union with God." Wherefore, "a soul must proceed [more] by not understanding than by desiring to understand; and by blinding itself and setting itself in darkness rather than by opening its eyes..." Chapter eight clearly explains this. If the "understanding must be blind to all the paths to which it may attain" there remains contemplation, which imparts the loftiest knowledge of God and yet remains secret and dark to the very faculty that receives it.[21]

In the ninth chapter, it is explained how faith alone is the proximate and proportionate means of union with God. And, although the virtue of faith is used as matter

[18] vii,3
[19] vii,7
[20] vii,13
[21] viii,6

of illustration, it cannot be doubted that contemplation is the positive element. Only contemplation can hush and put to silence the understanding, which must be pure and void of *all that can clearly be perceived*.[22] All that can clearly be perceived is divisible according to different types of knowledge, whether natural or supernatural in mode, corporeal or spiritual. Besides all the apprehensions that strike the intellect as clear, distinct and particular, there is another type of knowledge described as confused, general and dark. This tenth chapter is very important, being a keystone, as it were, uniting the half-arch of the first nine chapters with that other half-arch of the chapters to follow. Previous to this, St. John has been laying down general principles in the light of which he would judge all these types of knowledge which he now enumerates. His thesis is evident and clear, and it is important that it be kept in mind, for it may seem in the later chapters that the Saint has no longer contemplation but only faith in mind; the real elements of this night might be forgotten. But there is no reason to believe that the author departs from his thesis. The elements, for which we must not cease searching in what follows, are: *negative* — the night of the understanding, which means that the understanding must remain in darkness as regards all *clear* and *distinct* knowledge; *positive* — contemplation, which is given in faith, differentiated from the other types of knowledge by being *obscure* and *general*. To this contemplation, says the Saint, the soul must be guided, being emptied of, or at least detached from, all other apprehensions. The reader who is familiar with the chapters to follow knows that one by one the different classes

[22] ix,1

of apprehensions are discussed, and always the soul is exhorted to remain in the darkness which constitutes the negative aspect of this night. But, what about the positive element? It is always contemplation. If the Saint uses the term "faith," that must be taken to mean "contemplation which is given in faith." If we take "faith" as the theological virtue merely, we have truly become lost in the darkness, and no longer appreciate the sublimity of this night. I do not say that a person who has not yet reached infused contemplation cannot gather very profitable instruction from this second Book of the "Ascent," for, after all, much of the counsel as regards extraordinary things applies to beginners as well as to contemplatives. But I do maintain that this night of the spirit, as the Mystical Doctor conceived it, has for its positive element the serene and pure light of contemplation.

It was in chapter four that we saw unmistakable evidence of the fact that "faith" was to be taken as equivalent for "contemplation." It was in that chapter also, that the saint promised "to describe more minutely" [23] and "in detail" [24] at a later time what he spoke of there in a general way. Again in chapter eight he proved in a general way what he afterwards intended to prove "in detail," [25] as regards the proper means to Divine union, namely "faith" equivalent to contemplation. There is, then, a unity in this Book which we must not fail to recall when immersed in the latter part of this work, where it may not seem so evident that contemplation remains the positive element.

Beginning with chapter eleven, we begin to examine all the apprehensions of the understanding according to

[23] iv,1
[24] iv,6
[25] viii,1

the order of human cognition, *i.e.*, from exterior to interior. First comes the exterior senses in relation to natural
perception. But from these the soul was detached in the
night of the senses (Book One of the "Ascent") as the first
step toward contemplation. Next is to be treated the perceptions produced supernaturally (preternaturally) in
these senses, which is the object of chapter eleven. These
visions must be quenched in the night (negative element),
in order that the soul may remain in the purity of faith
(positive element).[26]

In chapter twelve, we begin to consider the apprehensions of the interior senses, and first comes its natural
apprehensions inasmuch as these may be used for spiritual
meditation. But meditation is only a remote means to
Divine union, and must therefore be abandoned (negative element), in order that the soul may practise the
proximate means which is contemplation (positive element). Having proved in chapter twelve the inadequacy
of meditation, the Saint in the three following chapters
treats of the characteristics and signs of contemplation, in
order that those who recognize in themselves the signs of
the proximate call to contemplation may resolve to journey wholeheartedly in this night. These chapters are very
useful in their description of the positive element, which
compensates superabundantly for the darkness of the
journey. If our author does not speak at greater length of
this positive element, that is because he is reserving it for
later consideration in the passive night, which is its
proper place.[27]

Chapter sixteen is concerned with the representations

[26] xi,4,8
[27] D.N., I.

in the imagination received from God or the devil. Of these forms the understanding must be emptied, preferring darkness to this kind of light. The positive element of contemplation is here described as a mouth-to-mouth communication of God to the soul, and as faith and "substance" and "dark light," by means of which it may attain to a participation of Divine Wisdom.

In the seventeenth chapter, the opposition between sense and spirit is shown.[28] Sense is all that knowledge which comes to the rational part of the soul through the channels of the senses; it is evident that the soul must remain "in complete abstraction from every sense,"[29] in order that it may operate according to "pure spirit." Pure spirit means contemplation, which is mentioned explicitly.[30] The following chapters continue to discuss corporeal visions, and in general the opposition between sense-knowledge and purely spiritual communion with God. The soul must be *emptied* and *detached* and *freed* from the apprehensions of sense (negative), in order that it may be able to soar to the "heights of dark faith" (positive).[31] "Purity of spirit in dark faith is the means of union."[32] "Dark faith" is an instance of how St. John sometimes unites both the negative and positive elements of this night in a single term. In the twentieth chapter, there is but one clue to this theme, but both elements are expressed in one sentence: "Wherefore, we must have confidence, not in understanding, but in faith."[33]

[28] Cf. the chapters above on "Sense and Spirit."
[29] xvii,5
[30] xvii,7
[31] xviii,2
[32] xix,14
[33] xx,8

ELEMENTS OF THIS NIGHT.

NIGHT OF THE UNDER-STANDING

Negative element: intellectual darkness, more or less complete

- Darkness of all clear and distinct knowledge received in the understanding by means of the senses ...
  - external senses
  - complete darkness
  - internal senses
    - { naturally A, I. supernaturally (in mode) II,xi.
    - { naturally xii supernaturally (in mode) xvi

Positive element: Intellectual light of infused Contemplation

- Darkness of all clear and distinct knowledge received directly in the understanding
  - Visions of corporeal substances, xxiv. ("dark detachment")
  - Revelations of the Creator, xxvi,1-10 (modified darkness of merely not desiring these)
  - Revelations of creatures, xxvi,11-18 (complete darkness)
  - Manifestations of secrets and mysteries, xxvii (complete darkness)
  - Successive words, xxix (complete darkness)
  - Formal locutions, xxx (complete darkness)
  - Substantial locutions, xxxi (modified darkness of merely not desiring them)
  - Spiritual feelings, xxxii (modified darkness of merely not desiring them)

the substantially supernatural LIGHT of CONTEMPLATION. xii-xv

The negation of such knowledge as is here discussed is not something to be lamented, since even the devil may have this *natural* knowledge.[34] Confessors ought to direct their penitents in faith, teaching them to void their understanding of extraordinary things, which are not necessarily associated with charity.[35]

Beginning with the twenty-third chapter, the question of purely spiritual knowledge received in the understanding without the use of the senses, comes to our attention. We had no difficulty in understanding how the senses must be set in darkness, because of their inferiority, or why the understanding itself must be voided of all rational and natural knowledge, since these are inferior to the positive means of union, namely, faith. Now that we take up pure intelligence, received directly in a "supernatural" mode, it may not be easy to admit the necessity of the negative element of this night. Must the intellect be deprived of purely spiritual apprehensions, which cannot come from the devil, but only from God?

Speaking in general, the Mystical Doctor says that we should disencumber the understanding (negative), leading and directing it by means of them into the spiritual night of faith (positive).[36] God, Himself, cannot be seen, ordinarily, in a clear vision in this life. Nevertheless, He can be perceived in some manner, by means of sweetest touches and union. It follows, therefore, that the understanding must remain in darkness (negative). But there is a kind of knowledge that is not clear and distinct: a dark

[34] xxi,8
[35] xxii,19
[36] xxiii,4

and loving knowledge, a dark and confused mystical understanding — the positive element of faith or contemplation, with which we are already somewhat familiar.[37] As regards the visions of corporeal substances, one must conduct oneself in a purely *negative* way concerning them, in order to make progress by the proximate and *positive* means — faith. "Pure faith and dark detachment" sums up both elements here.[38]

The second type of spiritual knowledge is revelations. Revelations of the Creator are most sublime, and receive the name of "pure contemplation" from St. John, and they come only to souls that attain to union with God, since they are a part of that Divine union to which the Saint is directing the soul.[39] It is not necessary, therefore, for the soul to behave in "the same negative manner" as heretofore. We see that the negative element of this night is somewhat modified here: all that is required is that the soul should neither desire to have these revelations, nor desire not to have them. The reason that the soul should not desire to have them, although they are so desirable in themselves, seems to be because they are above the capacities and free will of the soul, and depend absolutely on the good pleasure of God. The positive element in this instance is "pure contemplation" in which the soul burns with a most ardent love of God. The negative element is merely that the soul should remain humble and resigned as regards these favors granted to the intellect. If the darkness of this night is not so intense here, it is because, as

[37] xxiv,4
[38] xxiv,8
[39] xxvi,3,10

the soul approaches its perfection, the light of dawn begins to illumine and transform it.[40]

The revelations of created things is another matter. These are a source of danger rather than a means of Divine union. The two elements of the night in this place are: "a soul must journey by believing rather than by understanding"; ". . . seek to journey to God by the way of unknowing." [41] This is complete darkness of the understanding, in order that the soul may not be drawn away from the light of contemplation.

Another kind of revelation is that which comes through words, figures and similitudes. Because of these sensible means, the devil may meddle herein and cause great deception; complete darkness is the best security against so much peril. In this chapter, the Mystical Doctor does speak of the *virtue* of faith, since it is by Catholic faith that every other revelation must be judged. Here we must remember what we said previously concerning the theme of this book, lest we forget that contemplation is the positive element even here. The following is a good clue: ". . . preserve the merit of faith, in its purity and entirety, and likewise that it may come, in this night of the understanding, to the Divine light of Divine union." [42]

[40] A.,I,ii,5; II,ii,1; xvi,15; S.C., XV,23

[41] xxvi,11 and 18. When St. John writes in xxvi,18 that "Such knowledge as this, whether it be of God or no, can be of very little assistance to the progress of the soul . . . ," he is referring, not to the revelations of the Creator in the beginning of the chapter, but to the revelations of creatures. "Whether it be of God or no," means that such knowledge may have its *source* in God or the devil.

[42] xxvii,5

As regards the chapters on locutions, it will be sufficient for our purpose to give several quotations:

> ... in purity of faith, to Divine union with God.[43]

> ... abyss of faith, where the understanding must remain in darkness, and must journey in darkness, by love and in faith, and not by much reasoning.[44]

> ... faith, wherein is no clear understanding ...[45]
> ... all the wisdom of God in general, which is the Son of God, Who communicates Himself to the soul in faith.[45]

> ... legitimate and proximate means to union with God, namely, faith ...[46]

As regards the intelligence which overflows from spiritual feelings, only a modified darkness is necessary, to wit, a humble indifference as in the case of substantial locutions and revelations of the Creator, for all these are profitable means to Divine union.

From this brief review of the night of the understanding, we reach the following conclusions very important in determining the essence of this active night of the spirit. There are two elements in this night; one is negative, — the darkness of the understanding. This darkness must be complete in relation to some things which are not a proportionate means of Divine union or which may even hinder progress or be dangerous. The darkness is somewhat modified in the case of certain means which God may use to unite the soul to himself, being a darkness

[43] xxviii,1
[44] xxix,5
[45] xxix,6
[46] xxx,5

merely of desire for such favors. The positive element is
contemplation. The density of a shadow is in proportion
to the intensity of the light. In like manner, the depth and
darkness of this night is measured by the fathomless abyss
of faith or contemplation, which overshadows the rational
part of the soul and inclines the intellect rather to unknowing. This does not mean, of course, that the power
of reasoning is annihilated, but only that, as the veils of
distinct and clear things are drawn aside, the pure and
serene light of contemplation will flow into the passive
understanding; and on the other hand, the purer and
more general is the light of faith, the deeper is the darkness of the natural intellect. Only contemplatives can endure the fullness of this night.

Does this mean that this night (or this second Book of
the "Ascent") is only for contemplatives? No. Beginners,
too, should profit from this night, for it is just as necessary, and perhaps more so, for them to know what is
ordinary and what is extraordinary, what is safe and what
is dangerous in the spiritual life. Perhaps, one of the
greatest benefits of this work is that it will awaken many
souls to their own capacity for contemplation, which perhaps they were resisting, thinking it idleness and deception. Let the beginner remember but one thing: the
practise of spiritual meditation is not to be laid aside
until a soul has the habit of contemplation to replace it!
Meditation is necessary until the Holy Spirit calls the
soul to the prayer of quiet and repose according to the
three signs given by the Mystical Doctor. It seems at least
probable that God never refuses this grace to those who
have passed through the active night of the senses. Once
the soul has attained the habit of contemplation, rejects

all sensible means of communication with God, keeps aloof from revelations of created things, and remains humble, resigned and detached from even the loftiest intellectual communications of God, it is living in "pure spirit" and in the fullness of this night of the understanding.

CHAPTER XXXIV

Theological Explanation of this Night

Now THAT we have determined the elements of this night of the understanding, which is the essential doctrine of this book, we are in a position to examine the theological principles of that doctrine, thus adding weight and credit to so important a matter. We have already touched upon this, in considering chapters five and six, where St. John treats of the obscure habit of union and the theological virtues. But it will not be unprofitable to go over this ground again, briefly.

Who is there that can saunter through the woods in springtime, when the trees and bushes, stark bare sticks and twigs through a winter's unprosperous resign, begin to bud and blossom, to breathe and live under the warm rays of the sun; when every lightning cloud has been grounded in the moist earth, whose green blades slash through the dry mesh of last year's undergrowth; who is there, I say, that can watch autumn's whirlwind of seeds flying through the air, or lying on the earth, unsown, with the infant acorns and the aged, black oak leaves seeking a grave — and does not ponder the mysteries of life? Nature's countless seeds, thoughtlessly flung on rock and mire, are the future glory of wood and forest. What ineffable power, what mystic might, in the nigh invisible nugget of life! The seed, the root, the stem, the branch, the flower — who can signal their start, who can measure their pace, who can say what beauty shall bloom, or whether the storm shall break or the sun shall scorch?

So it is in the unseen world of souls. The soul is the seed of life, the root of thought and love. Its spiritual span has its sun and rain and storms. And not once only, but twice! Created in the world of nature, it may bloom with fairest grace in a region untrodden by the crowd. With doubled root of a twofold life, it may chose the main course of its future development. One root is that of nature, the other is that of grace. Two stems sprout from nature: thought and love, for future planning. Three stems grow from the root of grace: faith and charity with hope for future possession. Or again, faith is the one stem, hope is its branches and leaves, charity is its flower. Every Christian knows that faith is a participation of the Divine Truth, a light shining in the darkness of the world; the sighing wayfarer remembers that hope gives promise of eternal happiness; the vivacious, fruit-laden soul realizes that charity is the bond of union, the embracing of the Infinite Beauty.

But few, perhaps, realize the role of the sevenfold gift implanted with grace. The gifts of the Holy Spirit are qualities of soul, permanent habits that give the mind docility and the will flexibility, with reference to the Spirit of light and love. In the beginning, the soul relies on reason and meditated decision, remaining confident in its own virtues and perhaps inflexible in its attitude. Its powers of flexibility and responsiveness are not attuned to those external forces which alone can make it perfect. A flag pole is stiff, unbending and deaf to the wind, but a living tree is pliant, swaying with its leafy banners at the breath of a zephyr. That tree is in touch with the forces around it; it waits for the promptings of the spirit which blows where it will. So also the soul that lives the fullness of its gifts. It is alert, docile, responsive to the breathings of the Spirit Whose inspirations sway it as He wills, whether quietly and with little stir in the serene light of evening, or invisibly and secretly in the unknowing shadows of the night.

The gifts of the Holy Spirit are implanted with the root of grace. And as the sap increases with the growth of the plant, so the gifts increase with movements of grace, with the ascendency of faith, the branching-out of hope, and the flowering of charity. A marvelous plant is this! For the stem cannot grow nor the branches spread out, without the flower. It is as if the plant breathed through its flower, or as if the sap were poured into the branches and down through the stem and into the root by means of its flower-funnel. "And the more charity it has, the more is it illumined and the more gifts of the Holy Spirit are communicated to it, for charity is the cause and the means whereby they are communicated to it." [1] Paradoxical as it may seem, grace receives its increase from the very love to which it gives birth, much in the same way as the root, though first in order, cannot increase or retain life without the vegetation it supports.

What is the precise role of the gifts in our spiritual life? What do they contribute that faith, hope and charity have not already effected? According to St. Thomas, the gifts have a distinct and important part to play. Though these gifts could not exist apart from the virtues which they adorn, they nevertheless intensify the characteristic quality of those virtues in a way which those virtues could

[1] xxix,6

not develop alone. They give a new mode of action and development to faith, hope and charity. Have you ever seen a plant, which, if rooted up and shaken free from the earth, could lift itself up higher into the light and warmth of day in order that it might draw from above, and share with its roots, the life and strength which it no longer derives from them? But, what is impossible to a plant, that is given to the soul to accomplish, through the gifts of the Holy Spirit. In the spring of its spiritual life, the soul has its roots deep in the lowly soil. Even when its nature and activity are somewhat supernaturalized, there is still much in its stem and branches that savors of the earth. Faith retains much material imagery, and, fed by such earthly sap, strives in vain to ascend to the highest altitudes. No soil watered in this vale of tears can form a flower that will live above the clouds. Faith needs to be eradicated and shaken loose, as it were, so that with the cup of purest love, the soul may drink of light Divine and heavenly inspiration. Contemplation does just that. In infused contemplation, the mind and will forget their lowly sources of nourishment, shake off the clinging concepts of the barren clay, and drink in their life from the true font of wisdom and charity.

It is faith primarily that must be shaken loose from its imperfect attachments. Faith needs to be refined; it needs to learn how to drink in passively that Wisdom which will not commingle with the mire. As faith grows more refined in proportion to the growing influence of the gifts, especially wisdom, charity likewise grows more intense and pure. "For the purer and the more refined in faith is the soul, the more it has of the infused charity of God; and the more charity it has, the more is it illumined . . ."

The Holy Spirit communicates with the soul according
to its capacity. If the soul has not progressed beyond the
recollection of meditation, it receives from the Holy
Spirit only partial truths and checkered light, like the
little tree, which, canopied by the giants of the forest, can
obtain only patches of light mixed with shadows and
never basks in the full sunlight too far above it. These
partial truths are the images and reasonings of meditation, limited, particularized, distinct. When, through
the medium of the gifts, faith reaches the more refined
state of recollection in contemplation, the illumination
of the Holy Spirit is greater and fuller, befitting this state
of purest faith, although the soul is thus sometimes deprived of particular truths, just as the little tree will be
deprived of the beautiful shadows when it shall be able to
drink in the uncheckered sunlight. "And if you ask me
why the understanding must be deprived of these truths
[of meditation], since it is illumined through them by the
Spirit of God, and that thus they cannot be evil, I say that
the Holy Spirit illumines the understanding which is
recollected, and illumines it according to the manner of
its recollection, and that the understanding cannot find
any other and greater recollection than in [purest] faith;
and thus the Holy Spirit will illumine it in naught more
than in [purest] faith. For the purer and the more refined in faith is the soul, the more it has of the infused
charity of God; and the more charity it has, the more is it
illumined and the more gifts of the Holy Spirit are communicated to it, for charity is the cause and the means
whereby they are communicated to it." [3]

[2] xxix,6
[3] xxix,6

In these few words, (and be it noted, this is one of his charming ramblings) the Mystical Poet indicates his indebtedness to the doctrine of the gifts of the Holy Spirit. This paragraph could be fitted in well with his chapters on meditation and contemplation. Notice how skillfully he shows the influence of the gift of wisdom in contemplation, and the intimacy of Divine union thereby attained through this proximate and proportionate means:

> And although it is true that, in this illumination of truths [in meditation], the Holy Spirit communicates a certain light to the soul, this is nevertheless as different in quality from that which is in faith [contemplation], wherein is no clear understanding, as is the most precious gold from the basest metal; and with regard to its quantity, the one is as much greater than the other as the sea is greater than a drop of water. For in the one manner there is communicated to the soul wisdom concerning one or two or three truths, *etc.*, but in the other there is communicated to it all the *wisdom of God* in general, which is the Son of God, "Who communicates Himself to the soul in faith [contemplation]." [4]

This doctrine may be found in St. Thomas, as follows:

> Men are called the sons of God insofar as they share the likeness of the only-begotten and natural Son, as it is written: "Whom He foreknew ... to be made like the image of His Son, Who is Wisdom Begotten ..." And so, sharing the *Gift of Wisdom,* man attains sonship with God. [5]

[4] xxix,6
[5] S.T., II II, q.45, a.6

It may be well to note other traces of this doctrine in St. John:

> If these impediments and these veils were wholly re-moved . . . the soul would then find itself in a condition of pure detachment and poverty of spirit, and, being simple and pure, would be transformed into simple and pure Wisdom, which is the Son of God.[6]
>
> The Wisdom of God, wherein the understanding is to be united, . . . is wholly pure and simple. And as, in order that these two extremes may be united — namely, the soul and Divine Wisdom — it will be necessary for them to attain to agreement, by the mediation of a cer-tain mutual resemblance, hence it follows that the soul must be pure and simple . . .[7]
>
> . . . contemplation . . . mystical theology . . . *secret wis-dom of God;* . . .[8]
>
> . . . drinks of *wisdom* and love and delight.[9]
>
> . . . union with Divine Wisdom . . .[10]

This doctrine was foreshadowed even in Book One of the "Ascent." [11] In both these Books, too, there was fre-quent mention of the Holy Spirit, which also throws light on the Saint's use of the term "spirit" to designate the supernatural life in man, and also the opposition he no-tices between "sense and spirit," as we noticed in a pre-vious chapter.

Such is the sure and solid foundation of St. John's spiritual road — and carefree ramblings or poetic flights.

[6] xv,4
[7] xvi,7
[8] viii,6
[9] xiv,2
[10] xvi,5
[11] Cf. A,I,ii,4;iv,5; viii,1,2,4,6, and elsewhere.

O, let the little root rejoice! Let it send forth its two-fold shoot of natural and supernatural activity. May the stem of faith be strong and quick in upward flight; let hope sustain branch and leaf in every storm; may charity be pure and simple; may the gifts from above increase and mature the whole organism. And if, Little Tree, your rejoicing is not unmingled with sorrow, nor your sunshine uncheckered with shadows, be patient, calm and faithful. Be strong and unafraid in the unknowing night. Let the soft breezes of the Spirit caress you and sway you in the sightless shadows: this perfects you from blossom to root. As you take your place among the giants of the forest, forget the dancing shadows, let the Divine Husbandman uproot you and shake you free of that which is earthly. Breathe the pure air above the clouds, drink in undefiled wisdom, bask in the full light of God's Sun. This is perfection.

CHAPTER XXXV

Conclusion

I BELIEVE that the reader who has persevered in following me thus far will admit that the doctrine of St. John in this second Book of the "Ascent," mystifying though it may be at first sight, confusing to those who will not mull over it, profound and sublime to those who do not fear the mysteries of spiritual realities, is founded on firm psychological and theological foundations, and accords with the tradition of mysticism and the testimony of the saints. I have not regretted writing at such length on this part of the "Ascent," because a thorough understanding of the principles involved therein, will go far in giving the reader an insight into, and appreciation of, further writings of St. John, whether in this didactic work of the "Ascent" and "Dark Night" or in his descriptive and poetic pieces, "The Spiritual Canticle" and "The Living Flame of Love." If the reader has conceived admiration and love for the Carmelite priest, he will desire to go to the following books which complete the phases of the *one* night of the soul or the *one* ascent towards the summit of perfection.

Because it is necessary to take things piecemeal in the process of analyzation, one may easily become lost in the forest by going from tree to tree. In taking the measurement and testing the strength of the parts of a building, the beauty and symmetry of the whole edifice may not strike one until he has laid down the hammer and the

square, has forgotten about the lost nails and the spilt
paint, and, receding to some distance, takes in the whole
with a unity of view. I trust, then, that the reader will not
object if we step back together, and view as a unity the
doctrine covered so far, forgetting the little rough places
and the ramblings of our Carmelite friend.

The soul is a unity, simple and indivisible. This may
be seen, for example, in the way it utilizes all its powers
for its happiness and well-being. That a simple, undivided substance may have several distinct powers may be
a mystery to our feeble understanding, but nevertheless
it is true. The soul has corporeal and spiritual powers,
each and every one related in a hierarchy of purposes.
The unity of these powers, or the way in which they serve
a unity of purpose is a striking reflection and proof of the
oneness or simplicity of the soul. For example, the vege-
tative and locomotive powers of the body serve both to
maintain the senses in health and to bring them into
contact with material realities. And the senses are not each
independent. Their impressions of the outer world are
brought to the common warehouse or recording machine
of the imagination. The imagination unites the impressions of the exterior senses in itself, and stores them for
future reference. But neither is the imagination for itself
alone, but it serves the understanding, which draws out
of the sensible phantasms ideas that are purely spiritual.
Through the retentive powers of the memory, these ideas
are made a permanent possession to be recalled many
times. Again the imagination serves to clothe the ideas of
the understanding in tangible garments for the purpose
of communication with others. Finally, the will presides
over all the faculties as a queen, exercising and coordinat-

ing them to serve her objects, while she, on the other hand, being a blind faculty, depends on the senses, the imagination, the understanding and memory to guide her. So closely associated and mutually cooperative are our cognoscitive powers that we seldom reflect that each is distinct from the other. Rather we are conscious of a *oneness* of operation: a single, undivided soul is manifesting its powers in these various ways.

The powers and means of action are the life of the soul. Without them the soul is merely an essence. They must be taken into account, therefore, in any profound study of the soul's spiritual life. And this John of the Cross does, particularly in the "Ascent," which is divided according to these faculties. Not only does he treat of the separate faculties, but also of the manners in which the faculties may receive their knowledge, that is naturally, or in a way that is outside of nature, namely, supernaturally.

Besides this unity, there is another kind of unity in the soul: the tendency to operate in a single direction and to concentrate on a single object. An example will suffice to show what is meant. A young man who falls madly in love with the girl of his dreams, tends to forget and neglect all other things. Many other examples might be given. Due to the attractiveness of an object and the repetition of acts, the soul forms a habit which inclines it towards whatever most interests it. It is an undeniable principle that no habit can exist perfectly in the soul unless the contrary habit be entirely cast out. St. John has a philosophical formula to express this: *Two contraries cannot exist in the same subject.*[1] Opposing habits cannot exist together in a *simple* substance; insofar as one tend-

[1] A.,I,vi,1;iv,5

ency strengthens, the other must weaken. This would seem to be especially so when the habits themselves belong to different orders of being, as natural and supernatural habits.

From this it follows that a perfect habit of affection or devotion for one creature is contrary to like affection and devotion for another. St. John puts it this way: *Affection for creatures is contrary to affection for God.*[2] Stated in another way it comes to this: *Esteem for the creature means less esteem for God.*[3] The strength of the soul consists in its singleness of object, because a habit is not perfectly strong until its opposite is cast out: *There is strength in unity.*[4] These principles have greater importance for the soul when it considers that *God is transcendent*[5] and *love makes the soul like the object of its love.*[6]

All this may be summed up briefly as follows: *The unity of the soul demands a unity of operation and object.* This is to be understood, of course, as regards the perfection of habits. Now, we find that the soul's unity is reflected in the soul's faculties. If the soul tends to *one* object, its faculties are the means of thus tending toward it, and therefore the faculties, too, tend toward a singleness of object. This happens in two ways: first, they will habitually tend toward the same object; secondly, no faculty is capable of opposing acts at the same time.

This unity of the soul does not always bring it peace.

[2] A.,I,vi,1;iv,1,2
[3] A.,I,v,4,5; A,II,xi,4
[4] A.,I,x
[5] A.,I,iv,4
[6] A.,I,iv,3

Because of the distinct functions of the faculties, war sometimes flames up. When the object of the soul is material things, the corporeal powers are satisfied, and the spiritual powers may find satisfaction, too — for a time. But the supreme end and object of the soul is God. And there is the difficulty! The corporeal faculties cannot tend toward God as a proper object; they reach only material reflections of Him. And the strong inclination of the bodily powers toward material things must cause strife in the soul. In his present state, man is distracted by sensible things from the perfect knowledge of spiritual things.[7] The soul is more adapted to receive spiritual influences when withdrawn from corporeal things.[8] When the soul is totally inclined to the act of one power, man is abstracted from the use of other powers; this may happen in various degrees.[9]

The consequence of all this is that, if the soul will love God perfectly, it must cast out from itself the forms of created things, must no longer have affection for creatures for their own sake, must esteem God as its one, sole object, must withdraw from the use of those powers which hinder the perfect love of God, and gather strength in singleness of aim. The soul has but one will, and it must not divide and weaken that will with things less than God.[10]

But, how can the soul be united to God? The created things that we know through the senses are infinitely distant from God, and therefore they cannot be a means

[7] S.T., I, q.94, a.1

[8] S.T., II II, q.172, a.1, ad.1

[9] "Cum totaliter anima intendat ad actum unius potentiae, abstrahitur homo ab actu alterius potentiae." De Veritate, q.13, a.3.

[10] A.,I,xi,6

of union.[11] The theological virtues alone can unite the soul to God.[12] These virtues demand the root of grace in the soul.[13] In the second book of the "Ascent," we consider only the faculty of understanding. Faith is the proximate and proportionate means of uniting the understanding to God.[14] Faith causes darkness in the understanding in proportion to its purity and perfection; dark contemplation is the perfection of faith.[15]

God more properly communicates Himself to the spirit of man.[16] Spirit is of another order than sense.[17] Our natural faculties cannot reach the supernatural.[18] It is possible for the will to love supernatural objects only naturally,[19] and so fail to attain Divine union. Sense experience hinders spiritual operations.[20] Created forms obstruct the light of contemplation.[21] The reason is that the Wisdom of God has no mode or manner; neither is it contained within any particular or distinct kind of intelligence or limit, because it is wholly pure and simple. So the soul likewise must come within no distinct form or kind of intelligence.[22] The soul does not attain to contemplation all at once or immediately, but in God's plan

[11] viii
[12] vi; xxiv,8,9
[13] v
[14] ix
[15] iii,iv,xii-xv
[16] xi,2
[17] xi,2,3,4,12; xii,4,5; xvii,5
[18] xxix,7,8; xxxii,4
[19] xxix,11
[20] xi,7,11; xvii,8; xix,11
[21] xv,4,5
[22] xvi,7-11

CHART OF
"THE TOTAL UNION OF THE SOUL AND ITS FACULTIES
(IN THE 'ASCENT')"

THE SOUL

supernaturalized radically by grace (v)

and perfected through supernatural operations of its faculties, by means of the theological virtues (vi) and the gifts of the Holy Spirit (xxix,6 and elsewhere)

(Book Two) UNDERSTANDING (supernaturalized by faith; perfect faith is contemplation, xii-xv)

MEMORY (purified by hope, III,i-xv)

WILL (supernaturalized by charity, III,xvi-xlv)

nature of faith (and contemplation)
  a) obscure (iii,iv)
  b) proximate and proportionate means (viii,ix)

knowledge that may hinder the practise of perfect faith —
  a) in the exterior senses
    — natural knowledge (Bk. I)
    — supernatural mode (xi)
  b) in the interior senses
    — natural mode (xii)
    — supernatural mode (xvi)
  c) in the intellect alone (xxiii)
    — intellectual visions (xxiv)
    — intellectual revelations (xxv-xxvii)
    — intellectual locutions (xxviii-xxxi)
    — intelligence overflowing from spiritual feelings (xxxii)
  d) chapters xvii-xxii treat *in general* of the above, but especially of the supernatural modes of knowledge

it rises gradually from sense to spirit.[23] The Holy Ghost generally illumines the soul according to its habitual mode of recollection, increasing the virtues and gifts in it according to its love.[24]

[23] xvii; xxi,3
[24] xxix,6

One principle is of utmost importance; the understanding must rise above sensible knowledge to that which is purely spiritual and supernatural, namely infused contemplation. The more strong and habitual this contemplation becomes in the soul, the more perfect is the Divine union, at least as far as the understanding is concerned. Therefore, the soul must cast out contrary forms and all that hinders contemplation.

What are these contrary forms? What are those types of knowledge which may hinder this infused contemplation? With scientific precision, St. John classifies all the types of intelligence that may come to the understanding. (See accompanying chart.) One of these types of intelligence is general, confused and dark; this is supernatural, infused contemplation, to be desired above all else. This contemplation is the form which perfects the soul in Divine union. Since the simplicity of the soul will not permit two forms to coexist within it, it is necessary that the soul learn how to empty itself of all other forms. This is the work of these first two Books of the "Ascent": to empty the understanding of all forms contrary to contemplation. Beginning with that which is most exterior, St. John strives to lead the soul away from the forms of the world about us, and from the natural desires which it engenders. This is the object of Book One. In the second Book, he treats of the supernatural knowledge of the exterior senses; of the interior senses, whether informed by natural or supernatural modes of knowledge; and of the intellect insofar as it may receive intelligence in a supernatural mode. The senses are easily dismissed since, being of a lower order, they cannot be the means of Divine union. Union must be in the intellect, so far as knowledge is concerned. The knowledge which is of creatures cannot be a proximate means to Divine union, even when such knowledge is infused by God, and therefore all such intelligence should be set aside. The *clear* intelligence of God — that is, from God and about God — is profitable, but since the soul cannot attain to this of its own power, but rather the understanding would substitute its own natural operations, it is necessary to be detached from such intelligence, for God will send it according to His own good pleasure. Therefore, the soul must desire dark and confused supernatural contemplation alone, and prepare itself for this priceless gift.

Understood in the light of this doctrine, chapter seven has a magnificent appeal. Few souls utterly renounce themselves, or carry their self-denial far enough. Few there are who travel the narrow road and enter the gate of this kind of prayer. This is not the fault of the words of Christ, for they point to this complete detachment and spiritual night. The soul who imitates Christ perfectly will practise this doctrine, abandoning the consolations of the world, of meditation, and of visions, in order to attain to contemplation.

May God lead souls to understand this doctrine. Individual souls striving for perfection need it. And the world at large will profit by it.

THE ESCAPE

(of St. John of the Cross from his Toledo prison).

The spiders, spinning dreams abed,
Spied not the thin and linnen thread,
Long dangling from the stony height,
In silence plummeting the night.

Obscure the night. O fortune fair
That broke the web! Now groping where
The rope might fail, the wingless flee
Begins his flight. He falls — is free!

Deep peace and quiet flow and fill
The shadowed valley — not so still
The stellar glints that strike pellmell
Against the monastery bell.

Stumbling with bleariness, half-friar bent,
Haggard with weariness, crawls the ascent.
Is it the laggard's fate, slows down the race? —
Mountain of Carmel's weight, staggers his pace?

But his spirit, fleet and swinging,
Beats a rythmic march in ringing
Measures; rings, with joy consummate —
Far a-pealing from the summit —

Stanzas struck on flints of mystic
Light with nature's dint artistic,
Casting sparks in spirits ashen,
Kindling living flames of passion.

O prisoner at large, what plea?
What do you ask a world that's free?
What gift? Or what revenge? How must
Men pay for grief and pain unjust?

"Enclosed in dungeons narrow, dense,
Restrain, repress their restive sense
With chains of chastening distress:
Enlarge their souls with emptiness.

"Bind them whose galleons, storm-tossed,
Pursue the spectral hues — souls lost
Without, for having failed to find
Within, the treasures there unmined.

"Let the gates of loneliness clash to!
Dark rays of light unearthly, like dew
Upon the soul, remove the daze;
Restore the spirit's blinded gaze

With balm of shade, in night concealed.
O foolish souls that go afield,
With pleasure's flares or torch of Mars,
Through midday's glaze, in search of stars!

"Fast shackle them where darkness seeps
In solitude's unsounded deeps,
With leisure's links untaut around —
Their spirit-selves alone unbound! —

In caverns deep and inner cells
Where hidden life of spirit dwells
And breathes the silent peace of stars
And harmony of prism bars.

"O men who spin with habit-wires
The webs of glistening desires;
Enmeshed in joy's symmetry —
A gossamer of liberty! —

Forsake the freedom of the flesh;
Slip through the circling, wiry mesh;
Escape and journey in the night;
Return to faith's imprisoned light."

Setting of the Poem: "The Escape."

On the night of December 3, 1577, St. John of the Cross was taken captive from his little cottage near the convent of the Incarnation in Avila, and together with another Carmelite friar, removed to the ancient monastery of the Calced Carmelites in the same city. Carried off like malefactors and scourged twice, they were locked up in separate cells, as disobedient and obstinate subjects of the Order. St. John belong to the spirit of the Reform; his captors to the Mitigated Rule. We cannot go into details here, but suffice it to say that both sides thought that they were right, both clung to their opinion and refused to compromise in the misunderstanding and entanglements which had disturbed the Order of Carmel for the preceding five years. St. John, faithful to the spirit of St. Teresa of Avila, was adamant — obdurate in the eyes of those who retained him forcibly. His habit of the Reform had to be taken from him against his will, and it was with great secrecy and suffering that he was transported to the chief monastery of the Castilian Carmelites, in Toledo, where his friends of the primitive observance would be

unable to find him. Resolute before suffering and compromise alike, he was imprisoned in a cell where he
would endure the punishment meted out to rebels.

John of the Cross spent nearly nine months in his
prison at Toledo, which stood on the eastern and lower
slope of the city, and rose three stories high, with walls
of stone nearly three feet thick. The cell to which he was
committed was ten feet by six ("hardly large enough to
hold him, small as he is," Teresa said later when speaking
of her "half-friar"). There was no window looking out
toward the lofty mountains he loved — only a hole high
in the wall, through which reflected light came from an
adjoining room, sufficient, if the sun shone brightly outside, for him to read his Office, standing on a stool to
catch the rays. Rebelliousness was a very great crime in
that religious atmosphere, and it is, therefore, not a matter of surprise that he suffered cruel treatment, at least
for some months — scourgings, hunger, extreme fatigue,
burning heat, loneliness, harsh words. It was only to be
expected that John would be so weary and bent, after his
escape from the "web" of his captors, that he must, as it
were, crawl the ascent that brought him safely to the
convent of reformed Carmelite nuns in Toledo.

These months in jail were probably the most important in John's life. This is the period in which he en-
dured the dark night of the soul on which he later wrote
a commentary. Here he began the writing of that mystical
poetry which has brought him fame. He carried with him
in his escape a little note-book containing some of the
verses of his Canticle of Love, and probably also the eight
stanzas of "The Dark Night." But even without the note-

CONCLUSION   317

book those stanzas would be ringing in his heart as he fled in the night. When these months of suffering and loneliness were drawing to a close, John had attained to that perfection of love about which he was to write so well in days of freedom. In the night of his soul the dark rays of pure faith had illuminated his understanding; the emptiness of his faculties had been filled with the Divine light of infused contemplation; his spirit had mounted to the heights of consummate joy; the deep caverns of his being were overflowing with the hidden treasures of spirit. He wrote with faculties purified by God, and set in that peace and order which rays of light have among themselves on a prismatic chart.

From a high window overlooking the Tagus river John let down a rope made of narrow strips of bed-clothing and a tunic sewn together. This "linnen thread" being about nine feet too short, he fell and rolled down the steep bank of the Tagus. He had, therefore, to climb wearily up the bank and up the steep streets of Toledo to where he found refuge at the porter's lodge of the Car-melite nuns of San Jose, which ascent is symbolized in our poem as the "Ascent of Mt. Carmel." We can only imagine how weak and staggering his steps must have been, after his long months of physical suffering. But it is only physical suffering that slows his climb; his spirit is already on the "summit," his soul ringing with the joy and zeal of one who had attained the heights of spiritual life, his heart ringing with the substance of his poetry, which he desires all men to possess.

In "The Escape" St. John is questioned about his feel-ings toward the world in general, which was, at least remotely responsible for his pains. His answer, as we have devised it, is in substance culled and garnered from his biography and his works. Each one of us, transported back to the night of the escape of that great Saint, might imagine John of the Cross speaking to him personally.

APPENDICES

APPENDIX I

Normality of Infused Contemplation

There are many difficult and interesting questions in the study of mysticism. One of the most practical of these is this: Does mysticism belong to the normal way of sanctity? To restrict the question a little more, let us put it this way: Does infused contemplation, which is the positive element of this night of the understanding, belong to the normal way? I do not intend to launch out into an unrestrained discussion of this vital question, but I do not think it will be unprofitable to point out what is (or to put it mildly, what appears to be) the mind of John of the Cross in this matter. Let us, therefore, examine what proofs or indications there are in the second Book of the "Ascent" regarding the normality of contemplation, in order that souls may be encouraged on this road to perfect prayer and union with God.

First, let us agree on what we shall mean by the term "normal." If I should say that infused contemplation is "normal," I shall not mean that it is "common" or "usual." It is not! Perhaps, I had better be cautious, and say that it *appears* not to be. For, after all, as authors remark, it is not a matter of classifying a contemplative according to his state in life, nor is it always possible to tag a contemplative by his conversation, nor even by his views on prayer. Some may be contemplative, without realizing the fact. Still, it is safe to say that contemplation is not "common" or "usual," for the simple reason that the majority seem to have little knowledge or interest in it.

What, then, do I mean by "normal"? For one thing I mean that it is not extraordinary, as for example, prophecy or the gift of miracles. It is ordinary, that is to say, according to the *order* of things. It is normal, that is, according to *norms* and principles which are able to give it being. If a magician were to produce an oak tree or a rose bush in barren soil, right before your very eyes, that would be extraordinary and abnormal, because, according to the laws of nature, oaks and rose bushes do not come into existence in that way. But that which we may see in due season: the planting of the acorn or the rose-bush seed, the fertilization of the soil, the cool drafts of rain, the warm gaze of Mother Sun, the gradual development of the shoot, the branch, the leaf and blossom — these are normal because they have proceeded according to established laws and causes able to produce them. So with contemplation. It must be termed "extraordinary" and "abnormal" if it does not proceed according to spiritual laws, founded on true spiritual causes working in favorable environment. The acorn is a true natural cause, and its gradual growth into the oak is normal in nature, yet the abundance of acorns lavished on the earth yields only a very small percentage of mature oaks. So also, if contemplation be normal, it must not, therefore, appear to be the common and usual thing, for the soil of human nature barren in original sin, and the environment of the worldly spirit, are opposed to the growth of the contemplative organism.

I propose to point out certain trends of thought that indicate the normality of contemplation, that the reader may see for himself how St. John seems to take for granted that which has been questioned since his day. In the first chapter of the second Book of the "Ascent," St. John begins the exposition of the second stanza of his poem. It is important to notice here the natural transition from the preceding book on the senses to this book on the understanding. This is evident, first of all, in the poem, for it is the same lover or soul that, in the first stanza, left its house to go forth in search of its lover, as now, in the second stanza, descends by the secret ladder, in darkness and concealment. So, likewise in the commentary, the soul which goes forth in the darkness of the spiritual night is the same that has passed through the night of the senses, which was the way of sense-mortification and meditation. Later, St. John will say that he is speaking particularly to those who have begun to enter the state of con-

templation,[1] but that is because the night of the senses prepares the way for contemplation, and only the contemplative can
fully live the night of the understanding which follows that of
the senses. In the second chapter this is made still more evident
by the fact that the night of the soul is *one*, and whatever divisions of this night may be made in a logical manner, they are not
made for different classes of souls, but according to the faculties
and the progress of "the soul." Anyone who takes notice of this
term "the soul" in St. John's writings, cannot help but conclude
that "the soul" means the human soul as such in its essence and
powers: therefore, *every* soul, insofar as its radical nature is concerned. The unity of this night of the soul, and the natural
transition from the night of the senses to the night of the spirit
(as expounded in books one and two) is asserted, at least implicitly, in several places.[2] Add to this the fact that the goal described in Book One is no a less sublime one, but the very same
goal as in Book Two, as the student of St. John will notice for
himself, in such terms as "union," "transformation," "contemplation" and others.

In chapters three, four, eight and nine, St. John shows the
necessity and obscurity of faith. The Saint's treatment of faith is,
no doubt, unique. In treating of those chapters, we saw the concepts of faith and contemplation were associated together, placed
side by side, exchanged at will, scarcely distinguished, almost confused. So mystifying are his words at first reading, so closely associated his ideas of faith and contemplation, that two conclusions
are possible: Either the author of those chapters was himself
confused and insufficiently acquainted with his subject — but who
would accuse John of the Cross of that? — or, there is, according
to him, a relationship and transition from the virtue of faith to
that "contemplation which is given in faith." The latter thesis is
justified and proven in chapters twelve to fifteen. And indeed,
in chapters fifteen and seventeen, there is stated explicitly the
doctrine of the normal (though unusual) transition from faith to
contemplation, from sense to spirit. The modified darkness of

[1] vi,8; vii,13
[2] vi,6; xi,10; xii,1; xiii,1; xvii.

faith leads to the deep night of contemplation; contemplation is the perfection of faith. The normality of this transition is justified by the work of the gifts of the Holy Spirit, as explained by Thomas Aquinas.

In chapter five, our author goes backward, as it were, to the foundation or germ of the obscure habit of Divine union in the soul, that is, grace. It must be remembered that he is speaking of the germ of contemplation as it exists in the soul before blossoming in the faculties. The Divine union is one of "love and grace" with no hint of anything extraordinary in the sense of supernormal.[3] The terms "likeness," "conformity," "participation," "transformation," "illumination," *etc.* are employed by Christian theologians in general when speaking of normal Christian life. Notice how he contrasts this supernatural union with the natural union by creation, but there is not a shadow of contrast or distinction between "ordinary" and "extraordinary" Divine union.[4] In a context where there are undoubtedly the elements of contemplation and "the state of perfection," he refers to the Scriptural passage on regeneration and adoption which is indispensable even in the first instant of the supernatural life of all Christians.[5] If St. John meant to use this text only in an accommodated sense, he certainly left himself open to misunderstanding. Later, he speaks of the "capacity" of souls both in heaven and on earth, making no distinction between ordinary and extraordinary, but only a difference of degree depending on the will of God. Unless a soul attains to that measure of detachment and emptiness which is required for simple union, in conformity with its capacity, it never attains true peace and satisfaction.[6] How can this be, unless this union pertains to the ordinary course of spiritual life?

In chapter six, the Mystical Doctor speaks of the theological virtues. There is nothing here to indicate something supernormal, and yet the reference to contemplation is there. His reference to

[3] v,4

[4] v,3,4

[5] v,5

[6] v,10,11

what concerns beginners is to those chapters where he shows how the imperfections of beginners are eliminated by contemplation.[7]

To my mind, chapter seven is one of great force for our present thesis, which is that St. John regards infused contemplation as normal. Both before and at the end of this chapter, he insists that he is speaking particularly to those who are beginning to practise contemplation. He uses texts from the New Testament which nowhere find so satisfactory an interpretation as in this uncompromising doctrine. If there are few who enter into this night of contemplation, that is only because few have the courage and desire to enter it.[8] The wonderful teaching of our Lord, which is the source of his doctrine, seems to be less practised by spiritual persons in proportion as it is more necessary for them.[9] How different is THE WAY from that which many spiritual persons think proper! Many flee from this solid and perfect spirituality which the counsel of Christ points out for us. St. John wishes that he could convince spiritual persons that the narrow road of spirituality (which is described in the gospel, and used continuously by himself as a figure of the spiritual life) does not consist in a multiplicity of meditations or methods or consolations (for these belong to beginners only), but it is to be found in the suffering, self-denial and annihilation of this spiritual night, which is the sum and root of all virtues. All other meditations, communications or methods are of little profit. For progress comes only through imitation of Christ as practised in this spiritual night. Any other spirituality is inapt for progress, when the time comes to be contemplative in prayer.[10] In saying that this dark night is the *one* way of progress for those who are no longer beginners, does he not implicitly say that it is the *normal* way? But the positive element of this night is contemplation, which is therefore normal.

In chapter ten, the Saint makes a division of all the types of knowledge that can possibly enter the understanding, in order

[7] Reference to D.N., I,i-viii.
[8] vii,3
[9] vii,4
[10] vii,8

that he may lead the soul away from those kinds which may be unnecessary and even dangerous to progress. Is contemplation one of the types of intelligence against which he warns the soul? No, but rather this contemplation is the one thing to which he wishes to lead us, by detaching us from all the other means. Through all the following chapters, this principle is maintained, and St. John directs the soul past all other kinds of communications to the "contemplation that is given in faith," using sometimes the term "contemplation," but very often the term "faith" in the same signification.

Chapters twelve to seventeen give undeniable proofs of St. John's mind on this subject. He insists that meditation is only a remote means toward perfect union with God. He gives the signs by which a person may know when he is to pass on to contemplation. He tells why these signs are necessary. And a separate chapter makes it clear that the transition to contemplation is not made suddenly and irrevocably, but gradually as is the case with any habit. The saint does not overlook the fact that contemplation is a supernatural gift of God, but he makes it indubitably manifest that the root of contemplation is within the soul, and develops by an orderly process, with the light and inspiration of the Holy Spirit. The similes which are used to illustrate this development and transition were selected especially for their aptness to illustrate the continuity between meditation and contemplation. Meditation, he says, is a "journey" toward the "goal" of contemplation. What can be more continuous or normal than a journey toward a goal? Again, meditation is "labor," but contemplation is the "rest and peace" that follows successful labor. Meditation is an "act"; contemplation is a "habit" derived from repeated acts. Or again, just as intellectual knowledge progresses from particular facts to general principles, so the soul that makes progress ceases from "particular" acts, and becomes occupied in one act that is "general" and pure. In the same way that man passes from the "milk" of childhood to the "strong meat and wine" of manhood, so in religion man passes from "spiritual childhood" to "spiritual manhood." One must first peel off the "rind" or "husk" of fruit and food; afterwards one gives up this labor in order to partake of this "substance.' First, one takes "morsels" of a new kind of nourishment; later, the digestive system becomes stronger, and one may consume "substantial" amounts. All of these comparisons we spoke of in our chapter on the characteristics of sense and spirit. The reader may refresh his memory by turning back to the chart on page 203. St. John's seventeenth chapter reviews the matter well. One cannot help be convinced that contemplation is the normal flowering of principles planted in the soul by God and given increase by Him according to the soul's cooperation.

All of this is confirmed by what we said of grace, the virtues and gifts (ch. 34 above). In the theology of Thomas Aquinas, grace, the virtues, and gifts are a supernatural organism implanted in every justified soul by God, giving it the power to be united with Him through faith, hope and charity, imperfectly at first, but afterwards, through constant and unthwarted growth, perfectly — that is, in a manner not merely rational, but in a Divine mode, superhuman, superrational. This is normal development, according to St. Thomas.[11]

Of great weight in our evidence for the normality of contemplation is the aversion which St. John shows for the "extraordinary." [12] "Evangelical doctrine and reason" are the normal and sufficient means.[13] "If we leave this path, we are guilty, not only of curiosity, but of great audacity." [14] It is implicit in these pages that the normal way is "spiritual poverty and detachment, which is the dark night." [15] But if the dark night is the normal way to perfection, then contemplation which is the positive element of this night, must be normal.

Other parts of St. John's writings add plain evidence to this thesis, but this is not the place to speak of them.

[11] "Christian Perfection and Contemplation," Garrigou-Lagrange, O.P.
[12] xxi,1,2,4
[13] xxi,4; xxii,3
[14] xxii,7
[15] xxii,17

APPENDIX II

An Outline of Chapters According to Logical Sequence

The spiritual organism in general

> Chap. 5. The Divine union in the state of perfection, or the transformation of the soul in God, is a (mystical) union of grace and love. It is a total union of both the soul and its faculties, with the stress on love, since it is love that transforms the soul. Here it is considered as a habit of the soul, permanent and obscure. However, St. John speaks of the work of the faculties, because it is in this way that we come to know the habits of the soul.
>
> Chap. 6. Speaking now only of the faculties, these are perfected by the theological virtues. All these three virtues set the faculties (and consequently the soul) in darkness as to all things. (This darkness is the reason for speaking of an *obscure* habit of the soul.)

Means of union in the understanding only

> Chap. 9. The first of the spiritual faculties, the understanding, is perfected through the theological virtue of faith (and the gift of wisdom), for such faith is the proximate and proportionate means to Divine union. (Faith = contemplation.)
>
> Chap. 8. No creature nor any knowledge that can be comprehended by the natural understanding or the natural modes of the understanding, can serve as a means of Divine union. Here the author shows in a general way, as he will later in particular, how these different types of knowledge are not the road to union.
>
> Chap. 3. It is from faith (contemplation) that this spiritual night or obscure habit of the soul obtains its obscurity. This obscurity is now studied, since it will play such an eminent role in chapters to follow. (Both chapters 3 and 9 contain descriptions of the efficiency and obscurity of faith.)
>
> Chap. 4. If, then, obscurity is the necessary result of the proximate means which is faith, the soul ought to proceed voluntarily in darkness, in order that the supernatural light of faith alone (contemplation) may give it illumination. This demands detachment or darkness as regards all knowledge, whether received naturally or supernaturally.

Introductory {

Chaps. 1 and 2. Consequently, the spiritual part of the soul — understanding, reason, memory and will — is placed in darkness, being guided by faith and contemplation (not excluding hope and charity, nor the gifts of the Holy Spirit) which is to the soul a ladder and disguise. In this sense, St. John interprets the second stanza of his poem. Faith is the second part, or midnight, of the integral night of the soul.

This pure
and perfect
faith of
which he
is speaking
is none
other than
infused
contem-
plation
{

Chapters 12 to 15. Although St. John was describing faith in general, he is concerned particularly with contemplation. This is evident from the way he now treats of contemplation, although that is properly the subject of the passive night of the senses; and also from the fact that he has made other passing references to contemplation. (Cf. iii,6; title of iv; vii,13; viii,6; ix,2) Having been led to speak of meditation, he now shows that meditation must give place to infused contemplation.

Chap. 13. The three signs of contemplation.

Chap. 14. The fitness of these signs.

Chap. 15. Of incipient contemplation, or the transition from meditation to contemplation.

These three chapters are not properly the scope of the active night because contemplation belongs to the passive night. But, because of his anxiety to further the soul's progress, he thus treats of contemplation, in order that persons may know when and how to make this transition.

Chap. 10. Having shown that darkness is the necessary (negative) element of this night of faith (the positive element is contemplation), he goes on to make a division of all the types of knowledge by which the understanding might seek union with God. Since the understanding is the first of the spiritual faculties, and cannot be united with any object except through its act of knowledge, St. John is getting down to the root of the problem. Having made the divisions of knowledge, he states right off that the soul must be detached from all except obscure contemplation. Let it be kept in mind therefore, that infused contemplation is the road of union, and the soul is to be led past all other kinds of intelligence.

The types of knowledge are divided as follows:

Corporeal knowledge which is divided into ...

Knowledge of the exterior senses
- Natural (as treated in Book One)
- Supernatural. — these cannot be the means. (Ch.xi)

Knowledge of the interior senses
- Natural.—the natural apprehensions of the imagination cannot be a means of union because they are derived from created objects. The deficiency of meditation. The proportionate means is contemplation. (xii)
- Supernatural.—why they cannot be the means of union. (xvi)

Having explained the visions of both the senses and the imagination, St. John, in these five chapters continues the subject of supernatural visions. He also refers back to these chapters later on.

Chap. 17. The purpose of God in sending such visions. How God raises the soul from sense to spirit. Why these visions are to be rejected.

Chap. 18. Errors of penitents and directors as regards these corporeal visions.

Chap. 19. The above kind of visions, revelations and locutions though true and from God, may deceive. Proofs from Scripture. Therefore, the director should lead his penitent in faith.

Chap. 20. Proofs that the Divine locutions, although always true, are not always certain in their causes.

Chap. 21. Though God answers prayers for such things sometimes, He is not pleased that we should use such methods. The devil, too, enters into such things.

Chap. 22. It is not lawful under the New Law, as it was under the Old, to enquire of God by these extraordinary means. Now we have Christ and the Church.

All such visions should be communicated to the spiritual director.

Conduct of the director.

Chapter 23 begins to speak of purely spiritual knowledge received in the understanding without the aid of any bodily sense. This is divided into four kinds, as follows: Visions, revelations, locutions, and spiritual feelings.

Chapters 24 to 32 treat of these purely spiritual apprehensions.

Chapter 24. Intellectual visions. These are of two kinds: corporeal and incorporeal.

Chapter 25. Intellectual revelations. These are of two kinds:

Chapter 26. The first kind: intellectual knowledge or naked truths.

Chapter 27. The second kind: manifestations of secrets and hidden mysteries.

Chapter 28. He begins to speak of locutions and divides them into three kinds:

Chapter 29. The first kind: successive words formed by the understanding itself.

Chapter 30. The second kind: formal words.

Chapter 31. The third kind: substantial words.

Chapter 32. The intelligence that overflows from spiritual feelings.

Chapter 7. This chapter seven is a fitting conclusion to this book, being a forceful exhortation or appeal to the reader to follow his doctrine, and enter into this spiritual night.

APPENDIX III

Certain Explanations of Terminology

A critical examination of the text of this second Book of the "Ascent" has shown that there are two elements that go to make up this night of the understanding: the one negative, the night of our natural modes of knowing; the other positive, the light of contemplation, truly supernatural knowledge, to which the night, as it were a shadow, must correspond in depth and intensity. Next we saw that the doctrine of St. John is based on the supernatural foundation of grace, virtues and gifts. Now it is the doctrine of the gifts that accounts best for both the negative and positive elements of this night.

The gifts are those permanent qualities in the soul which dispose it to be swayed or impressed in a way unusual to human experience. Persons just beginning on the spiritual road receive the enlightenment of the Holy Spirit by means of their reason illumined in faith. This is the *human* way. The higher way of the gifts receives the Divine light unmingled with the operations of reason and natural understanding. There is for man a twofold manner of movement: reasoning, which is within him; and God, Who is extrinsic to him. The gifts of the Holy Spirit are as sails which gather up and utilize the breathings or inspirations of the Spirit Which blows as It will. St. Thomas explains this twofold movement as follows:

> Now it is evident that whatever is moved must be in proportion to its mover. And the perfection of that which is to be moved (insofar as it is to receive motion), consists in a disposition whereby it is disposed to be *well moved* by its mover. Hence the more exalted the mover, the more perfect must be the disposition whereby he that is to be moved (or inspired) is made proportionate to his mover. We see, for example, that a disciple needs a more perfect disposition in order to receive a higher teaching from his master. Now, human virtues perfect man according to his powers of reason. But if man is to be moved *directly by God*, he needs higher perfections to prepare him for such movement. These perfections are called gifts

... those who are moved by Divine instinct ... are moved by a principle higher than human reason.[1]

Let it be noticed how this echoes in St. John:

> ... the Holy Spirit illumines the understanding which is recol-
> lected, and illumines it *according to the manner of its recollec-
> tion* ...[2]

According to St. Thomas, the gifts dispose man to accomplish
acts in a *superhuman manner;* gifts transcend the virtues because
they operate above the *human manner;* the gifts perfect the virtues by elevating them above the *human manner.*[3] And the faith
of which St. John speaks is not merely the virtue, but the virtue
perfected by the gift of wisdom. In the light of this doctrine, we
are in a position to judge certain terms which might have puzzled us, previously.

§ 1 MODES AND MANNERS.

Various phrases, using the words "ways," "modes," and "manners" occur frequently in these chapters on the understanding.
We shall see how they are perfectly explained by the doctrine of
the gifts. The gifts raise man above the human *manner* of operation to a superhuman *mode* due to the passive infusion of the
Holy Spirit. Consequently, all that is done without the gifts, or
at least without their influence preponderating, must be done
according to human modes, ways and manners. All that is set in
motion according to those permanent qualities in the soul which
are special gifts, will be done in a Divine way, and therefore will
lack those human modes, ways and manners. In the following
quotation, the word "manner" might well have taken the place
of the human operations enumerated:

> And thus a soul is greatly impeded from reaching this high estate
> of union with God when it clings to any understanding or feeling
> or imagination or appearance or will or *manner of its own,* or to any
> other act or to anything of its own ... [4]

[1] In susbtance from S.T., I II, q. 68, a.1.

[2] xxix,6

[3] Cf. "Christian Perfection and Contemplation," Garrigou-
Lagrange, O.P., p. 276.

[4] iv,4

Likewise in the following, changing "manner" to "way":

> Wherefore, upon this road, to enter upon the road is to leave the road; or, to express it better, it is to pass on to the goal and to leave one's own *way*, and to enter upon that which has no *way*, which is God. For the soul that attains to this state has no longer any *ways* or *methods*, still less is attached to such things or can be attached to them. I mean *ways* of understanding, or of experience, or of feeling; although it has within itself all ways, after the way of one that possesses nothing, yet possesses all things.[5]

That is equivalent to saying that this is the road of the gifts. Yes, for the Holy Spirit gives power to become the sons of God in a perfect way, to those who are born of God, and not of the will of man, wherein is included every "way and manner" of judging and comprehending with the understanding.[6] If the soul retains any "method" of its own, it is "a method whereby the spiritual faculties are voided and purified of all that is not God, and are set in the darkness of" faith, hope and charity.[7]

This road to God does not consist in a multiplicity of meditations nor in "ways and methods" of meditation, but rather in the self-annihilation and docility proper to the superhuman mode of the gifts. All "other methods" are so much wandering about in a maze . . .[8] For, although the "forms and *manners* of meditation" are necessary to beginners, souls cannot in "such a *manner*" reach the goal of contemplation, yet, sad to say, many cling to "those palpable *methods*" and that "earlier *manner*" — the human mode of the virtues. It is fitting and necessary that those who aim at further progress should know how to detach themselves from all these "methods and manners." [9]

Coming to the chapter on supernatural apprehensions in the imagination, one of the reasons for rejecting these is that the soul may be "detached, free, pure and simple, without any *mode* or *manner*, as is required for union." Why does Divine union demand this? Because Divine union, and the act of contempla-

[5] iv,5
[6] v,5
[7] vi,6,7
[8] vii,8
[9] xii,5,6,8

tion, demand that the soul be elevated above the human modes and manners of beginners. The imagination is a human mode of operation; therefore, these apprehensions of the imagination are according to "certain *modes* and *manners* which are limited." But the Wisdom of God, with which the soul is to be united, cannot be contained in any mode or manner, being wholly pure and simple.[10]

Chapter seventeen throws much light on this matter. One of the principles enunciated here is: "Omnia movet secundum *modum* eorum." "God moves all things according to their *mode*."[11] This is equivalent to saying that the Holy Spirit illumines the soul according to the manner of its recollection, as was said above.[12] In order to raise up the soul from its own depth of lowliness to the height of His loftiness, God does it according to the *mode* of the soul's own operation, and "its own *method* of understanding." In this chapter, it is made clear that sense operation is the mode and manner and method of human nature, above which the sevenfold gift elevates the spirit.

The soul's attachment to this human mode and manner of understanding is a frequent cause of deception in the matter of extraordinary communications of God, because God in His locutions, visions, *etc.*, does not always limit Himself to our manner and way of understanding.[13] If God communicates with certain souls in extraordinary manners and methods, it may be merely because of the weakness of the soul. For God gives to each "according to his manner," but He is not always "pleased with their methods." [14] In these chapters on the extraordinary and modally supernatural, St. John is, of course, exhorting the soul against extraordinary and unlawful means of communicating with God, but he continually points out the dangers and emptiness of the soul's own manner and method of understanding — which im-

[10] xvi,6,7
[11] In this chapter "nature" or "method" is equivalent to "mode."
[12] Cf. xxix,6
[13] xviii,2,8,9; xix,1,3,4,8,10,12
[14] xxi,2

perfection is obviated, as we said, by the supernatural mode of the gifts.

These terms do not occur so frequently in later chapters, and they are not always used in the sense I have indicated. Nevertheless, their frequent use in the treatment of the sense-faculties clearly shows that St. John had in mind the wide difference between the soul's own mode of action and the superhuman manner of the gifts.

§ 2   PARTICULAR AND DISTINCT

One must not be surprised that St. John, in his exposition of spiritual life, should place so much importance on certain terms, as for example, "particular and distinct." The Mystical Doctor is writing from the psychological point of view; the "Ascent" is a psychological method of perfecting the faculties of the soul, and as a necessary consequence, the soul itself. This method has a special value, in that it eliminates the danger of placing perfection in external actions or regular observance (though these have their importance). In the study of the understanding especially, we must see the importance of such terms as serve to classify the soul's operations.

Psychologists tell us that the object of the understanding is not any *particular* truth, but *universal* truth. The child does not ask one "why" and then remain silent; all too obviously there is in the growing mind, an instinct or power that must explore farther and farther, and never says, "Enough." The understanding seeks truth *in general*, just as the will seeks good *in general*, and can never be satisfied with any particular good. In the natural order, of course, there are only *particular* and *distinct* truths, and *particular* and *distinct* good things, limited by their very essence as creatures. The natural understanding and the natural will, it may be said, have no adequate objects really existing. For universal truth and universal good do not exist in concrete, objective reality, except in God. In the natural order, then, there would be a kind of frustration, since the natural faculties cannot see and embrace God, as He is, without intermediary.

What is impossible to the natural intellect and will, has been made possible to the soul and its powers through grace, virtues and the gifts. Grace gives the soul the radical power of seeing and loving God as He is in Himself. The virtues of faith and love differentiate this power, dividing to the understanding the power of progressing towards the vision of God by faith, and to the will the faculty of attaining to Divine union even while on the way. The understanding's object of truth *in general* is now verified in Divine Truth Itself, of which faith is a participation. And the will's object of good *in general* is not without hope, since even now the soul may attain to Infinite Good, of which charity is a participation. The object of our understanding and will, in the supernatural order, is the Essence of God, in *clear* and *distinct* vision. I say "clear and distinct," not because we shall fully comprehend that which we shall see, but because we shall see it in face-to-face vision. In this life, however, we do not enjoy the *clear* and *distinct* vision of God.

The point I wish to make is this: since we cannot understand God in this life *clearly* and *distinctly*, it follows that our knowledge of Him must be *general* and *confused*. Our knowledge of creatures is naturally *clear and distinct;* but, though God is mirrored in creatures it is only in a *general* and *confused* or vague way, because His infinite perfections are so imperfectly mirrored therein. Another important principle follows: the more clear and distinct our knowledge is, the closer is its relationship to creatures, and the farther it must be from God. From this we may enunciate the following: that mode of uniting the understanding to God will be the more proper which is general, confused and dark. For this is more in accordance with the universal object of the will — even naturally considered — and also in accordance with the infinite transcendence of the Divine nature.

In a previous chapter, when speaking of the characteristics of sense and spirit,[15] we showed how all sense knowledge must be particular and distinct because the senses are directed to particular objects distinctly perceived. And since our understanding depends on the senses for its ideas, therefore all our natural understanding is related to particular and distinct objects. In contemplation, which is the proximate and proportionate in-

[15] Cf. chapter 20 above.

telligence of God (insofar as is possible in this life), intellectual light strikes the understanding as general, indistinct, confused, dark. By the very fact that it transcends all natural knowledge, it is above all that is clear and distinct — pure, simple, truly supernatural, general. This obscure contemplation, therefore, is the one type of knowledge which satisfies the tendency of the intellect to truth in general, as also the transcendence of the Divine nature. St. John is concerned with the latter. The wisdom of God, he says, has no mode or manner, nor can be contained with any *particular* or *distinct* kind of intelligence or limit, because it is wholly pure and simple. In treating of sensible knowledge, the terms "mode and manner" are associated very closely with "particular and distinct." The modes and manners to which he is referring are the human modes and manners of which he spoke above. But human knowledge, even enlightened by faith, may be characterized as "particular and distinct." The gifts of the Holy Ghost elevate the soul above the human mode and therefore above all particular and distinct knowledge that may come through the senses. The gifts have a function which is higher in order than either meditation or corporeal visions.

It is easy to admit the inferiority of particular and distinct knowledge of the senses. But what shall we say of the particular and distinct, purely spiritual knowledge of the understanding, in which the senses have no part? This spiritual knowledge is of four types: visions, revelations, locutions, and the intelligence that overflows from spiritual feelings, all of which are infused into the understanding "clearly and distinctly." [16] In classifying all the types of knowledge that could possibly enter into the understanding, St. John said that the soul must be lead to obscure contemplation, and be detached from all other types of knowledge including the purely intellectual apprehensions which we are now considering.[17] Why is this, since these spiritual visions, *etc.* come to the intellect without any of the modes and manners of sense, and in a passive manner, *i.e.*, independently of the soul's

[16] xxiii,1
[17] x,4

activity? Before treating of these one by one, the Saint says that 'he understanding ought to be disencumbered of them.[18]

Here we shall only treat of general principles, and not examine the different kinds of clear and distinct knowledge. There are three main reasons why the soul ought to be detached from these. First, because of the deception that may result, or other evil results, or the interference of the devil. All other evil results follow from the deception of the soul, and such deception sometimes follows from the weakness of the understanding, sometimes by the devil. But the devil can only succeed by deceiving the understanding, which he accomplishes through suggestion and sensible means. All the reasons, then, are resolved in one: the weakness of the natural understanding. In this is to be seen the importance of the night of the understanding, for neither the devil can deceive, nor the understanding be hindered from Divine union, except by "particular and distinct" knowledge. But if the soul remains in the night of detachment from all things, in humility and resignation, those favors which God wills to work in it, even though they be clear and distinct to the understanding, cannot be resisted by the soul, nor can they fail to enrich the soul according to God's good pleasure.

Now, if all the reasons of this night resolve themselves into that of the weakness of the natural understanding, how is this to be explained? Two important principles are to be invoked, which the Mystical Doctor has stressed and repeated again and again. First, on the part of God, it is to be remembered that the Divine Nature cannot (at least ordinarily) be seen in this life. Whether naturally or supernaturally, "the understanding in its bodily prison has no preparation or capacity for receiving the *clear* knowledge of God; for such knowledge belongs not to this state, and we must either die or remain without receiving it." [19] It is possible, as we know, to have manifestations of God, certain lofty degrees of knowledge which instruct us about His attributes. These are infused ideas, more or less clear and distinct, but still never relating to the *particular*, but only to God, and so lofty

[18] xxiii,4
[19] viii,4

that the soul can speak of it only in *general* terms. In these perceptions, God is not "experienced *manifestly* and *clearly*, as in glory." [20] This is not the consummated union of the next life, for "the Wisdom of God, wherein the understanding is to be united, has no mode or manner, neither is it *contained within* any particular or distinct kind of intelligence or limit," because of His transcendent perfection.[21] If a soul lean upon any experience or knowledge of its own, "however great this may be, it is very little and far different from what God is; ... in this life, the highest thing that can be felt and experienced concerning God is infinitely remote from God and from the pure possession of Him." [22] That is why certain visions, though purely spiritual, "inasmuch as they are of creatures, with whom God has no proportion or essential conformity, cannot serve the understanding as a proximate means to union with God." [23] That is why the soul ought to desire "to remain in emptiness and darkness as to all things, and to build its love and joy upon that which it neither sees nor feels, neither can see nor feel in this life, which is God, Who is incomprehensible and above all things." [24] Since therefore, God cannot be experienced *clearly* and *distinctly* in this life, it follows that everything that we do experience with clarity and distinction must be less than God. The soul, therefore, that will remain in darkness to all clear and distinct knowledge, in order that it may be united to God alone, is safe against all hindrances to Divine union, for every obstacle presents itself to the understanding with the aforesaid clarity and distinction which is proper to created and limited things.

Secondly, on the part of the understanding, the soul is always in danger of knowing and loving *naturally*, instead of supernaturally as in contemplation. We have already dealt with the dangers that come to the understanding through sense knowledge: in setting aside *particular* and *distinct* apprehensions, we

[20] xxvi,3,5
[21] xvi,7
[22] iv,3,4
[23] xxiv,8
[24] xxiv,9

cannot help but exclude all that comes through the senses, for these are always directed to a particular and distinct object. However, when we considered the purely intellectual apprehensions of the understanding, we saw that some of them were directed to *particular* created objects, but others, though clear and distinct were directed towards God, and gave the soul lofty perceptions of His attributes. As desirable as such perceptions are, St. John says that they should not be desired, but rather that a soul ought to be detached from them. There are two reasons for this. First, since the understanding of its own natural power cannot reach them, it is vain to strive after them. Secondly, the understanding has a natural tendency to introduce its own action, which remains in the natural order. Certain passages found here and there, are of universal application, and ought to be remembered by every spiritual person:

> For, inasmuch as this illumination which it receives is at times very subtle and spiritual, so that the understanding cannot attain to a clear apprehension of it, ... the understanding ... forms reasons of it own accord. ... For since, at the outset the soul began to seize the truth, and then brought into play the skillfulness or the clumsiness of its own lowly understanding, it is natural that it should change its way of thinking in accordance with its intellectual capacity, ..." [25]

> [There is danger that the soul may] busy itself with things which are *quite clear* and of little importance, yet which are quite sufficient to hinder the communication of the abyss of faith, wherein God supernaturally and secretly instructs the soul, and exalts it in a way that it *knows not*. ... We must therefore not apply the understand to that which is being supernaturally communicated to it, but simply and sincerely apply the will to God with love. ... For if the ability of the natural understanding or of other faculties be brought actively to bear upon these things which are communicated supernaturally and passively, its imperfect nature will not reach them, and thus they will perforce be modified according to the capacity of the understanding, and consequently will perforce be changed; and thus the understanding will necessarily go astray and begin to form reasonings within itself, and there will no longer be anything super-

[25] xxix,3

natural or any semblance thereof, but all will be merely natural and most erroneous and unworthy.[26]

But there are certain types of understanding so quick and subtle that, when they become recollected during some meditation, they reason in conceptions, and begin naturally, and with great facility, to form their conceptions into these words and arguments, and think that without doubt they come from God. Yet they come only from the understanding, which, with its natural illumination ... is able to effect all this, and more, without any supernatural aid ... such persons are greatly deceived, thinking that they have attained to a high degree of prayer ...[27]

When the locutions [and this will be true of all intellectual knowledge] proceed from the brilliance and illumination of the understanding only, it is the understanding that accomplishes everything, without that operation of the virtues (although the will, in the knowledge and illumination of those truths, may love naturally).[28]

Wherefore, in order not to go astray on their account nor to impede the profit which comes from them, the understanding must do nothing in connection with these [spiritual] feelings, ... and not interfere by applying to them its natural capacity. For, as we said in dealing with successive locutions, the understanding, with its activity, would very easily disturb and ruin the effect of these *delicate* manifestations of knowledge, which are a delectable supernatural intelligence that human nature cannot reach or apprehend by its own efforts, but only by an attitude of receptivity. And thus the soul must not strive to attain them or desire to receive them, lest the understanding should itself form other manifestations.[29]

Let us sum up these principles:

1. God has no proportion or conformity with creatures. He is above all things; He is incomprehensible and cannot be contained in any human mode or manner, or any distinct and particular intelligence or limitation.

2. The understanding, in this life (at least, ordinarily) has no capacity for receiving the *clear* knowledge of God. The highest

[26] xxix,7
[27] xxix,8
[28] xxix,11
[29] xxxii,4

experience of God in this life is infinitely remote from the pure possession of Him.

3. However, the understanding may receive communications from God, some of them very lofty, general, subtle, delicate, confused or dark, which serve as a means to Divine union.

4. The intellect has a tendency to bring into play the skillfulness or clumsiness of its own lowly understanding. Thus it is natural that it should change its way of thinking in accordance with its intellectual capacity, and to busy itself with things that are *quite clear,* but of little importance, which things are sufficient to hinder infused, obscure contemplation. The soul ought not to apply its understanding to that which God communicates to it supernaturally and passively, for its imperfect nature cannot reach them. Rather the communications of God will be modified and changed by the capacity of the understanding. Consequently, there will no longer be anything supernatural but only merely natural understanding and love. Some types of understanding are so quick and clever with natural reasonings that they begin with great facility to substitute their own thoughts derived merely from natural illumination without any supernatural aid, and these souls may mistake this for high degrees of prayer. But in such cases, the intelligence proceeds from the understanding itself, which is able to accomplish this by its own power. From such natural illumination and knowledge, no supernatural virtue, but only natural love, can result. Thus the understanding disturbs and ruins the *delicate* manifestations of God. Wherefore, the understanding ought not to apply its natural capacity to the communications of God, lest it should of itself form other manifestations, for it cannot reach or apprehend them by its own efforts, but only by an attitude of receptivity.

Our conclusion is always the same: the soul should choose the dark night of contemplation, "wherein is no *clear* understanding ...," wherein "is communicated to it all the wisdom of God *in general...*" [30] This is what we read in the beginning: "But the soul must be voided of all such things as can enter its capacity,

[30] xxix,6

so that, however many supernatural things it may have, it will ever remain, as it were, detached from them and in darkness." [31]

§ 3. SUBSTANCE

The word "substance" and the corresponding adjective "substantial" occur many times in John of the Cross. It will not be without profit, therefore, for the reader to try to form a precise idea of what is meant by substance. First, it may be well to remark that many mystics have spoken of God's action in the substance of the soul. It is true, of course, that God can and does have contact with the very substance or essence of the soul: first, by creating and preserving the soul in its natural being; St. John speaks of this as "substantial or essential" union which is merely natural [32]; secondly, by the supernatural union of grace. But, when some mystics speak of substantial union, they refer to a very intimate, supernatural action of God on the will and intellect, for the soul does not understand and love except through these faculties. This union is very intimate or profound, let it be noted, and thus sometimes God's action is therefore described as being at the roots of the faculties, or some other such expression. The whole purpose of such unique description is to make it clear that the soul is not united to God merely through the work of the senses as intermediaries. But the Divine union is immediate, *i.e.*, without the external operation of sense.

In an earlier chapter, we noted that the saint used "substance" in opposition to "rind," "husk," and "morsels" which pertain to sense operation. Contemplation, which is above sense was called pure spirit and substance. "Rind," "husk," is accidental to the inner substance. Always in the back of St. John's mind are the philosophical concepts of substance and accidents. Substance is that which has its own existence; accidents can exist merely as a modification of substance. Our senses know only the accidents of being; substance itself cannot be communicated to the senses. [33] That is why the substance of God can never be known through the senses, whether in meditation or corporeal visions.

[31] iv,2

[32] v,3

[33] Cf. S.C.,xix,4,5

The rind and husk of images, forms and figures are accidental to the substance of spirituality, for if the senses cannot attain to the substance of a natural object, much less can they attain to supernatural and spiritual objects. That is substantial spirituality, therefore, which attains to God without the mediations of sense operation, which is precisely the case in infused contemplation, which is "substantial and loving quiet." [34]

We may consider in this matter three orders of being: God, created things and the soul. God, of course, has no accidents, but is pure substance without modification or possibility of change. The soul is a substance having certain accidents which are its powers and qualities; thus intellect and will are accidental to the very being of the soul. In created objects, there are both substance and accidents. We can come into immediate contact with the accidents only, by means of our senses. How well we experience this in the Holy Eucharist!

In speaking of Divine union, therefore, that kind of union will be most substantial, in which the substance of the soul is united to the Divine Substance. Now, the knowledge and love of God through discursive means, that is, by reasoning on the images and forms that we see around us, is not an immediate union. Any union of the senses or the natural understanding must be through the intermediation of created things, whose own nature we do not perceive directly or substantially. For a substantial union with God, these created intermediaries between the soul and God, must be eliminated. But, in contemplation they are eliminated, for no external object comes between the soul and God, and hence, contemplation is a contact with the Divinity, a union of substances. Does this mean that the soul is united to God without the use of its faculties? No, for the soul is united with other substances by intelligence and love; even in the very substance of the soul, union consists in the radical power of knowing and loving. But that will be "substantial" union, on the part of the soul, which will unite it to another substance without the need of intermediaries. Friend is united to friend by a handshake or an embrace, not by letters or pictures. So the

[34] xiv,4

soul is united to God, when intermediaries have been eliminated.

But how are intermediaries eliminated? By the actuation of those powers in the soul which do not require intermediation. The outer senses, the imagination, the intellect insofar as it requires sense operation, cannot be united to God immediately, and must therefore remain in the darkness of night as far as the Divinity is concerned. But insofar as the intellect can receive knowledge of God directly from Himself, and the will can be united directly to Him by infused love, there is possibility of substantial union. The *substance* of understanding is given to the intellect, stripped of *accidents* and imaginary forms. In this we see the basic idea of "substance" and "substantial." God gives *substantial* intelligence to the passive intellect without any need for those *accidents* which are the proper object of the active or natural intellect.[35] Substantial knowledge, according to St. John, is intelligence far removed from all sense and accidents; it is the touch of pure substances.[36] It is the touch of God's supernatural power on the passive intellect of man with corresponding effects in the will and soul.

In some places in the "Ascent," the term "substantial" is used with doubtful meaning, which however is cleared up by our definition above, namely, that is "substantial" which is opposed to accidents and the corresponding knowledge of the senses. For example, referring to the visions of St. Paul and Moses, it is said that "these visions that were so substantial" were given outside the limits of natural communication, which means that there were no intermediaries, since St. Paul knew not whether he was in the body or out of the body.[37]

Again, St. John says that the meditation and recollection of certain persons turns out to be nothing, and to have the "substance of no virtue," and it is plain in the context that their own natural understanding is at fault, because it reasons naturally and makes a purely natural meditation with knowledge received in the ordinary human fashion, *i.e.*, by means of the senses and the

[35] S.C.,xiv and xv,14
[36] S.C.,xix,4.5
[37] xxiv,3

accidents which are their object. But all natural knowledge is merely accidental to the substance of that which is truly supernatural.[38]

Substantial words are a good example of the case in hand. These locutions or words are called substantial because they produce vivid and substantial effects upon the soul, impressing upon the soul substantially that which the words signify. The locution itself is merely concomitant or accidental. If God should say to the soul: "Love thou Me," the soul would then have within itself the substance of love for God.[39] In the communications of God, therefore, there is a nice distinction between that which is the substance of supernatural good, and that which is merely an accident. It is easy to see that an infusion of God's love would be just as valuable to the soul though unaccompanied by external words, just as the substance of fruit is not less valuable when one removes the accidents of rind or skin.

It is to the "Divine and *substantial* union of God" that the Saint wishes to lead the soul.[40] For this purpose, it is necessary that the understanding be disencumbered even of purely spiritual apprehensions that are clear and distinct, in order that the soul may travel in the night of faith (or contemplation). Here is definite proof that the substance of the spiritual life is attained by means of obscure contemplation. For although the soul which attains to this contemplation has no longer any of the ways and methods of imagination and reasoning, still the way of contemplation contains within itself the "substance" of all these lesser means.[41] Souls who do not know how to detach themselves from accidental means, and to govern themselves according to perfection of the theological virtues, are unable to reach the "substance and purity of spiritual good." [42]

[38] xxix,8
[39] xxxi
[40] xxiii,4
[41] iv,5
[42] vi,7

§ 4. DIVINE TOUCHES

"Divine touches" is one of those terms which occur frequently in the works of John of the Cross, and it is well, therefore, to have an accurate idea of its meaning. The Mystical Doctor uses this picturesque idea with rare poetic beauty (in the "Living Flame," for example), but not without good theological foundation. Thomas Aquinas says that, in justifying the soul, God *touches* it, and causes grace in it. The idea of touching, therefore, means in this instance to cause something, as when a fire touches dry wood, it causes it to burn like itself. Again Aquinas says that the soul *touches* God by knowing and loving Him.[43] According to this, God touches the soul even for the first infusion of grace, and the ordinary Christian life is one of *contact* with God.

Is this the meaning of St. John, or does he use the term in a more restricted sense? From an examination of the various types of "touches," it is clear that St. John does not apply the term to every infusion of grace, but only to those communications of God which are above the natural mode of the senses and the active understanding. In other words, the touch of God is independent of the soul's activity: it awakens powers which no other object can awaken. It will be noticed that the term "substance" and "Divine touch" are related. We said that the "substance" of the soul was not the essence of the soul alone, but also the roots of the faculties where the accidents of things and the senses could not touch. But where the accidents and the senses cannot penetrate, the Divine Substance is present, touching the substance of the soul with its passive faculties, and awakening it to sublime acts of knowledge and love. It is the "substance" of the soul that receives the Divine touch; the sensual part is too base for this delicate and sublime touch. I wish to show two things as regards these touches: first, that they have to do, not only with the essence of the soul (grace), but also with the intellect (supernatural light) and with the will (charity); secondly, that they cause in the soul only those operations which are not directed to accidents and natural concepts.

[43] De Veritate, q.28, a.3

First, it is to be noticed that St. John maintains the principle that the soul acts through its faculties and not through its essence. I believe this evident throughout, but in particular where he says that the "lofty and most delectable knowledge of God, and of His virtues ... overflows into the understanding at the touch which these virtues of God effect in the substance of the soul." [44] Again, it is clear that, in touching the soul, God can actuate either the understanding or the will or both together.[45]

Speaking now of clear and distinct contemplation, "these lofty manifestations of knowledge [are] equivalent to a certain *contact* with the Divinity.... this touch of knowledge and delight is nevertheless so sublime and profound that it penetrates the substance of the soul." These touches of God, which have the intellect for their primary object, enkindle the soul with lofty perceptions of God's attributes, enkindling the will with love, filling the soul with virtues and blessings. The soul cannot attain to these perceptions by any imagination or thought or will of its own. God must work them in the soul without making use of its own (active, natural) capacities.[46] Here is evident what we said: first, the substance of the soul does not exclude altogether the faculties of intellect and will; secondly, Divine touches are concerned with that which is above the natural capacities.

Turning now to the spiritual feelings of the soul which have to do primarily with the will, it is to be noticed that these do not come to the soul because of any good works, meditations or spiritual exercises in which the soul may be engaged at the moment.[47] Both the feelings and the intelligence that overflows into the understanding are produced *passively*. This supernatural intelligence, like the feelings which precede it, are so high that "human nature cannot reach or apprehend [it] by its own efforts, but only by an attitude of receptivity." [48]

What we have said is even more true in the case of obscure

[44] S.C.,xiv and xv,12
[45] D.N.,II,xii,5-7; xiii,1,2
[46] xxvi,5-8
[47] xxxii,2
[48] xxxii,4. Cf. S.C.,xxv,5,6

contemplation because therein the understanding is darkened, not only as regards the accidents and sensible knowledge of things, but of any clear and distinct knowledge whatsoever. For, since God Himself dwells substantially in the soul by His creative power, He can communicate with the soul in a sublime and dark manner by means of "substantial touches of Divine union." This is a touch of the divinity, a kiss with the mouth of the soul, high above all that is sensible.[49]

For this obscure contemplation has regard to naked substance, and is free from accidents, which is the reason why it is dark, since, as Dionysius says, contemplation is a ray of darkness.[50] In the "Living Flame," this contemplation is described as touches or anointings of the Holy Spirit, and such is their delicate and subtle purity that they are disturbed by "the slightest act which the soul may desire to make on its own account." [51] The "Living Flame" is, of course, concerned with the highest perfection, and there are, therefore, many references to Divine touches, all of which confirm our thesis, namely, that these "touches" are the union of the substance of the soul together with the deeper powers of its faculties, and the substance of God, without any creatures acting as intermediaries.[52]

§ 5.   RELATIONSHIP OF THE ABOVE TERMS.

We have considered the meaning of such terminology as "ways, modes, and manners," "particular and distinct knowledge," "substance," "touches." All of these, when properly understood, are very useful to the spiritual person, because they designate the virtual parts or operations of the soul, specifically distinct from one another, and also those different types of knowledge or objects known, which correspond to the powers of the soul. We saw that "modes, ways, methods and manners" referred to the natural processes of human knowledge, what is known as the natural or rational or human mode of knowledge. Such knowledge, we

[49] D.N., II,xxiii,11,12. Compare A.,II,xvi,9
[50] S.C., xiv and xv,14,16.
[51] L.F.,iii,41
[52] Cf. L.F., ii,16-20

know, is derived from external things in the world by means of the senses and natural understanding, and is therefore "particular and distinct." The senses do not reach substance but only accidents — forms, images and figures. Above this natural mode of knowledge is that which God infuses into the soul. Obscure contemplation, for example, is a knowledge of God given directly to the passive understanding. It is substance free from accidents — forms, figures and images. When supernatural knowledge of God is communicated, it is infused into the "substance" of the soul, and this communication may be called a "Divine touch," since there are no intermediaries between the soul and God.[53] The "substance" of the soul does not exclude the passive understanding and will, but demands them in its fullness. Imagination, meditation, reasoning do not penetrate to the "substance" of the soul, but only the Divine presence and "touch" can do that. The Divine touch is, therefore, superrational and superhuman. It is one with the Divine breath to which the gifts of the Holy Spirit make us flexible and docile. The Divine touch, to speak more familiarly, is the inspiration of the Holy Spirit, entering the depth of our spirit where the gifts abide, and giving the soul that superrational and superhuman mode of movement in which the supernatural organism reaches its perfection.

Touched by the finger of God, the little plant opens its flower to the full rays of the heavenly sunlight, and drinks in the illumination and warmth that will make it flourish with more than natural life, even after it has been pulled up by the roots and shaken free of its former manner of existence.

§ 6. "NATURAL" AND "SUPERNATURAL."

One of the causes of confusion in ordinary readers is St. John's use of the terms "natural" and "supernatural." As a rule their meaning can be easily determined from the context, at least by those who know the different meanings of these names. When, for example, a chapter deals with visions of the imagination, the sense of "supernatural" may be taken as "preternatural." But let us distinguish the different significations that these two words can have. "Natural" in the usual sense of the word refers to

[53] Compare L.F., ii,20 with A.,II,xvi,7

what is proper to our human nature unaided by grace; all are familiar with this usage. Entirely above the order of nature we have the supernatural order of grace. Grace is essentially super-natural, that is, above nature according to its very essence. The theological virtues, the gifts of the Holy Ghost and the infused moral virtues are esssentially supernatural. (I use the word "essential" and not "substantial" to avoid confusion with St. John's use of "substance.") These two orders of natural and supernatural being are absolutely distinct — and the matter would be comparatively simple, if there were not another category of effects that is called "supernatural" for another reason.

I say "effects" designedly; for the reason that such things are called "supernatural" is because nature is unable to effect them in itself, although it is capable of receiving them from an outside agent; in other words, though the operation itself has only nat-ural being, it must be effected by the intervention of God or a spirit. It is called "supernatural" because the mode of its pro-duction is above the natural process; it is "supernatural' in the *mode* of production, and, therefore, only *modally* supernatural. For example, the imagination is able to form images of external objects by means of the external senses. Such images are natural in their very being and also in the way they were produced in the imagination. But let us suppose that a person born blind has never seen external objects. He would have the capacity of re-ceiving images in his imagination, but he would have no way of bringing vision into his interior. Now, if God were to produce a vision of external objects in his imagination, He would effect a natural image or vision in a manner above the natural laws of attaining such imagery. The image or vision would be natural in essence, but "supernatural" in mode of production. It is in this sense that St. John sometimes uses the term, in relation to both the senses and the intellect, as we have seen. The distinction is important, because "supernatural" intervention of an outside cause does not necessarily raise the effect itself above natural being. Thus what is received "supernaturally" by one person might be apprehended naturally by another, as when a man sees in a vision his brother miles away while another person standing near the brother sees him in exactly the same appearance.

That which is modally supernatural brings us no more than what human nature is capable of, given the right conditions. But grace, the supernatural virtues and gifts, being essentially supernatural, lift us above ourselves and make us participate in Divine life. What a difference, then, between the content of these two terms! If St. John seems not to distinguish explicitly between them at times, his doctrine makes it abundantly clear how much he esteems the supernatural powers of the soul above those pre-ternatural phenomena which he urges his readers to reject.

There is another use of the word "natural" which we may well examine here. In treating of faith we saw that, although infused and intrinsically supernatural, this light of faith may be received in two ways: either as reflected in the images of earth, or in a dark, confused and general manner. The latter is wholly super-natural, which is why it causes darkness and indistinctness in the natural understanding. The former uses the imagery of this world to convey analogical knowledge of Divine things. Now, because of the natural forms (though illumined by faith), St. John sometimes speaks of this mode of knowledge as "natural" (Cf. A.,II,xii,3). His meaning is that faith uses our natural concepts to convey Divine truth. He does not mean that meditation is *merely* a natural process, but only that in mediation we use natural imagery and ideas, though they are illumined by faith. Such meditation might be called supernatural in essence but nat-ural in mode; it cannot equal infused contemplation, which is entirely above our natural knowledge, being supernatural both in essence and in mode.

The accompanying chart will help to make these distinctions clear. The two divisions "a" and "b" are only natural in essence, the difference between them being extrinsic. The divisions "c" and "d" are supernatural in essence, but they, too, are dis-tinguished according to mode. St. John's distinction between "a" and "c" or "d" is always clear (for example, A.,II,v,3). The distinction between "a" and "b" is also plain, for the latter is always caused by an outside agent, and St. John advises the soul to reject it. If our author does not always distinguish between "c" and "d," may it not be that he regards these two as forming one organic whole, so that the soul progresses gradually and normally from one to the other? This is nothing else than to say that the supernatural or superhuman mode of the gifts is normal to Christian life. Thus we have another proof that contemplation is normal. Notice in A.,II,v,3 how St. John distinguishes clearly between "a" and "c-d"; yet he makes no great effort to distinguish between "c" and "d" in the rest of that chapter, except implicitly, by his practical counsel for making progress. His doctrine consists in this, that by gradual elimination of all that is natural, the soul should reach that which is wholly supernatural.

The following examples may illustrate the distinctions found in Book Two of the "Ascent." In A.,II,xv,4, St. John means to say, it seems me, that when "a" and "b" have failed the soul, then it will live according to "c" and "d." In A.,II,xvi,4 it is said that the devil uses both "a" and "b." In A.,II,xvii,3 and 4, God is said to bring the soul from the lowest extremity, "a," to the highest, "d." In A.,II,xxvi,12, it seems merely a question of the state of grace being distinguished from the spirit of prophecy; Balaam had "b" without "c-d," while the holy prophets, apostles and other saints had "b" together with "c-d."

CHART OF "NATURAL" AND "SUPERNATURAL."

NATURAL
in essence
(e.g. our human
nature)

    a. natural also in mode of operation (according to ordinary laws of nature)

    b. supernatural in mode of operation (by intervention of an outside cause. E.g. visions, prophecy, etc.)

SUPERNATURAL
in essence
(e.g. grace,
infused
virtues,
gifts)

    c. natural in mode (due to use of natural images and ideas, though illumined by faith)

    d. supernatural mode (knowledge above and independent of our natural images and ideas. Entirely infused by God. E.g. infused contemplation)

NOTE: The soul is called *active* when it is acting by its own natural powers, and *passive* when it is in operation through the intervention of a force above nature. The soul is *passive* in every supernatural act, even though the act be supernatural only in the mode of operation, as in "b" above (cf. A.,II,xxiii,1). Much more is the soul passive in regard to the light of faith, which is essentially supernatural; however, insofar as faith uses the natural mode of imagery and ideas, as in "c," writers speak of the soul as active, and thus St. John speaks of the soul's activity, and even labor, in meditation. Since "d" is supernatural both in essence and mode, the soul cannot receive infused contemplation except *passively*, as St. John often remarks.

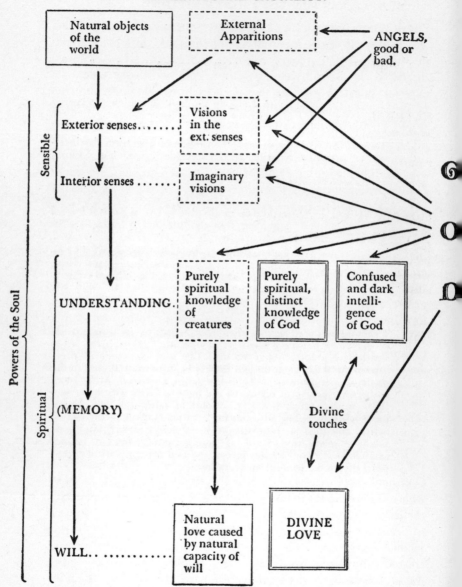

CHART OF NATURAL, PRENATURAL AND
SUPERNATURAL CAUSALITY.

Natural objects of the world

External Apparitions

ANGELS, good or bad.

Sensible

Exterior senses.......

Visions in the ext. senses

Interior senses ....

Imaginary visions

Powers of the Soul

Spiritual

UNDERSTANDING..

Purely spiritual knowledge of creatures

Purely spiritual, distinct knowledge of God

Confused and dark intelligence of God

(MEMORY)

Divine touches

WILL.. ....

Natural love caused by natural capacity of will

DIVINE LOVE

EXPLANATION OF THE PRECEDING CHART

There are four kinds of causality, represented in this chart, which may affect the spiritual life of the soul: the world, angels, devils, God. Our natural knowledge is that which has its source in the world. The arrows show how this knowledge enters the exterior senses, proceeding thence to the interior senses, and then being transformed into spiritual ideas by the understanding, stored up by the memory, and as the completion of the human process, eliciting love in the will. All this is in the purely natural order, whose progress is indicated between the two single-lined squares. This is the first cause which is nature alone. The second kind of causality is that of angelic spirits. Both good and bad angels, by their ordinary powers, can effect the external world and the corporeal senses of man, as is frequently evident in John of the Cross. External apparitions are a preternatural (outside the causes of nature) manifestation which affect man's eyes, ears, *etc.* in the same way as natural causes. It is evident then that such visions, *etc.,* — *in themselves* — cannot bring the soul any greater than a natural good, apart from the work of God. Visions, locutions, *etc.*, in the exterior senses, are preternatural (supernatural in mode only) in this, that they are caused without the presence of an external object; such causality may come from the angels or the devils, or directly from God. Imaginary visions are those which are caused in the imagination without any work of the outer senses. Even the devils, working on the natural faculty, can cause them. It is evident, therefore, that these, *in themselves,* cannot produce a supernatural good in the soul. All this is in the corporeal or sensible order.

Coming now to the spiritual faculties, only the causality of God may enter directly here, for the Creator's causality is everywhere. There are three kinds of intelligence in the understanding: the natural (derived from the sensible faculties); the preternatural (supernatural in mode. Infused directly by God, even when they relate to creatures. The intelligence which relates to natural, created things requires no more than natural intellectual light); the supernatural (which is above the natural power of the understanding, and requires that God should elevate its potency). The supernatural intelligence may be divided into distinct and confused; both are intimately related to Divine love.

We have then three kinds of knowledge or intelligence: the natural, the preternatural (broken-lined square), and the supernatural (double-lined squares). The first two are alike, being in essence merely natural; the third is supernatural in substance. The purely spiritual knowledge of created things (*e.g.*, prophecy) can *in itself* be the source of no more than a natural love, as if such knowledge had come through the senses.

Since only Divine love is of profit to the soul as regards the future life, it is evident then that only the supernatural intelligence of spiritual visions of God and the dark intelligence of infused contemplation are profitable to the soul, among all the knowledge outlined in the chart, although all these kinds may be caused by God Himself.

The intelligence and love which is above all natural forms and images, even infused, is called by John of the Cross "Divine touches," because they require the Divine causality, not merely in the natural part of the soul, but down deep in the substance of the soul where God has implanted new, Divine potencies.